The Unveiling

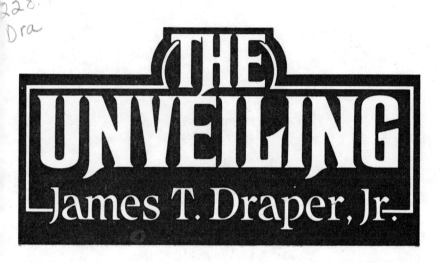

THE UNVEILING

James T. Draper, Jr.

BROADMAN PRESS
Nashville, Tennessee

© Copyright 1984 • Broadman Press
All rights reserved.
4215-04
ISBN: 0-8054-1504-1
Dewey Decimal Classification: 228
Subject Headings: BIBLE. N.T. REVELATION
Library of Congress Catalog Card Number: 83-25229
Printed in the United States of America

Library of Congress Cataloging in Publication Data

Draper, James T.
  The unveiling.

  1. Bible. N.T. Revelation—Sermons. 2. Baptists—
Sermons.   3. Sermons, American.   I. Title.
BS2825.4.D7   1984   228′.07   83-25229
ISBN 0-8054-1504-1

DEDICATION

To my grandson, *Kyle Draper,*
whose arrival
has brightened
the aging process
for me

Contents

The Unveiling

1

The Consummation
of the Ages
Revelation 1:1-8

The Book of Revelation was written to show God's servants the things which must shortly come to pass. Revelation is God's vivid reminder that he has a plan for this earth. The threads of prophecy run throughout all Scripture. Wherever we pick up the sacred Word of God, we will find strands of truth that relate to the end times.

But here in the Book of Revelation, it is as though God drew all these threads together and wove them into a beautiful, detailed tapestry for us. We see the apostasy of the faith and the rapture of the church.

We see wars, famines, pestilences, the coming of the beast and the false prophet. We see persecutions without parallel in history. We see the Battle of Armageddon and the golden age which follows. The eternal destinies of men are vividly painted for us in this richly descriptive book.

The setting alternates between heaven and earth. The reason seems to be obvious—God's ultimate purpose is to have his will done on earth as it is in heaven. Revelation shows that there is no power in heaven, on earth, or in hell itself that can frustrate the fulfillment of God's plan. God's kingdom is going to be fulfilled whether men like it or not. The Book of Revelation is a bold declaration of the inevitability and the invincibility of the purposes of God.

Revelation demonstrates the unity of the Bible. There are 404 verses in this book and 285 direct quotations out of the Old Testament. There are over 550 references to the Old Testament. In contrast, the Book of Matthew has only 92 references to the Old Testament; and the Book of Hebrews, considered to be the most Jewish of all New Testament books, has only 102 references to the Old Testament. Revelation, like no other New Testament book, has a distinctive Old Testament flavor.

There are four basic approaches to interpreting Revelation as follows:

(1) The teachings of the Book of Revelation lie in the past. It simply refers to events in John's own day when the people were under persecution. This view holds that all the prophecy was fulfilled historically at that time, so it has nothing to say to us about future events. We cannot accept this view.

(2) This book is a chronicle of the major events of the history of the church. The whole book is built around the history of the church. While Revelation has certain implications, understandings, and revelations about the history of the church, this approach is not an acceptable approach to interpreting the book, either.

(3) The whole book is symbolic. Everything is written in figurative language and the struggle depicted is not a real physical struggle. It is a spiritual struggle, a spiritual hostility, a spiritual battle, and there is nothing physical involved. We must reject this approach also.

(4) It had historical value for the people in John's day but its primary emphasis is on future events. Beginning with the fourth chapter, we are talking about some events that have not yet happened. This is the appropriate way to approach the study of the Book of Revelation. We will view it as a book of eschatology, dealing with last days, the consummation of the age. We will view it as a book that deals with the end of time

and with the events that surround it. With that in mind, let us begin our examination of this exciting book.

Comfort

> The Revelation of Jesus Christ, which God gave unto him, to shew unto his servants things which must shortly come to pass; and he sent and signified it by his angel unto his servant John: Who bare record of the word of God, and of the testimony of Jesus Christ, and of all things that he saw (vv. 1-2).

The key word in these two verses is *comfort*. The Book of Revelation was written sometime around 95 AD during the reign of Domitian, the emperor of Rome. He was one of the most cruel, wicked rulers ever to sit upon the throne. He fit quite well into the pattern set by the brutal Nero before him.

But Domitian went a step further. He demanded to be worshiped as God. Domitian said, "I am God, I am Lord." He commanded people all over the Roman Empire to bow down and worship him as Lord and as God.

The Christians refused to do that. A great period of persecution was launched against the church because of the Christian refusal to bow to the emperor. Public ridicule was heaped upon them. Economic boycott, imprisonment, exile, and even death were part of the persecution they suffered.

Revelation was God's answer to that reign of terror. God was saying to these persecuted Christians who were driven throughout the Roman Empire, "I want you to view life and history from a new dimension. I want you to see in a way never before seen that I am still on the throne."

The outlook appeared bleak and circumstances dreary, but God was still on his throne. Revelation was written to give comfort to those who were under tremendous persecution then, and to offer hope for Christians of all centuries.

Notice what is to be revealed in this book: "the revelation of Jesus Christ." The first five words of the book teach us its purpose. It is to exalt Jesus Christ.

If we want to understand the Book of Revelation, then we must realize that it is a book about Jesus. He is the key to the book. Jesus Christ is more fully revealed and exalted in the Book of Revelation than anywhere else in Scripture.

When we study this book, we will not set any dates or put any plans in concrete. Sometimes we look at the study of eschatology as we would a football team. We must know all the strategy and all the game plan so that when the time comes and the signal is barked, we will know the move!

That is not so with Revelation. Eschatology is the drama of Jesus Christ. All we have to do is to be there. We do not need to know the game plan. We do not have to understand every detail. Our part is to be obedient, subservient, and to worship him.

He is the one who will initiate the action. If we try to chisel in granite plans of the second coming and the surrounding events, we may be wrong. But if we will focus on Jesus and keep him at the heart of our study, the book will unfold. View after view is given about the glorious Person whose praises fill all of heaven.

The very word *revelation* is the Greek word *apocalupsis* from which we derive our English word *apocalypse*. It has been borrowed for movies, book titles, etc. and it simply means to unveil or to expose to view. The Book of Revelation is not meant to be obscure. It opens the door and helps us understand, unveiling what God has given to us.

It is a revelation of "things which must shortly come to pass" (v. 1). The word *shortly* does not necessarily mean near in point of time. It speaks of rapidity or speed of execution. Once a series of events are set in motion, they will come quickly, rapidly. That is the meaning of the word *shortly*.

"He sent and signified it by his angel unto his servant John." The word *signify* is a word which speaks of signs and symbols.

Someone asks, "Do we believe that the Book of Revelation is symbolic or literal?" The answer is yes! It is both symbolic and literal. There are many symbols in the Book of Revelation.

In this first chapter, we see symbols of the church called lampstands. We have a picture of the messengers called angels.

We have a symbol in chapter 8 of the prayers of the saints symbolized by the smell of sacrifices rising to God.

There are many symbols in the book, but do not be misled; the symbols represent fact and reality. They are not merely symbols of vague and mystical things, but of hard, concrete reality.

One half of all the symbols are explained in the book. For instance, the lamps represent the churches, stated in the first chapter. The stars represent the angels. The incense odor is the prayer of the saints, etc. The book explains itself.

When we come to a symbol, let the book tell us what it means. If the Book of Revelation does not tell us, then we look somewhere else in Scripture. The first rule of hermeneutics, of interpretation is to let the Bible be its own interpreter. If we do this, we will find it very consistent.

The revelation of Jesus Christ is from God. John is not the originator, God is. But it is also a revelation from John because it says that John "bare record of the word of God and of the testimony of Jesus Christ, and of all things that he saw" (v. 2). What a great definition of inspiration!

If we want a clear picture of whom the inspiration of the Bible is, it is Jesus Christ—from God and whomever the writer might be. God used human personality to bring that revelation to us, but it originated with God, and is given to glorify Jesus Christ. This is the comfort given.

Congratulations

"Blessed is he that readeth, and they that hear the words of this prophecy, and keep those things which are written therein: for the time is at hand" (v. 3). *Blessed* means "happy" or "congratulations." There is a great happiness prescribed for those who read and who hear. If we just hear the Book of Revelation, we will be blessed. The Holy Spirit said we will be blessed if we read and hear the words of this prophecy.

We have before us a wonderful thing. Though there is a blessing in reading all of the Bible, Revelation is the only book which specifically promises a blessing to those who read it and hear it.

It may seem difficult at times, but so constant are the glimpses of Jesus Christ in his glory, and so consistent is the picture of the will of God, and so glorious is the ultimate consummation, that just to hear it brings blessing and happiness to a troubled heart.

He also says that blessed are those who "keep those things which are written therein" (v. 3). We must give attention and consider carefully the teachings of this book because "the time is at hand" (v. 3).

What does that mean? It means that the end time, the second coming of Christ, must always be viewed as imminent. Throughout the Christian age there has been an anticipation of his return.

If we view it as something lost in the distant future, beyond our time, there will not be the sense of urgency and the desire to communicate the gospel around the world.

But if we live in an understanding that the time is at hand, that the beginning of these events is upon us, that this event hangs over every age that has ever lived, we will have a real sense of urgency about the proclamation of the gospel.

All God has to say is "Now," and the events will start. Let us consider what God says in order to better understand that which soon may come to pass.

Congregations

> John to the seven churches which are in Asia: Grace be unto you, and peace, from him which is, and which was, and which is to come; and from the seven Spirits which are before his throne; And from Jesus Christ, who is the faithful witness; and the first begotten of the dead, and the prince of the kings of the earth. Unto him that loved us, and washed us from our sins in his own blood, And hath made us kings and priests unto God and his Father; to him be glory and dominion for ever and ever. Amen (vv. 4-6).

Seven represents completeness or perfection of the Holy Spirit, but here it refers to seven different churches, and we know that because he names them.

It is interesting that he did not say "John to the church in Asia." He used the plural. We have a tendency to talk about the church in Korea or the church in America. But the Bible always talks about churches. From its inception, the original order of the church was congregational. There is a sense in which all believers are a part of a great spiritual fellowship that we call the universal church, but the concept of the church in the New Testament is local congregations. To be committed to the church in general is to be committed to no church in particular, and that is heresy.

Whatever God is going to do, he is going to work through the local churches. That is why Jesus is seen walking through the candlesticks as we will see in the next chapter. He does not always have to work through *this* church. He can move through another church.

There are some churches where Christ has moved the

candlestick; God has just decided not to strive anymore. He doesn't have to use *us*, but he will use *a* church.

"Grace be unto you, and peace" (v. 4). It is interesting to notice that grace and peace always come in that order in the New Testament. We never have peace until we experience grace. Until we experience the presence and the cleansing, forgiving power of Jesus Christ, we will never know peace. Peace comes only through the grace of God.

Two points about this chapter are amazing. Revelation, first of all, deals primarily with judgment. This is a book of solemn warning and imminent judgment, yet God begins by talking about grace. He will speak of judgment but he offers grace. Men can have what they desperately need but do not deserve. Grace is offered to them.

For that reason, the converts of that dark and dreadful age to come will probably outnumber all the converts who have ever committed their lives to Christ throughout all of history. John said out of this great tribulation there came multitudes which no man could number who had washed their robes in the blood of the Lamb and who loved not their lives unto death. That is grace.

So in a book of judgment, he offers salvation, deliverance, grace. And then peace. The Book of Revelation deals with the opposite of peace. There is bloodshed and war, the noise of strife, carnage, and conflict, earthquake and famine, pestilence and woe. It tells us of purges and persecutions, with blood flowing in crimson tides. It tells us of the crash of an empire, of anarchy and opposition, of terror and despair, of war in heaven and on earth.

Thunders roll, stars fall from heaven. Plagues issue up from the abyss. Demons take control of human affairs. Armies are marshaled by the millions, yet God starts the book with one word: *peace*. What a beautiful offer.

The exciting fact is that grace and peace win. When the

book is over, the thunder is quiet, and the strife is gone. Peace prevails.

This grace and this peace are offered by the Triune God. Notice it says, "From him which is, and which was, and which is to come" (v. 4). That is a description of God himself. God the Father is he who transcends time, who cuts across all ages. It is backed by the authority of the eternal God himself.

Then it says, "From the seven Spirits which are before his throne" (v. 4). The word *seven* here speaks of completeness and perfection. It simply speaks of the omnipotence and sovereignty of the Holy Spirit. This blessing is secured and sealed by the Holy Spirit as well.

"And from Jesus Christ" (v. 5). The blessing of grace and peace to those who will respond is guaranteed by God the Father, God the Holy Spirit, and God the Son. What a wonderful security.

The words of verses 5-8 are incredibly beautiful. They are vividly descriptive of Jesus Christ and his return. He is called, first of all, "the faithful witness." Jesus Christ reveals to men all they ever need to know about God. His witness is sufficient.

In the Old Testament, God was known by his name. When God would provide something for his people, they would call him a name which spoke of his provision. For example, they might call him Jehovah who provides or Jehovah my salvation or Jehovah my rock, etc. Whatever the experience of men, they would give God a name.

But Jesus gave witness to a new name. The name that Jesus gave is that tender, lovely, intimate, heartwarming name *Father*. Man had never called God "Father" until Jesus came and revealed through his faithful witness the name *Father*.

Jesus witnessed to the horror of sin. People had some concept of sin as they watched an innocent animal writhing in pain while being sacrificed on a Levitical altar in Old Testament times. But people never understood sin until they saw the horror of God's son, Jesus Christ, hanging on a cross. Sin broke his body and his heart when he hung on that cross. He was a faithful witness to the horror of sin.

He was also a faithful witness to the need for righteousness. In the Old Testament, there was a challenge for right living but people apparently never fully understood the righteousness that God wanted from them until they heard Jesus preach the Sermon on the Mount and interpret the righteousness of faith.

He witnessed to the nearness of judgment. Jesus talked more about hell than he did heaven. He warned men of impending judgment. He was a faithful witness.

He was "the first begotten of the dead" (v. 5). The Greek literally says, "the first begotten from the dead." It speaks of the resurrection of Jesus. He was not the first one ever to be raised from the dead, but he was the first one ever raised who did not die again. He was raised incorruptible.

The whole fifteenth chapter of 1 Corinthians speaks of the incorruptible body that shall be ours. Jesus was raised in his glorified body and because he was, we have the ultimate guarantee of our own resurrection. He was the first begotten from the dead.

The Greek word for "first begotten" is *protōkos*. It refers to priority, to sovereignty. He is the leader of all who will rise from the dead through him to everlasting life.

He is called "the prince of the kings of the earth" (v. 5). That does not mean just a prince among princes. The word *prince* means ruler. He is the ruler of the kings of the earth. Christ is in control. He permits certain latitude of earthly leaders, but his ultimate purposes are moving inevitably toward their conclusion.

"Unto him that loved us, and washed us from our sins in his own blood" (v. 5). "Loved us" is in the continuous present tense. It means that he loved us, and he still loves us. "Washed us" is in the past tense which says "it is done." We have been washed, we have been cleansed, and it stands as a completed act, but he keeps on loving us.

The American Standard translation says, he "loosed us from our sins." If we view it as washing, then sin is seen as a stain, and he cleanses us from it. If we view it as loosing then sin is a chain, and he frees us from it.

It is a beautiful picture. We are forgiven. We are loosed, we are washed in the past in that moment when we were saved. But he keeps on loving us with everlasting love.

"And hath made us kings and priests unto God and his Father" (v. 6). The word *kings* is in the singular and should perhaps be translated "kingdom" of priests. It speaks of our position as we are a kingdom of priests in him. Grace elevates. He has bestowed upon us the majesty of the kings and priests of this earth.

Some time ago, we inaugurated the new president of Baylor University. That was impressive. I had on a robe with three stripes on each sleeve, and we walked from Pat Neff Hall down to Waco Hall.

Lining the way as we went, there were 148 flags representing the 50 states and the 98 countries in which Baylor graduates live and serve today. Then we marched into that hall to a majestic orchestra and pipe organ. It was something for this country boy!

It was most impressive to see the honor bestowed upon a man inaugurated as a president. I could not help but be deeply moved because I had just been studying this passage. All the honor that comes to a president, a king, or one who rules is nothing compared to what Jesus Christ has made me to be.

All the glamor and honor of a royal wedding in London or an inauguration in Washington fades into insignificance when we realize that the grace of God lifts us and bestows upon us power with men and power with God. He has made us kings and priests.

"To him be glory and dominion for ever and ever" (v. 6). It is all to give glory to Christ. That is why we are saved. That is why we worship together. That is why we serve together.

Climax

> Behold, he cometh with clouds; and every eye shall see him, and they also which pierced him: and all kindreds of the earth shall wail because of him. Even so, Amen. I am Alpha and Omega, the beginning and the ending, saith the Lord, which is, and which was, and which is to come, the Almighty (vv. 7-8).

John could not wait until the last chapter to tell us that he won. He is coming back with clouds, victoriously, visibly. What a day that is going to be!

When God led the children of Israel, he led them with a cloud. When he dwelt among them in the tabernacle in the wilderness, he draped his shoulders with a cloud. When he left Mount Olivet to ascend back to glory, he did it in a chariot of clouds. When he comes again, he will come draped majestically with a cloud about his shoulders.

He will come visibly for the Scripture says, "Every eye shall see him" (v. 7). That means every eye of every age shall see him. Jesus, in Matthew 26:64, told Caiaphas that he would see him. Caiaphas is dead but when Jesus comes Caiaphas is going to see him. There will be tremendous victory in his return.

It will not only be a visible return but a victorious one. The Scripture says, "All kindreds of earth shall wail because of him" (v. 7). They will all be busy getting ready for Armageddon. When he comes it will all be over and they shall wail because of him. Those who have opposed him shall wail at his victorious return.

He shall be declared omniscient, for he says, "I am Alpha and Omega" (v. 8). Those are the first and last letters of the Greek alphabet. The alphabet is an ingenious method by which we capture all the knowledge and wisdom of a civilization and keep it for posterity. That is how we write books and all the methods we use to keep the composite knowledge of our world.

He is saying here that Jesus Christ is the *a* and the *z*. He is the final source of all knowledge, the final source of all understanding and all wisdom. He cannot be deceived, he cannot be disputed, he cannot be discredited. He is omniscient, Alpha and Omega. He is the beginning and the end, meaning he is omnipresent.

It is spoken of here in terms of time, but the same is true in terms of space. Wherever there is a beginning and wherever there is an ending, there he is. He is the one "which is, and which was, and which is to come, the Almighty" (v. 8). Verse 4 has already spoken about God who is and was and is to come.

Finally, he is called "Almighty." There is no higher name than that in human language, and it is applied to Jesus Christ, our coming Lord. If we want to understand Revelation, we must understand that it is about Jesus. He is the key to the book, and the climax is that he shall come visibly and victoriously back to earth.

2
The Revelation
of Jesus Christ
1:9-20

The tribulation spoken of here is not the Great Tribulation he describes later (chapters 4–18). He was experiencing tribulation with them as Rome had unmercifully persecuted the church. Many of them had already been killed.

Witness

"I John, who also am your brother, and companion in tribulation, and in the kingdom and patience of Jesus Christ, was in the isle that is called Patmos, for the word of God, and for the testimony of Jesus Christ" (v. 9).

John was a prisoner on the isle of Patmos, exiled because of his witness for Christ. His commitment to Jesus caused him to be punished.

This reminds us that in this age of grace, we have the opportunity to speak for Jesus, to declare the Word of God. It is our privilege, our greatest opportunity, to express to a world who Jesus Christ is and what his word declares. This is a witnessing age in which we are privileged to give such a witness for Jesus Christ.

Every Christian ought to give himself to that task. Everyone of us ought to be living witnesses for Christ. We ought to confront the skepticism and the paganism of a lost world with lives that prove the validity of the gospel we proclaim.

John identified with those to whom he wrote: "who also am your brother, and companion." He is our brother, our companion. We are in this thing together. We are part of the same assignment. God has given us the same privilege and we are companions "in tribulation."

This is not the great tribulation that he talks about later. But in all ages, those who have dared to live for God have always suffered persecution and tribulation. Paul said, "All that will live godly in Christ Jesus shall suffer persecution" (2 Tim. 3:12).

The church, in the day when Revelation was written under the terrible reign of Domitian, was a church in tribulation—under great stress. John said, "I am with you in it. I am with you in the patience and kingdom of Jesus Christ."

I believe this patience and kingdom of Jesus Christ is a spiritual kingdom. He was talking about those of us who are in the family of God, those of us who share the same assignment under God. We are in the kingdom and patience of Jesus Christ.

"In the isle that is called Patmos" (v. 9). John was in exile. He spoke out too often, and they got rid of him. They were smart enough not to make a martyr out of him, they just sent him away.

So there he was, separated from his loved ones, marooned on a barren, rocky island. What a terrible thing! But it won't be long before John shouts, "Glory!" God opens the door of eternal truth to him and what seems to be a bitter, disappointing experience, a persecution and a tribulation, God turns into the greatest experience of his life. He shouted "Hallelujah," and praised God. He gave us an unprecedented, unparalleled picture of Jesus Christ.

Sometimes we go through experiences that are dark and dismal. Sometimes there is heartache and disappointment. Life moves on, and we find that the things we have clung to have changed and are not what they used to be.

But in the midst of discouragement and despair, we must not let Satan rob us of what could be the greatest experience of life. For it is in those dark moments that God may reveal the greatest thing about himself to us. So it was with John. What a blessing!

Worship

I was in the Spirit on the Lord's day, and heard behind me a great voice, as of a trumpet, saying, "I am Alpha and Omega, the first and the last: What thou seest, write in a book, and send it unto the seven churches which are in Asia: unto Ephesus, and unto Smyrna, and unto Pergamos, and unto Thyatira, and unto Sardis, and unto Philadelphia, and unto Laodicea."

And I turned to see the voice that spake with me. And being turned, I saw seven golden candlesticks; And in the midst of the seven candlesticks one like unto the Son of man, clothed with a garment down to the foot, and girt about the paps with a golden girdle.

His head and his hairs were white like wool, as white as snow; and his eyes were as a flame of fire; And his feet like unto fine brass, as if they burned in a furnace; and his voice as the sound of many waters. And he had in his right hand seven stars: and out of his mouth went a sharp two-edged sword: and his countenance was as the sun shineth in his strength.

And when I saw him, I fell at his feet as dead. And he laid his right hand upon me, saying unto me, "Fear not; I am the first and the last: I am he that liveth, and was dead; and, behold, I am alive for evermore, Amen; and have the keys of hell and of death" (vv. 10-18).

This is a beautiful description of worship. John said, "I was in the Spirit on the Lord's Day" (v. 10). There are two phrases, one in verse 9 and one in verse 10, that seem to relate. In verse

9 he says he was in the isle called Patmos. In verse 10 he says he was in the Spirit.

Well, where was he, in the isle or in the Spirit? Both! He was worshiping.

Every true Christian lives in two locations, in a specific place physically and in a spiritual place, in heavenly places. We have our citizenship in two countries. There is a human, earthly environment in which we live and a heavenly environment in which we live.

Paul in Colossians 1:2, talked about Christians who were "in Christ," but were "at Colosse." Where were they, in Christ or at Colosse? Both. They had an earthly address and a heavenly address. We need to remind ourselves not to exclude one or the other. Do not overemphasize one of your addresses.

If we are going to emphasize that we are in Christ and do not realize that we also live in Colosse or Euless or Irving or Dallas, then we become mystical in our approach. We become otherworldly and disinterested in what is happening at our earthly address.

But the opposite is true. I believe the opposite is the problem today. We do not live enough for eternity. We emphasize so much that we live at a location here that we do not have time for eternity. That is materialism.

One extreme is mysticism, the other extreme is materialism. We must be careful not to emphasize one to the exclusion of the other.

John was in the isle of Patmos and in the Spirit on the Lord's day. There are several possible interpretations of "the Lord's Day." Some think it refers to Sunday, the first day of the week. Some believe it refers to the day of the Lord, meaning that God had transported him to a place where he was able to see the events that shall climax in the last days.

I suggest that he was in the Spirit on Sunday and God gave

him a glimpse of the Day of the Lord. He was worshiping on Sunday. He was talking to God, praying to God, and God gave him the experiences described in this book.

What did he see in this worship experience? "I . . . heard behind me a great voice, as of a trumpet, Saying, I am Alpha and Omega" (v. 10-11). He had already said that earlier in this chapter. It is a reminder that everything man can know about anything is found in Jesus Christ. He is the perfection, the completeness, the source of all human wisdom and human knowledge.

"What thou seest, write in a book, and send it unto the seven churches which are in Asia" (v. 11). The ease of travel and the roads that tied them together made it logical that these would be the ones he would choose. I believe there were seven churches, but I also believe he chose to illustrate the truth that is revealed with the number seven. Conditions that existed in those churches also exist in the churches today. They help us to examine our own hearts and lives.

"And I turned to see the voice that spake with me. And being turned, I saw seven golden candlesticks" (v. 12). The Book of Revelation has much symbolism in it, but it also explains itself.

In verse 20, he speaks of the mystery of the seven stars and the seven golden candlesticks. Then he explains it. The seven stars are the angels of the seven churches. The seven candlesticks are the seven churches. So he saw seven churches.

"And in the midst of the seven candlesticks one like unto the Son of man, Clothed with a garment, down to the foot" (v. 13). Then through verse 16 he is described.

Let's start with the candlesticks, "lampstands." A lampstand does not originate light. It only conveys it. If we have a lampstand, we must get light from somewhere else to shine from the lampstand. The lampstand itself does not have any light. The only limitation to the brilliance of the light that stands on the lampstand is the yieldedness of the lampstand.

In other words, the light that we have is the light of Christ. If we have anything to offer to the world, it is nothing of ourselves, but the light of God. Jesus said, "I am the light of the world" (John 8:12). "You are the light of the world. You are to be a reflector of his light."

Here is a lampstand, a church, which exists for the purpose of giving light. The church should not confuse or cloud the issue. There ought not to be an uncertain sound that comes from the voice of the church. There ought to be light.

He called them "golden" lampstands. Gold, in the Word of God, is always a symbol of the glory of God. Here are seven golden lampstands. The terminology tells us the church is to give light to a dark world and glory to God. That is our purpose. We are to give the glory to God and to reflect his light.

The "Son of man" is Jesus Christ. The term *Son of man* is an Old Testament term that was always used to apply to the Messiah. It is a prophetic term. When Jesus claimed to be the Son of man (and that was his favorite name for himself), he was picking up an Old Testament reference to the Messiah.

Here he is seen in the midst of his churches, where he ought to be always. Where God's people are gathered together, Jesus should be in their midst. They are to reflect him. Their attitudes, actions and words to each other and to the world are consistent with Jesus Christ, who is in the midst of the candlesticks.

Christ is the head and the central power of the church. Christ is in the church, and Christ loves the church. If we love Jesus, we will love the church also because that is where the heart of Christ is.

He was clothed from head to foot and had a girdle about his chest. The average person in that day did not dress like that, only a priest or a judge. Jesus is dressed as a King and a Priest walking among the lampstands.

What was Jesus doing? A letter to one of the churches tells us that he was trimming the lampstands, making sure they gave good light. But he was not just maintaining the lamps. He was evaluating them—judging their fitness for service. He had the golden snuffers with him to snuff out the light and remove the lampstand, if necessary. Jesus was very critically, carefully examining the life of these churches. We will see that more as we get into the third chapter.

"His head and his hairs were white like wool, as white as snow; and his eyes were as a flame of fire" (v. 14). Look at Daniel's view of the coming Messiah: "I beheld till the thrones were cast down, and the Ancient of days did sit" (Dan. 7:9).

We take "white hair" to denote the aging process. That is not what this passage means. It refers to the agelessness of Christ, "whose garment was white as snow, and the hair of his head like the pure wool: his throne was like the fiery flame, and his wheels as burning fire" (Dan. 7:9).

Compare those verses in Daniel to these in Revelation. Revelation says that his hair was white as wool, white as snow; his eyes were as a flame of fire, etc. This is a description of Jesus Christ, the agelessness of Christ himself.

The white symbolizes the absolute purity and the absolute righteousness of Jesus Christ. The only way we can be cleansed from the foulness and the evil of our sin is through Jesus Christ, even as Isaiah 1:18 declares. His shed blood alone can cleanse us from the vileness of sin.

"His eyes were as a flame of fire" (v. 14). The Greek says that his eyes literally "shot fire." He was indignant about something. Whenever a church is not what it ought to be, it arouses the indignation of Jesus Christ. We do not get too upset about it. We get accustomed to our compromise, apathy, and indifference.

It infuriates Jesus. He is indignant about it. Flames of fire come from his eyes. In other words, Jesus Christ, the returning Lord, has X-ray vision. We cannot hide anything from him. We may be able to hide things from everybody else, but we cannot hide anything from him.

A fire refines and proves; it tests the metal which is being examined. Everything is exposed by his piercing eyes. No one can escape his scrutiny.

It is easy for us to compare our church to other churches. But it is a fearful and sobering thing to go under the X-ray vision of Jesus Christ. In that light, we do not fare as well. When we are willing to bring our lives and the life of our church before the X-ray vision of him whose eyes are flames of fire, revival will come.

John spoke more about his feet. His robe went down to his feet but did not cover his feet: "And his feet like unto fine brass, as if they burned in a furnace; and his voice as the sound of many waters" (Rev. 1:15).

Brass is a symbol of two things in the Bible: judgment and strength. Remember when God brought judgment upon the children of Israel, he sent fiery serpents into the camp. And when the deliverance came, he said, "Put a brass 'serpent' on 'a pole' " (Num. 21:7-9). That was a sign of deliverance and of the judgment of God.

It is always this way through the Word of God. The fine brass is a symbol of strength and endurance, of the firmness of God's judgment.

His feet were not bound. That means an unfettered, holy walk as well as the powerful triumph of judgment in the person of Jesus Christ.

His voice was as "the sound of many waters" (v. 15). Have you ever stood by a waterfall? It is difficult to hear anything else. The waterfall is overwhelming.

God is largely silent right now, but when God does decide to speak everything else will grow silent. The sound of many waters is going to come.

God may be in a period of chosen silence today as far as this world is concerned, but when he comes to speak, all of the world's people will have their voices drowned out in the presence of God.

"And he had in his right hand seven stars" (v. 16). Those seven stars indicate complete control over the forces that shape the destinies of men. The stars, verse 20 says, refer to the angels of the seven churches.

The word *angels* is *angelos* in the Greek. It is translated "angel" and "messenger." Sometimes it refers to a heavenly or supernatural messenger, sometimes to a human messenger.

I personally think the angel he is talking about here is the pastor. According to Ephesians, God gives pastors as gifts to his churches. They are his messengers; and if a church is to be what it ought to be, the messenger of God needs to be held in the right hand of the Son of man.

"Out of his mouth went a sharp two-edged sword: and his countenance was as the sun shineth in his strength" (v. 16). That two-edged sword is a reference to the Word of God. The word of God in Hebrews 4:12 is described as a sharp two-edged sword. A sword will either save us or slay us, depending upon how it is used. If we need protection, a sharp sword can protect us. On the other hand, someone can attack us with a sharp sword and kill us.

The Word of God will either save us or slay us. We have come to a day when men take great delight in passing judgment on the Word of God. But the Word of God they pretend to judge will one day slay them. The Word of God that goes from his mouth will either confirm faith or reveal falsity. Nothing can stand before God's Word.

"His countenance was as the sun shineth in his strength"

(v. 16). This is the last picture we have before John fell down before Christ.

We cannot look at the sun. Our natural eye cannot stand it. There is a good reason. The sun is too brilliant. One pound of heat will raise 20,000,000 tons of rock by 2500 degrees centigrade and turn it into incandescent lava. But the sun is losing weight by radiation at a rate of 4,200,000 tons per second!

No wonder we cannot look at it. We cannot look at a force so brilliant, so bright, much less approach it. So it was with the apostle John.

When John saw Jesus, he said his countenance was as the sun; and he knew exactly what to do. "When I saw him, I fell at his feet as dead" (v. 17). What else could he do? When we approach a force so strong, so bright, there is nothing to do but fall at his feet as dead. He sensed it instantly and fell before Jesus.

We can curse with the name of Jesus. We can take the name Christian and make a mockery out of it. We can make such a mockery that none of our neighbors will go to Jesus because of us.

We can take Jesus lightly and flippantly today, but when he comes he will come with a countenance as bright as the sun, and the only response will be to fall at his feet.

"And he laid his right hand upon me" (v. 17). The right hand has always symbolized supreme authority. In a court of law, we are required to raise our right hands. There is something, even in our secular culture, about the strength of the right hand.

"Fear not; I am the first and the last: I am he that liveth, and was dead; and, behold, I am alive for evermore, Amen; and have the keys of hell and of death" (vvs. 17-18).

Jesus has the keys of death and to hell. We do not have to walk the lonesome valley by ourselves. He told us not to fear. He is still in control. He has complete mastery over death and hell, and all of the forces that would oppose us.

Is it any wonder that we want to break forth in "Hallelujah, what a Savior"? The picture of worship is complete. John views the coming Messiah and falls on his face in worship before him.

Waiting

Write the things which thou hast seen, and the things which are, and the things which shall be hereafter; The mystery of the seven stars which thou sawest in my right hand, and the seven golden candlesticks. The seven stars are the angels of the seven churches: and the seven candlesticks which thou sawest are the seven churches (vv. 19-20).

The Lord's return is always imminent. It is not always immediate. It was imminent in John's day but in looking back, we see it was not immediate. But John lived in a holy expectancy of the imminent return of Christ. The Christ who John worshiped was in absolute control. He was the one directing the drama. John viewed his coming as near, and so must we.

But while we wait, there must be an intelligent waiting on him. There must be a seeking after fresh light from his Word. That is why he writes to the seven churches. While we wait, let us apply this to our lives.

Peter said that because we understand our times, we should live soberly and righteously in this present world (1 Pet 4:7). We wait with intelligence, not flippantly, carelessly, or in apathy. Let us ask God for understanding these days while we anxiously wait for his return. Pray that we can be a people to whom he can say, "Well done, you served me as I told you. Enter into the joy of your Lord" (see Matt. 25:21).

3

Ephesus:
Loss of First Love
2:1-7

Ephesus was a very wealthy and cultured city. It was on a great highway. Travelers going to and from Rome to the east would more than likely come through the city of Ephesus.

It was a very corrupt city. The cult of Diana was very prominent. Ephesus had hopelessly mingled religion and magic. The great temple of Diana, one of the seven wonders of the ancient world, was a center of pagan worship in Ephesus.

Ephesus was also a strong center for the worship of the Roman emperor, with an abundance of religion. Today, we have an abundance of religion. There is not much difference between liberal theology, seen in churches that shun the fundamentals of the Christian faith, and the pagan worship of Ephesus.

In this wealthy, cultured, corrupt city, there was a church, a good church. The word *Ephesus* means "desirable" and this was a desirable church. If it had been written up by the Baptist press of that day, it would have been a five-star church, one that topped the charts in all the standards of excellence. It was a busy, achieving, aggressive church.

The Lord Jesus writes a letter to each church. In each of these letters, he introduces himself as the one who is writing with a different description. When we get to the end, we will find these seven introductions give a comprehensive view of the One who is our King of kings and Lord of lords.

He is described here as the one who "holdeth the seven stars in his right hand, who walketh in the midst of the seven golden candlesticks" (v. 1). As the One who holds the messengers in his hands and the One who walks among the churches, and who knows and understands all about them, he writes to the church at Ephesus.

Regular Activity of the Church

Unto the angel of the church of Ephesus write; These things saith he that holdeth the seven stars in his right hand, who walketh in the midst of the seven golden candlesticks; I know thy works, and thy labour, and thy patience, and how thou canst not bear them which are evil: and thou hast tried them which say they are apostles, and are not, and hast found them liars: And hast borne, and hast patience, and for my name's sake hast laboured, and hast not fainted (vv. 1-3).

He recognizes the regular activity of this church: "I know thy works, and thy labour, and thy patience" (v. 2). When he uses those three words, he is describing a church that is standing up to the task, that is doing its job.

Works, labor, and patience are words that indicate that a real service is being rendered. It was not just talk. This was a busy church. They really did minister to the people in the community.

The word *works* speaks of actual service rendered. People's lives were really being touched. The word *labour* indicates that painful effort was required to produce the works. These were sacrificing, ministering people. They were full of good works.

They had a magnificent, aggressive program. They were not a country club for preserving the life of a few saints. They were an aggressive and active congregation of saints.

This description is more impressive when you realize it was Jesus who said it. This was not the pastor's evaluation. It was not the deacon's recommendation or a study committee that came back with an approval. This was Jesus who walks among the churches, who understands, sees, and knows. He said they were a working church, a patient church, and a labouring church. That was the verdict of the Lord of the church.

They were also standing for the truth. "Thou canst not bear them which are evil" (v. 2). This was a church with convictions; they stood for moral purity. They could not bear those who were evil.

More than that, it was a church that would not tolerate theological heresy. "Thou hast tried them which say they are apostles, and are not, and hast found them liars" (v. 4). The church at Ephesus stood on the fundamentals of the faith. They gave themselves to the truth of the Word of God.

They were standing up to the test: "hast borne, and hast patience, and for my name's sake hast laboured, and hath not fainted" (v. 3). This speaks of their posture in the face of opposition and hostility.

Every church that is a true church will rub the community wrong. The world is never going to accept a church that dares to be like its Lord. Here were people who faced the opposition and hostility of the world about them and bore it patiently for the sake of the Lord.

They did not grow weary or faint. They stayed with it. They had a great reserve of strength. They were persistent in their faithfulness and untiring in their service, and God commended them for it! Now these were the regular activities of the church. We could not expect a better combination than that.

You see now why it would be considered a five-star church. Outwardly, everything was great. It was standing for the truth.

It was known to be evangelistic, conservative, and compassionate. It was everything we say a church ought to be.

Ruinous Attitude of the Church

> Nevertheless I have somewhat against thee, because thou
> hast left thy first love. Remember therefore from whence
> thou art fallen, and repent, and do the first works (v. 4-5).

Then he talks about the ruinous attitude of the church. In one simple sentence, the picture changes. Here is a church that was doing everything right but for the wrong reasons. There is a way to stand for God in an ungodly way. This church had given itself to the outward expressions of serving God but had left its first love.

They had lost their passion. The furnace was still there but the fire had gone out. They simply did not love the Lord like they should. This one large debit consumed all the credit Jesus had given them. The word *left* is a strong word. It really means "abandoned," "forsaken."

They had completely forsaken that first fine flush of enthusiastic love they had for the Savior. They had yielded to the ever present temptation to put all emphasis on sound doctrine and practice but to forget the Lord. In that process they had lost their love for Christ, without which all else means nothing.

Sometimes it is possible for us to be so busy being Christians that we forget about the Lord. We forget why we are doing what we are doing. This was the problem with the church at Ephesus. Everything looked great, but the Lord of the church said, "You do not love me like you ought to. You have forsaken your first love."

What is "first love"? It defies analysis. There is no way to describe it. Remember when you first fell in love? How did you know you were in love? Someone described it as an itch all over that can't be scratched. I do not know how you know you are in love; you just know it.

But one thing is plain: first love is an abandonment to love. It is ardent; it burns like a flame. And it consumes everything else. When you really love, everything is affected by it. Love gives itself, that does not have any calculations.

Jesus said, "You used to love me like that with a reckless abandon, an enthusiasm that cannot be described. You used to love me with a consuming love. You have forsaken that." We need to learn this truth: activity in the King's business cannot make up for neglect of the King.

Where is our first love? It is not our doing that lightens the world. It is not our rituals and ceremonies that help men and women. It is not even our orthodoxy that lifts the world. It is our love for Christ and each other.

Sometimes we think we have problems, but our problems as Christians come back to one simple thing: we have left our first love. We do not love Jesus as we ought.

Why would a Christian husband forsake his wife and destroy his home? When asked, he says, "I don't love her anymore." That is not the problem.

The real reason is that he does not love Jesus as he used to love him. He is not near enough to Christ. If he were, he would love his wife even as Christ "loved the church and gave himself for it" (Eph. 5:25).

Why would a wife leave a husband and say, "I don't want to be a part of your life anymore." When asked, she says, "I don't love him anymore."

But the real problem is, she does not love Jesus like she used to love him. If she did, she would respect and love her husband like the church loves Christ.

So much is conditioned by our desire for comfort. We are more concerned for the trappings of religion than for the relationship that makes it possible. It is not "church" that brightens the heart. It is not even our fellowship with other Christian people that makes the difference. It is our fellowship with Christ and that comes through our love for him.

Do you realize the implications of what Jesus is saying? Is it possible for us to do all the things we ought to do and still abandon him? We can be faithful in church. We can be active in the outward evidence of religion and still not love Jesus.

All of our service that is not motivated by our love for Christ is worthless. We are not here to cater to our own needs but to fulfill a commission that can only be fulfilled through our love for Christ.

Jesus said, "You are working hard, you have patience; you have labored and toiled, but you don't love me like you ought to." They had lost their passion. Consequently, they lost their genuineness.

"Remember therefore from whence thou art fallen" (v. 5). He described them as fallen. Here was a church that seemed like anything but a fallen church. But Jesus told them they had fallen. In one terse, tragic statement he summed up the whole problem. Their service had become mechanical. Their worship had become routine. They did not have the old fire from above. There was no place for emotion. Cold and regular, without love, was their approach.

The enemy of the church is formalism: getting into a pattern and doing it because we have always done it. Doing something as an end in itself is a tremendous threat to the life of any church.

Worship is like a telescope. It is not something to look at; it is something to look through. Our purpose is to be genuine, fresh, eager, and alive in our relationship with God.

That had gone out in Ephesus. Their devotion was gone. That spirit of giving all for God regardless of the cost was gone. But they could hate! "But this thou hast, that thou hatest the deeds of the Nicolaitans, which I also hate" (v. 6). They could hate, but they had forgotten how to love the Lord.

It is amazing how much work can be done without love and even without the Spirit of the Lord. God forbid that we should ever be able to do what we do without him, that anything we do could be done without his presence and power. Here was a church that had forsaken its first love and lost its realness.

Rigid Admonition to the Church

Repent, and do the first works; or else I will come unto thee quickly, and will remove thy candlestick out of his place, except thou repent. But this thou hast, that thou hatest the deeds of the Nicolaitans, which I also hate. He that hath an ear, let him hear what the Spirit saith unto the churches; To him that overcometh will I give to eat of the tree of life, which is in the midst of the paradise of God (v. 5-7).

Notice the rigid admonition Jesus gave. He said three things to this church. He reminded them that love has to be paramount. No love, no life—that is the rule.

"If you don't recapture this love, I am going to remove the candlestick—take the light out of the midst of you—and will give it to someone else." If we have no real love for Jesus Christ in our hearts then the reason for the church's existence has vanished away.

A church without love for Jesus is useless. It gives a wrong impression of what Christianity is all about. It will be removed. That is Jesus' conclusion.

But he gives an admonition that is encouraging because the condition does not have to remain. It can be changed and he gives three steps. Remember, repent, return or repeat those first works.

The word *remember* is in the present imperative. It literally means "keep on remembering." God never intended for us to forget what it was like before we were saved.

Keep on remembering how it was when you met Jesus. Keep on remembering how fresh that relationship with him really was. For every Christian there is a subtle temptation to become mechanical in our approach to God. For everyone of us there is also that terrifying temptation to forget what it was like before we met Jesus and to forget the freshness of his love for us.

Through submission to the Holy Spirit, we must continue remembering. Do we remember a time when we loved Jesus with such enthusiasm and warmth that just to think of his name would bring a lump to our throats, tears to our eyes, and joy to our hearts because of how precious he was to us?

Jesus says this is the first step to getting back to first love— remember. Get in a quiet place and come to the Lord. Look into his face and say, "Lord Jesus, I remember the day when you meant everything to me, when you were my very life. Nothing in this world was more precious than you were." The thrilling flush of a newfound conversion and experience with Christ must be guarded by remembering.

The Lord said, "Repent." This is in the aorist tense, and means a sharp break with evil: a point where we stop. Judgment is not irrevocable if we repent. Our lives can be turned back to God. There can be renewal and rejuvenation.

The Christian who is unwilling to yield all of his life, his talents, his capabilities to Christ has a love problem. Our favorite excuse is to blame someone else. "I don't come to church because I don't like so and so." The real problem is a love problem, nothing more than an excuse.

Nobody can make us a certain way. People may encourage us or pressure us but we ultimately are the ones to decide. Wherever we are with God, we got there by ourselves. Face the responsibility and repent: "God, here I am, here is where I stand. Oh, God, forgive me. Change me; I don't want to be this way."

Then he said, "Do the first works" again (v. 5). This is also in the aorist tense, and it speaks of a specific act. What did we do when we first met the Lord? We confessed our needs to him.

We confessed we wanted him to be Lord in our life. We repented of our sins. Do it again. Do the first works. Return to him.

There is a tremendous cost when we lose our first love. Not only is there misery in our hearts, but there is the unspeakable grief that we have offended and hurt the one we really love the best. Do not remain with a lost love. Repent and return to him.

He said an interesting thing in verse 7. Up to now, he had talked in the second person plural—you plural, all of you. In verse 7, He speaks in the singular. "He that hath an ear, let him hear what the Spirit saith unto the churches" (v. 7).

Churches do not repent as groups, but as individuals. That is the only way a church gets back to its first love, when people in the church get back to their first love. While this admonition is addressed to the church at Ephesus, it is for individual repentance, not corporate repentance. He calls for each person to face the truth, for each Christian to come back to God himself.

The "church" cannot come to God for us. The warmth and the fellowship of a church cannot suffice for our need for God. We can come to him and have that warmth in our hearts, not just rub shoulders and sit in the same room with it. That warmth can be in our hearts and lives.

"To him that overcometh will I give to eat of the tree of life" (v. 7). Overcoming is something we ought to be interested in. Life sometimes does collapse around us, but there can be an overcoming. John tells us: "Whatsoever is born of God overcometh the world: and this is the victory that overcometh the world, even our faith. Who is he that overcometh the world, but he that believeth that Jesus is the Son of God?" (1 John 5:4-5).

Overcomers are people who live by faith, people who come to God in trust and faith. There is victory and peace. There is the overcoming Spirit. The failing can be corrected, the enthusiasm revived when first love is rekindled.

4

Smyrna:
Persecuted Church
2:8-11

T he church at Smyrna was a church under pressure, a suffering church, a church under tremendous persecution. The word *Smyrna* is the word that is translated elsewhere in the New Testament *myrrh*. The kings gave to the infant Jesus gold, frankincense, and myrrh.

Myrrh was a gum resin from a scrubby little tree. One could make perfume out of it, or one could make oil that the priests used in the anointings of the religious ceremonies. Or it could be used to make an embalming fluid. It was a very bitter substance.

It is interesting that the name of the city where this church was located is Smyrna. The very word means "bitter," symbolic of the fact that Smyrna was a church suffering horribly. The people were afflicted, oppressed, and persecuted. It was a difficult place to maintain a Christian testimony because it was probably the most persecuted and the most afflicted of all the New Testament churches.

Comfort

And unto the angel of the church in Smyrna write; These things saith the first and the last, which was dead, and is alive; I know thy works, and tribulation, and poverty, (but thou art rich) and I know the blasphemy of them which say

45

they are Jews, and are not, but are the synagogue of Satan
(vv. 8-9).

To the church under pressure, suffering and afflicted, Jesus
wrote: "These things saith the first and the last, which was
dead, and is alive" (v. 8). The original literally meant something like this: "I became a corpse, yet I live."

It was a reference to tremendous power. In spite of death,
Jesus lives. He is the one who knew what they were going
through because he experienced it. He is the first and the last
and in spite of death, he still lives.

Here is a letter to all people who have faced disappointment
and persecution, who have lived under the oppressive hand of
suffering and sorrow, who have known the devastation of
depression and despair. It is a letter for us today.

There was not a word of condemnation to this church. Jesus
did not condemn the church. In most of the letters, he
complimented the church, then followed with a condemnation. He complimented the church at Ephesus so much, then
said, "I have somewhat against thee" (v. 4). But to this church,
there was not a word of condemnation.

Satan learned a great lesson on Smyrna. He is very powerful
but he is not omnipotent, not God. He is very smart, but not
omniscient. He is very fast, but not omnipresent.

In this era, Satan had his headquarters in Pergamos. From
Pergamos emanated all of the power of Satan around the
earth. Satan cannot be everywhere and does not know everything. He thought if he persecuted the church, he could defeat
it. He thought if he put pressure on the Christians, they would
fall apart. He thought he could stamp out the Christian faith if
he put pressure at the right point.

For approximately 250 years, Satan persecuted the church.
But the church reached its greatest numbers in proportion to
the population of the world during this age of persecution.

Satan learned a lesson and moved to his most cunning tactic—what we face in America today: indulgence, endorsement, and acceptance. He has found that to be a far more devastating tool against the church.

How wonderful was the comfort that Jesus gave this persecuted church: "I know thy works, and tribulation, and poverty, (but thou art rich) and I know the blasphemy of them which say they are Jews and are not, but are the synagogue of Satan" (v. 9).

He began with one of the most comforting phrases anyone could ever hear. "I know." In the Greek language, there were two basic words which we translate "to know." One meant to know by observation. I know, for instance, that if you swing at a nail with a hammer and miss the nail and hit your hand, that is going to hurt. I know because I have seen people do that, and I have seen the pain on their face. I know by observation that it hurts.

But the other day, I was staking up a tree in my front yard. I had a piece of steel I was hammering into the ground. When I swung at it, I missed and hit my hand. I know that the hammer hurts when it hits your hand, not because I observed it somewhere else but because I felt the sting on my own hand: I experienced it.

There is a difference in observation and experience. The word which Jesus used here means to know by experience. Jesus knew what they were going through because he was going through it with them; he had experienced it.

Here is a word of comfort from our Lord Jesus Christ to every believer. Whatever we face, whatever threatens, oppresses, opposes, persecutes, torments, or attacks us, Jesus knows. He is there with us.

Hebrews 4:15 says, "For we have not an high priest which cannot be touched with the feeling of our infirmities." That means that whatever touches me touches him. Nothing hurts me that does not hurt him. When I hurt, he hurts. When I am oppressed, he is oppressed. Whatever comes to me, Jesus says, "I know because I share it with you." What a word of comfort that is to our hearts.

"I know thy . . . tribulation" (v. 9). He is going to describe the things that oppress these people. The word for "tribulation" is *thlipsis.* The word *tribulation* does not mean much to us. We think of inconvenience or maybe a little discomfort.

But this word is a word that could be used of the stone that grinds wheat until it becomes a powdery flour. Or it could be used to describe the pressing of grapes until the juice flows freely. It could be used of a man being slowly crushed to death under a great weight.

Jesus said, "It is as though the torment you are under is pressing you even to death. I know your tribulation." They were under tremendous pressure of persecution, sorrow, and death. They were an afflicted, tormented people.

Did you ever feel your life, your hopes, your dreams were being crushed? Jesus knows and understands. He knows our tribulation.

"I know thy . . . poverty" (v. 9). The word he chose to use here means actual "beggary." They were not just poor in the sense they had enough to eat and did not have anything extra. They did not have anything. This word means absolute destitution. They were the poorest of the poor. They were people who had absolutely nothing as we will see in a moment. They had nothing of this world's goods.

The early Christians were largely poor people. Just as persecution cannot stamp out the church, neither can poverty. The real question is: can the church survive prosperity? It may not be able to stand the pressure of prosperity. These were people who were absolutely, abjectly poor.

Someone has observed that the early churches were marked by material poverty and spiritual strength. Churches today are marked by material wealth and spiritual weakness.

"I know the blasphemy of them which say they are Jews, and are not, but are the synagogue of Satan" (v. 9). Normally, the word *blasphemy* refers to slander against God. But the word can be translated "slander against man." In this context, the scholars are almost universally agreed that it refers to blasphemous, slanderous, libelous statements that were made about the Christians.

For some reason, the Jews in Smyrna were more hostile towards the Christians than in most other places. They were hostile in every place, but here there seems to have been a more intense hostility and hatred toward the Christians.

The Jews in Smyrna, which Jesus called the synagogue of Satan, circulated libelous, slanderous statements about the Christians and inflamed and incensed the pagan population until Christians would have their property taken from them.

If they acknowledged Christ, they would be fired from their jobs. They were reduced to abject poverty because of the slander of those Jews. And Jesus said, "I know, I know."

Jesus knew persecution firsthand. He suffered under the oppressive weight that sought to destroy him. He knew poverty. "The Son of man hath not where to lay his head" (Matt. 8:20). God knows where we are, the pain we feel. God knows the pressure we are under, the despair and depression with which we live. What a comfort that God knows. He does not condemn our suffering. He does not condemn our persecution and sorrow. He says, "I know. I am with you in this. I know it from my own experience. I hurt when you hurt." Praise God for a Savior who knows our pain, our hurt, our circumstances of life.

Continuation

"Fear none of those things which thou shalt suffer: behold, the devil shall cast some of you into prison, that ye may be tried; and ye shall have tribulation ten days" (v. 10). You would expect, after his talking about knowing what they are going through, that he would say, "Cheer up, it is going to get better."

Instead, he said, "Cheer up, it's going to get worse." There will be a continuation of persecution. We have a distorted view of Christianity. We have the idea that blessing is material provision. If God really blesses us, we will not have any sicknesses or accidents, hostility or opposition; everything will be just wonderful. The only trouble with that is that it just is not so. That is our judgment, not God's.

Jesus said, "Fear none of those things." It is natural for us to shrink from the kind of suffering he just talked about. Nobody enjoys that. Notice he does not say, "Fear not what you have suffered," but he said, "Fear not that which you *shall suffer*.

"The past was bad enough, but brace up and do not be afraid of what lies ahead. The road ahead is rockier still. The suffering ahead is even heavier yet. Whatever you have experienced in the past is preliminary to what is coming ahead."

He told them that they would be cast into prison. That does not mean they would just be thrown into jail. The Roman Empire did not have any concept of imprisonment as a punishment for a crime. They did not believe the state had the responsibility of taking care of criminals. They put one into prison only to await a trial or an execution.

One did not get a sentence of twenty years in the Roman Empire. He might get a fine. He might get exiled, or he might get executed. That was just about the range of the penalties that were imposed by law in the Roman Empire.

When Jesus said that the devil would cast some of them into prison, he was talking about the whole gamut of difficulties they would face. There would be harassment; there would be accusations, slander and trial, exile, fines, and execution. Prison was the epitome of all the sufferings that lay ahead.

Why do we suffer? Why does a Christian face such pressure? He only gives one reason in this passage: "that ye may be tried." No great philosophical pronouncement—he simply said that the testing, pressure, and suffering comes in order that they might be tried.

In other words, the church must be tested. The chaff has to be separated from the wheat. The test of our faith is not what we receive when we have health, when everything is going the way we want it to. The testing of our Christian character is what happens when the roof falls in, life collapses around us, and suffering comes. What then?

Jesus says we must be tried. The time is coming when pressure and suffering will be thrust upon us, and the only answer Jesus gives is to test us. In this day of easygoing discipleship, we need to hear Jesus say, "Don't be afraid of what you will suffer because you must be tried."

We do not know much about that. We have not really suffered. Here was a suffering church, and Jesus offered no relief from the suffering, but he offered them assurance that he would go through it with them.

"Ye shall have tribulation ten days" (v. 10). Some think the "ten days" refers to the great era of persecution that went on during this 250-year period. There were ten great periods of persecution and purging of the Christians.

More than likely, however, it means that God is going to limit that which is going to happen to them. It will be heavy and hard, and the suffering will be real, but there will be an end. With daylight there will be a new day. Fear not that which lies ahead.

Those who understand know that following Jesus Christ is not a panacea to comfort and to cater to the whims of the selfish individual, but it is a means of bringing glory to God.

Since it pleased God through the sufferings of the captain of our salvation to make him perfect (Heb. 2:10), then we, too, shall expect to walk through the valley of suffering.

Conquest

"Be thou faithful unto death, and I will give thee a crown of life" (v. 10). Persecution is not the end of the story. He comforts those in the midst of it, but he also calls for conquest of it. Rather than urging us to exercise the energy of the flesh, being faithful to death is anchored in the faithfulness of our Lord Jesus Christ.

In the fifth verse of the first chapter, he called Jesus Christ the one who is faithful. The same word is used here. Jesus is saying that the faithfulness of the saints rests upon his faithfulness. We are victorious because he is victorious. We triumph because he has triumphed. We shall live because he lives. He is the victory. It is a call for us to depend upon him, to let him be our strength and courage. There is conquest for those who trust in Christ.

"I will give thee a crown of life" (v. 10). I do not believe the crowns that are given to us are crowns to be worn on our heads. According to Revelation 4:10 the crowns that are given to the Christian are crowns to be placed at the feet of our Savior for his glory, for his honor.

Notice that he made no commendation of this church. The commendation was silent. There was no word of complaint but also no compliment. The silence was more eloquent than language.

Jesus was saying to these saints that their spirit under pressure satisfied his heart. The way they had responded to the tremendous pressure, suffering and sorrow, was pleasing to him. The real strength of Christian character is revealed under pressure.

Are you overwhelmed with sorrow? with pressure on your soul? In the midst of it are you longing to hear his voice? Instead there is nothing but silence? The silence may be a sign, not of disapproval, but of approval.

Look up. Do not be cast down. If in the midst of suffering there is no voice, it may be that the silence of our Lord is his highest commendation for you. And that silence speaks of the provision that he has made.

But there was not just silence. There was that little parenthesis: "(but thou art rich)" (v. 9). The word *rich* is the word we get our word *plutocrat* from. "You are the real plutocrats. Smyrna says you are poor, but you are rich. Smyrna says you are destitute, but you are rich."

It is as though Jesus were saying, "I know your poverty because I have shared it, and I know your wealth because I have given it to you." What a tremendous compliment to the church: rich in Christ.

5

Pergamos:
Satan's Throne
2:12-17

Pergamos was a city that was very distinctive. It was the capital city of the Roman Province of Asia, at least through the end of the first century. It was not a great commercial city. There were no vast trade routes, no huge harbors. It was not a city that was known for its commerce or trade.

It was a religious city. What distinguished Pergamos was that religion seemed to thrive there. There was an ancient saying that whenever any weird idea was expelled from one place, it would always end up in Pergamos.

Pergamos just seemed to thrive on religious ideas. It had many religious institutions and organizations, and was given over almost entirely to wealth and fashion. It was a very high class place.

The church we see here was one that lived and served in the shadow of Satan's headquarters. I wonder where his headquarters are today? He has always loved luxury, wealth, and worldliness. I have an idea that it is somewhere in the Western world, probably in the United States. In that day the Lord said that Satan set up headquarters in Pergamos.

Because Pergamos was an imperial city, the center of emperor worship, a city that understood authority and the chain of command, Jesus introduced himself as the one "which hath the sharp sword with two edges" (v. 12).

In ancient times, the highest symbol of authority was the sword. The sword represented the greatest authority that people knew. When one talked about the sword, one talked about absolute authority. The one who carried the sword, it was said in ancient times, had the right of life and death. He had absolute authority.

Jesus introduced himself to a city which was a political headquarters as the one with the sword. He is the one in charge, who has absolute authority.

Dedication

"I know thy works and where thou dwellest, even where Satan's seat is: and thou holdest fast my name, and hast not denied my faith" (v. 13). Notice the dedication of this church. Here was a church in the shadow of Satan's throne and Jesus noted their dedication.

Imagine the peril of being a member of a church close to Satan's headquarters. The headquarters of Satan is a strategic place where he can best use his influence. That has always been in the great centers of worldliness and greatness.

Jesus told them he realized they were located near Satan's throne, yet they were a faithful, working, dedicated church.

The world is forever the enemy of God. That which is material, that which is sensual, that which is built on lust is forever against the things of God. Behind every appeal of mammon lurks Satan. In that circumstance was this church. Jesus said, "I know your works; I know where you are located."

"Thou holdest fast my name" (v. 13). To hold fast the name of Jesus means they were loyal to the person of Jesus Christ. The name is the symbol of the person. Always in Scripture the name of God, of Christ, represents his character. This church confirmed Jesus Christ as Lord. They confirmed his honor, his glorious nature, his holy character, his redeeming power. They held fast the name of Jesus.

More than that, he said, "hast not denied my faith." Notice that he says "my" faith, not "your" faith. That means that they had not denied the purpose for which Jesus came. They acknowledged his accomplished purpose. They had complete confidence in his mission and atoning work.

Here was a church that had not denied the faith of Jesus Christ. They had not turned their backs on the gospel. His name marks the glory of his person. His faith marks the perfection of his purpose. This church held fast to his name and had not denied his faith.

Détente

> But I have a few things against thee, because thou hast there them that hold the doctrine of Balaam, who taught Balac to cast a stumblingblock before the children of Israel, to eat things sacrificed unto idols, and to commit fornication. So hast thou also them that hold the doctrine of the Nicolaitans, which thing I hate (vv. 14-15).

But there was a problem in Pergamos. It is a problem that exists today, perhaps more strongly than ever in history. Notice their détente. Détente means an easing of friction between two parties. It means compromising so as not to muddy the waters.

The church was faithful; it believed in Jesus Christ right in the shadow of Satan's headquarters. It was a strong church, an orthodox church. They had not denied his faith but they were tolerating false views.

They had a false sense of charity and had established a détente with evil. They tolerated what ought to be expelled. They had come to a compromise with error.

The church did not hold false doctrine. It was a proper,

orthodox, fundamental church. But it held fellowship with those who did. That was the thing which Jesus attacked.

What did they allow in their fellowship? First of all, they allowed the doctrine of Balaam. Balaam was called by a king to curse Israel (Num. 22—23). Every time he opened his mouth to curse Israel, he blessed Israel. It became frustrating for Balaam. He was offered money to curse Israel but he could not do it. He absolutely failed.

On his way home, he thought that really was not a bad deal. He could make some money on the side if he could prophesy like that. Though he could not curse Israel, he came back and counseled Israel to compromise the purposes of God, to inter-marry with the Moabites.

He did not try to change their theology or to curse the nation. He just encouraged them to compromise the purposes of God. He polluted the people socially and spiritually.

The end result is seen in verse 14, a "stumblingblock" before the children of Israel, and it resulted in eating things sacrificed to idols and committing of immorality. They taught that orthodoxy gives a license to sin. Believe the right things, and one can do anything one wants to do. We have conviction about the same of Jesus. If we are safe in that orthodox belief, we think our conduct does not matter.

That was the doctrine of Balaam. It was to compromise the things of God. It was to believe the right things but to deny them by the way in which they lived.

People were so conservative and so fundamental and so orthodox in their beliefs, yet they began to buy this philosophy characterized by the wisdom of the world. It was an attack on the standards of separation that God expected Israel to main-tain.

The doctrine of the Nicolaitans was very similar. No one really knows for certain what that doctrine was. Apparently it promoted sensual conduct, carnal and fleshy appetites, and a compromise of the purity, holiness, and standards which God had given.

Notice the problem: the church believed the right things, but they tolerated those who had the doctrines of Balaam and of the Nicolaitans. They tolerated false teaching. Here was their détente. God never intended for the church to tolerate error.

We have a similar situation today. Christian people across the nation are saying that we need more pluralism. Believe what you want, they say: it is a big world; there is a big God who has a big heart and room for all of us.

That is what they said in Pergamos. That was the complaint Jesus raised. "You have become so broad-minded, accepting everything that you really don't hold to anything. You have no depth, no sense of conviction, because you have tolerated those things which by their very nature destroy what you say you believe."

It is possible for us under the guise of being broad-minded to tolerate teachings that if put into practice would destroy what we believe. That does not make sense and is not acceptable to God.

Direction

"Repent; or else I will come unto thee quickly, and will fight against them with the sword of my mouth" (v. 16). Notice the direction he gave. "Repent." He was not talking to the people who held the doctrine of Balaam or of the Nicolaitans. He was speaking to the church. He was telling the church to repent. How could the church repent? They were not guilty of believing those things.

Exclude those people from fellowship, Jesus said. Do not give them false security. They were wrong; they were destroying what the church believed, so the church should remove them. That is the only thing they could do. Jesus said to the church, "Exercise discipline."

We tolerate people today under the guise of love. Jesus said that if we really love them, we will exclude them. And if we do not exclude them, he will come and fight against them.

Do we realize the danger of someone who fights against the things of God, the danger of someone in the fellowship of the church who stands for that which contradicts the doctrine and gospel of our Lord Jesus Christ?

Jesus said, "You as a church had better repent and act on this matter, or I will come and work against them. You judge them, or I will judge them. They are in a place of death, and I must act if you do not." Christ will come himself and will remove from the church that which the church refuses to remove.

Delight

He that hath an ear, let him hear what the Spirit saith unto the churches; To him that overcometh will I give to eat of the hidden manna and will give him a white stone, and in the stone a new name written, which no man knoweth saving he that receiveth it (v. 17).

The hidden manna typifies the spiritual food provided by God in his Word. He is talking about individual feeding, not a church function. Manna was divinely supplied but had to be humanly gathered. God gave it, but the people had to gather it.

That is a beautiful description of the Word of God. All the truth is gathered in this Book. For many people it is hidden manna. God has given it; we must gather it. God's Holy Spirit will apply it to our hearts.

There are many ideas about what the white stone means.

There is no question that the whiteness represents the purity and the holiness of God. So it represents that which is ours in God. The new name doubtless represents the name that a believer receives in Jesus Christ.

There were some beautiful uses of the white stone in ancient times. Sometimes a white stone was given to a man after a trial when he was acquitted. That stone symbolized that he was not guilty.

Sometimes, after battle, the victor on return from the battlefield would be given a white stone which represented victory. Sometimes a person who was finally granted citizenship would be given a white stone which signified his new status.

Sometimes, two friends would take a white stone and break it. Each would write his name on that stone. The stone would signify their friendship and would be passed down from generation to generation.

Perhaps years and years later, two of their descendants might meet for the first time and discover that each of them had half of a white stone that fit together. Immediately they would have the basis for a lasting friendship.

When we apply that to our Christian faith, what a beautiful thing a white stone is. The white stone after a trial of acquittal speaks of our justification, when through Jesus Christ we are judged righteous. The white stone of victory signifies the triumph of the child of God over all enemies.

The white stone of citizenship indicates our free entrance into the city of God. The white stone of unending friendship indicates our relationship with our Lord. When we obey him we get a white stone with a new name and hidden manna that God shall give. What a beautiful promise to the church!

But it must be very clearly understood that the church of Jesus Christ must not tolerate within her borders those who lower the standards of truth. It is not a question of holding the truth; the church at Pergamos did that. It is a question of the right application of the truth. Truth never excuses sin. Error will not be suppressed by compromising with it. It is always sinful to countenance evil among believers. It is not enough to be grieved or shocked by. The guilty one must repent and forsake his evil way.

If there is no repentance, the church must expel the error. The present tendency to minimize sin in our midst has reduced the spiritual tone of the church to a weakened and emaciated condition.

It should not be done legalistically but lovingly and firmly. The church that dwelt near Satan's throne was in greater danger from within than it was from without.

It is ever that way. The enemies of truth and of God in our day are largely within the church! The peril is inside. It is the weakness, the compromise, the détente with evil that is our direst danger today.

Jesus said, "Take your firm stand and I will give you hidden manna and a white stone with a new name written upon it."

6

Thyatira:
Jezebel's Jewel

2:18-29

Thyatira was the least important of all the seven cities yet it received the longest letter. It was not a great commercial city or a center of worship. There were temples there, but it was not a key center of worship.

It was built in a broad valley, originally as a garrison of soldiers to protect the city of Pergamos. When the enemy would come to attack the cities of Asia, Pergamos, being a fortified city, wanted to have some warning and thus set a garrison at the place that became Thyatira.

If the enemy came, they would fight them at Thyatira and send word back that the enemy was coming. The city was a diversion to protect citizens further up the valley.

For that reason, Thyatira was wiped out quite frequently and often had to be rebuilt. Its greatest significance was its trade unions. Lydia, the first convert in Macedonia, is said to have been a seller of purple from Thyatira (Acts 16).

There were many splendid products that were produced in or came through Thyatira. Historically, we know very little about the city, and its importance is not strategic.

A problem had begun to develop in the churches. We saw it when we looked at the church at Pergamos. The problem of toleration—allowing heresy to coexist with the truth in the church—had become a major problem, a problem of tremendous proportions in the church at Thyatira.

In the church, there was a woman whom John called Jezebel. No one wants to be called Jezebel. We all know what that connotation is. Jezebel was an exceedingly wicked woman in Old Testament times. She was a leader in corrupting the nation of Israel morally, socially, and spiritually (see 1 Kings 18:4).

Jesus, in writing this letter, was writing to a church who had within its fellowship, either as a member or at least as a great influence, a woman of tremendous significance. He addresses her as Jezebel.

She apparently claimed absolute authority. She claimed to have special insights into the deep things of God. She was perverting the truth as it was being taught in Thyatira.

It is interesting what Jesus says about himself in this letter. It is always interesting what we say about Jesus, but it is even more interesting what Jesus says about himself.

He says three things about himself as he introduces this letter to the church at Thyatira. "Write; These things saith the Son of God" (2:18). He has not yet called himself the Son of God in these letters.

He is writing to one who claims to have infallible and absolute authority. At the very outset he makes clear that she is not dealing with an apostle or a prophet, but the Son of God. He speaks as one with divine authority. He establishes his authority over this woman in the church.

"Who hath his eyes like unto a flame of fire, and his feet are like fine brass" (v. 18). There is nothing more penetrating, more consuming, than fire. Everything yields before it. Everything melts in its heat. It penetrates through and sweeps away obstructions. Jesus said, "My eyes are like that."

We need to be constantly reminded that the eyes of Jesus Christ pierce the masks we throw up. They search the inner recesses of our hearts; the hidden things of our souls. There is no escape from the eyes of the Lord. He is one who knows it all.

His brass feet speak of judgment. Brass is always representative of the strength and firmness of judgment. With our feet we stay on the move, so there is activity and action. He is speaking of firmness, strength of judgment in action. He has already described himself as the one who walks among the golden candlesticks, seeing, knowing, judging. His is an active judgment.

Sin must be judged. God cannot be silent in its face. If the guilty people of Thyatira or America or Russia or any place do not repent and come to Christ, they must face him in judgment. That is the picture he gives of himself.

Tenacity

"I know thy works, and charity, and service, and faith, and thy patience, and thy works; and the last to be more than the first" (v. 19).

Thyatira was a growing, going, and advancing church—a tenacious church. They stood by the faith. They kept on and did not get weary. They started out well and got better and better. There was a spiritual tenacity about this church that is most commendable.

This commendation is unprecedented. He complimented this church. He said, "You are a working church, and I know your works, and the last works are even better than the first." In verse 25 he says, "But that which ye have already hold fast till I come."

He told the church at Ephesus that they needed to go back and do what they used to do. He told the church at Thyatira to keep on doing what they were doing. "Hold fast, you have the truth. You are going in the right direction. Stay with it." This was a church that was busy and active serving God.

The words are very beautiful. He said, "I know your works

and your love." They were a loving church. At Ephesus, they were a busy and a working church, but they had lost their first love for the Lord. But this church was a loving church, full of loving service.

The word for service is *diakonian* from which we get our word *deacon*. Many people serve God with their teeth gritted and with an attitude of having to do it. Some people sing in the choir like that, some teach Sunday School like that, some preachers preach like that, some give of their possessions like that, some witness to the lost like that. But not at Thyatira! That word *service* meant loving, tender, compassionate service. They hurt when people hurt, and they cared about the needs of others. With rejoicing they ministered to the needs of those people. What a beautiful description!

Then he called them a church of faith. The Greek word for "faith" speaks of faithfulness, steadfastness, dependability, reliability. Here was a church he could count on. It was known that they were going to do the right thing. They were faithful, and from that faithfulness came a patience and fortitude. Under pressure they maintained tremendous balance and patience before God.

When he got through describing all that, he said again, "and thy works." They were not slipping backwards. They were not even standing still. They were a church that was steadily pressing onward in their faith.

Tolerance

Notwithstanding I have a few things against thee, because thou sufferest that woman Jezebel, which calleth herself a prophetess, to teach and to seduce my servants to commit fornication, and to eat things sacrificed unto idols. And I gave her space to repent of her fornication; and she repented not.

Behold, I will cast her into a bed, and them that commit

adultery with her into great tribulation, except they repent of
their deeds. And I will kill her children with death; and all the
churches shall know that I am he which searcheth the reins
and hearts: and I will give unto every one of you according
to your works (vv. 20-23).

The thing Jesus had against them was their tolerance.
Ephesus would not tolerate evil, but she had lost her love.
Thyatira was strong in love but tolerated evil. Those two
extremes still exist today. They have never left the church.

There is always the tendency to be orthodox, strong and
committed to truth while failing to love the Lord with all our
hearts, minds, and souls. Or we may love the Lord so
completely and fully that we do not stand for the truth.

Let's look at Jezebel's contribution to the world. She led her
husband, Ahab, away from God. But her real evil was bringing
into Israel the worship of Baal. She did not have a quarrel with
those who wanted to worship God. Her only quarrel with
Jehovah was with his "monopoly."

So she set up temples and altars to Baal side by side with
altars to Jehovah. Many of those who worshiped at the altar of
Jehovah in Israel also worshiped at the altar of Baal. Thus, she
compromised and polluted the people.

That was exactly what was happening in the church at
Thyatira. We have seen the commendation of Jesus to it. It had
a wonderful heart with a great spirit and a great vision for
reaching the world and ministering to those around it.

But it had begun to tolerate, and little by little to encourage,
condone, and endorse Jezebel who taught that one could
serve God and do things contrary to his purpose.

Thyatira was a great union city. Unlike unions in America,
these trade unions put pressure on their members not just to
organize as craftsmen but to come together in great feasts.

These feasts often included acts of idolatrous worship to
pagan gods. Then, after they had eaten and drunk, they would

end the evening with a wild, licentious, sexual orgy. It was all part of their union responsibilities.

The Christians in the first century refused to endorse any lord but Jesus. All that would be required of the Christians to keep the emperor happy and the pagans happy was to be willing to bow down and say, "Caesar is Lord." They could not do it. Jesus Christ had died for them. They had no lord but him. The early church refused even token acknowledgment of false deity.

Yet in Thyatira, Jezebel came along and encouraged them to endanger the very thing they claimed to worship. The church there tolerated her teaching. She encouraged them to worship God but also to link themselves to that which was against God.

We are living in a very tolerant age. Everybody has a right to say what they want and believe what they want to believe. We want to be very tolerant in America today.

Dawson McAllister said, "It is fashionable today to be searching for the truth, but when you find it, you are a bigot." In this pluralistic society, there is no such thing as narrowness; we are going to be broad. We are going to embrace everybody.

But toleration can be sin. There is an exclusiveness that must belong to the church. Somewhere God's people have to take a stand for God, and we have to say, "We will not comply with anything that is opposed to Jesus Christ. He is our rule and authority. We measure our lives by Jesus and his word for us and will not compromise that stand."

In Thyatira they probably reasoned that there was an element of truth in what Jezebel said. All heresy has to have truth in it. It is a measure of truth that holds it together. Everybody would reject heresy if it were completely false.

The most dangerous heresy is the heresy that sounds the most like the truth. Jesus condemned this church, and his strongest language is reserved for these people. For here was Jezebel firmly established with the approval of the congregation.

It is not unchristian to oppose heresy. We are told today that if we say something is untrue we are being unkind, unchristian, and that Christianity is never unkind.

Jesus said, "Behold, I will cast her into a bed, and them that commit adultery with her into great tribulation, except they repent of their deeds. And I will kill her children with death" (vv. 22-23). The Lord is outraged at this. Such toleration is unchristian.

Today the voice of the prophet is silenced. No one wants to hear the prophet. It is bad for business. And the church has become a thermometer instead of a thermostat. God intended for the church to control the temperature of the society around it.

We were never intended to be thermometers simply reflecting the atmosphere about us. We were intended to create atmosphere, and the great tragedy today is that the church is so much like the world. We are not different. There is seldom anything distinctive about the church.

Jezebel refused to repent and Jesus condemned her and those that committed adultery with her to great tribulation. He is not talking here just about physical immorality.

This is a reference to the spiritual adultery of those who will not stay true to God. He is saying, "Those who participate in this doctrine, I am going to see they suffer greatly because of it."

"But," one says, "God has not done anything." Do not misinterpret God's silence, his patience. Whenever God's judgment is delayed, it is always to give us an opportunity to repent.

If God were not trying to get America to repent, he would have destroyed us before now. His delay in judgment is always for the purpose of drawing us to him. God is outraged, and yet he still talks of repentance.

"I will kill her children with death" (v. 23). This refers to the second death, eternal death. Regardless of what church one belongs to, if he does not know Jesus Christ he will participate in the second death.

All of the unbelievers of all of the religious affiliations, regardless of whether they be churches or that which is against the church, will be cast into the lake of fire (Rev. 20:15).

Salvation in the Scripture is always according to faith, but judgment is always according to works. We get into heaven by grace through faith, not because of our works. But when judgment comes it will be according to works. And God who knows perfectly, who sees everything, will judge perfectly.

Triumph

But unto you I say, and unto the rest in Thyatira, as many as have not this doctrine, and which have not known the depths of Satan, as they speak; I will put upon you none other burden. But that which ye have already hold fast till I come. And he that overcometh, and keepeth my works unto the end, to him will I give power over the nations: And he shall rule them with a rod of iron; as the vessels of a potter shall they be broken to shivers: even as I received of my Father. And I will give him the morning star. He that hath an ear, let him hear what the Spirit saith unto the churches (vv. 24-29).

To paraphrase, Jesus said, "The problem is too severe for any of you to handle so I will not ask you to step in and do something about it. You just stay faithful. Stay away from the heresy. Don't link your life with it. Don't participate in it. Just keep yourself pure from it."

He mentioned the depths of Satan (v. 24). That could mean many things, but it probably means all the strategies of Satan, all the tricks of Satan to keep us away from God.

Some have suggested that it refers to the heresy that nothing one does with his body can destroy his relationship with God in his heart; so it is all right to be immoral, licentious, and to be compromising physically. That is because the strength of one's faith will be shown by the fact that nothing one does can destroy his relationship with God. That is a very subtle form of heresy.

The depths of Satan may refer to the great strategies of Satan not discouraging our participation in religion. Satan is very religious. He goes to church as much as anybody. And he does not care if we join the church, profess Christ, and do good works as long as we will allow into our lives that which neutralizes our faith. That is the great depth of Satan.

He encourages us to take our stand in the church, believe the right things, be fundamental, be orthodox, but also to compromise. We will build into our lives those things that will neutralize our faith.

"But that which ye have already hold fast till I come" (v. 25). There are a lot of things we can do to stand for God in our society. But we need to hear Jesus say, "Whatever else you do, hold fast till I come. Stay true to me. Do not compromise. Do not be less than you ought to be."

Then he makes a beautiful promise. "He that overcometh, and keepeth my works unto the end, to him will I give power over the nations: And he shall rule them with a rod of iron; as the vessels of a potter shall they be broken to shivers: even as I received of my Father" (v. 26-27).

He speaks here of prominence and power in the millennial kingdom. He has already talked about that in the first chapter of Revelation: "hath made us kings and priests" (v. 6). He has already promised power, but look at the promise of verse 28: "I will give him the morning star."

What is the morning star? He tells us in the twenty-second chapter: "I, Jesus have sent mine angel to testify unto you these things in the churches. I am the root and the offspring of David, and the bright and morning star" (22:16). Jesus said, "I am going to give you myself."

If we possess Jesus, we possess everything. We possess everything we need, everything we want, everything we long to have in Jesus. Jesus is the only way to true greatness and true power. Everything men strive for is found in Jesus Christ.

He wrote to a church in Thyatira that was loving and standing firm in its faith, but they were tolerating that which would destroy it. And he said to them, "Hold fast until I come, stay true, obedient, and strong and I will give you the morning star."

7

Sardis: A Corpse and Didn't Know It

3:1-6

S ardis was one of the great cities of antiquity, the capital city of a great empire. The Greeks referred to it as the greatest of all cities. It was a city of great strength with a wonderful reputation as an unconquerable fortress.

However, it was a city of the past. It was a city that lived on its reputation. Sardis simply lived on its ancient prestige rather than its present attainment.

It was a city of failure, still known as a city of strength. It was conquered twice in its history, primarily through carelessness. Sardis had three walls that were virtually perpendicular, which dropped from the side of the city. Only one avenue gave a smooth approach to the city and it was easily defended.

There was no way that anyone could conquer the city by scaling the walls unless the guards and the watchmen did not do their jobs. Twice in history, Sardis was conquered by an enemy due to lack of vigilance by those who were supposed to guard the city.

Sardis spoke of unfulfilled promises. It lived one life on its reputation, but another life in reality. It was a city that spoke of life but really lived in death.

Jesus introduced himself as the one who holds the seven Spirits of God and the seven stars. That is a reference to the omniscience of Jesus Christ. The seven Spirits of God refer to the fullness—completeness—of the power of God through his Holy Spirit. Seven is the divine number for completeness, for fullness.

Jesus is saying, "I am the one who has all fullness within me. I am the one in whom resides the power and the presence of the Holy Spirit. I am the one who has the sevenfold spirit of God."

The stars—the messengers, the angels of the church—are held in the hand of the Savior. That is a tremendous comfort to pastors as we realize the responsibilities assigned to the pastors of churches.

The church at Sardis holds a tremendous warning for us today. Sometimes a Bible passage may not seem to relate to us in late twentieth-century America. But we can identify with the message Jesus gave this church.

This message has no good word. In all of the others, Jesus complimented the church. He told them what was good about their church, and then followed the commendation, generally, with a condemnation. Here there is no commendation. Some have said there is a short one when he said, "I know thy works;" but if we read the complete sentence, we find he says that their works do not amount to anything. Instead, the letter begins with a condemnation.

Reputation

> And unto the angel of the church in Sardis write; These things saith he that hath the seven Spirits of God, and the seven stars; I know thy works, that thou hast a name that thou livest, and art dead (v. 1).

Notice the reputation of the church. This is important. We live in a day of "super churches." There are thousands of churches, but here and there are churches who by reputation rise to the top; who by reputation are spoken of in the media;

and who by reputation are spoken of in Christian circles.

"I know thy works, that thou hast a name that thou livest" (v. 1). In previous letters, "I know your works" had been a comforting phrase. When he spoke to the churches, they were comforted by the fact that the Savior knew all about their working and striving for him. Here it is no comfort. It is, indeed, the trumpet blast of terror.

He has been tender up until this point, but here he says with a condemning judgment, "I know your works." They had a reputation of being a going and growing church. If we had a list of the ten fastest-growing churches in Asia Minor, they doubtless would have been at the top of the list.

They did everything right. They were a standard, busy church. They appeared to be flourishing. They were a progressive church. From outward appearance, there was nothing that seemed to be lacking. It was a beehive of activity. The machinery of organization was well oiled.

Reality

"I know thy works, that thou hast a name that thou livest, and art dead" (v. 1). Man's evaluation is not always the same as God's. The church needs to consider what Jesus says about it rather than what men say. We are too prone to be concerned about what we think of each other rather than what the Lord thinks about us.

Notice the reality concerning the church at Sardis. When the Great Physician pronounced death, we can be sure it was dead. It was not the opinion of a neighbor, not the opinion of someone in Pergamos or Philadelphia.

The Lord of the church said, "Your reputation says life, I say death. You are dead." What appeared to flourish was actually dead. Have you ever seen a tree with the heart decayed and eaten out? Even though that hole is there, and there is an emptiness inside that tree, there are many green leaves.

A tree will fool you sometimes. It may appear to flourish long after its heart is gone. A church can be like that. The church at Sardis was. It gave every evidence of growing and moving forward. But Jesus made a startling and terrible statement: "You are dead." Here was a church that was dead and did not know it. The Lord Jesus Christ looked at the heart, the inward recesses, and sought life there. He looked to see what was on the inside.

Jesus is not so concerned about the pretenses we make, the activities we engage in, the promises we make or even the apparent performance of those promises; rather he looks at the heart.

Remember the pathetic picture of Samson in Judges 16:20. After his hair had been cut and his strength had left him, Delilah wakened him and said the Philistines were coming. He went to fight them with great confidence. He had always been champion over the Philistines.

But sadly, he did not know that his strength had left him. He had always fought the Philistines in the Spirit of God but now he fought them in his physical strength and was conquered and captured.

So it is with the church. What a tragedy for a church to be dead, and not even know it.

What are the signs of life in a church? There are many. One is growth. I am not speaking of just numerical growth. There are many kinds of growth that do not mean increased numbers.

There will be growth within the life of the church family. Those who are living and serving through the church will be growing in their faith. They will be maturing in their witness, they will be sharing the Lord more effectively and giving themselves more completely to him. The law of life is the very opposite of stagnation. It means growth. A living church is a growing church.

A living church will have compassion, love for each other, and love for the lost. It will have unity. Division and schism is a sign of decay and death.

When a physical body starts to die, normally the various organs of the body cease to function together. One organ will stop functioning, stop cooperating, stop filling its place in the body. The body dies through the disintegration of the unity of that body.

A living church, in which the Spirit of God lives and moves, is a church united on the things of God and on the mission and purpose of the church.

Another evidence of life is emotion. There is nothing wrong with it. Don't be afraid to feel your faith. I weep, I sing, I laugh, I mourn. That is a sign of life.

Only the dead have no tears, no laughter, no music, no sorrow. That is all a part of living. There is emotion in life.

What are the signs of a dead church? Everything goes back to the past. When a church lives in the past, its reputation and its history, that church is dead. When a church is more concerned for form than life, for ritual than heart, it is dead.

When we are more concerned about church activities than that God be glorified through those activities, our church is dead. When a church loves systems more than Jesus and more than it loves people, it is dead. When it is more material than spiritual, it is dead. A church is either growing, or dying.

To the church at Sardis, Jesus said, "You have a reputation that you live, but you are dead." The same thing can happen to an individual. When we talk about the attitude of a church or the direction of a church, we are talking about the composite total of the attitudes of the people in it.

If a church is dead, its people are dead because *we are the church. We* are the instruments God uses.

Everyone of us needs to examine our hearts in light of the message that Jesus gave. He goes into more detail in verse 2:

"I have not found thy works perfect before God."

That means he looks at the works and life of the church. He scans, scrutinizes, and searches the life of the church. He knows everything we do, collectively and individually.

And Jesus said about the Sardis church, "It is a church that does not have works that are perfected before God." Perfect means "complete" or "to fulfill the purpose for which it was created." He was saying that their works never fulfilled the purpose that God intended.

What a sad thing for a church! When we sing, when we pray, and when we worship together it is in order for us to commune with God, to praise and glorify God. How sad if we just go through the motions and never realize the purpose of that worship, never really glorify or praise God. Our works are incomplete.

Many people feel if they just show up on Sunday, they have paid their dues to God. Those works are not perfected before God. We must do more than simply give lip service to the things of God. Somewhere, somehow, there has to come an understanding that to be a Christian is going to require everything we are and have, that everything in our beings belong to him.

Being a Christian is a way of doing everything in life. When I commit my life to Christ it is a total commitment, not a token commitment. Then, it will not be said that our works are not perfected before God.

Here was a church that went through the motions, did all the right things, had a great reputation. The Great Physician said, "You are dead."

Remedy

Be watchful, and strengthen the things which remain, that are ready to die: for I have not found thy works perfect before God. Remember therefore how thou hast received

and heard, and hold fast, and repent. If therefore thou shalt
not watch, I will come on thee as a thief, and thou shalt not
know what hour I will come upon thee (vv. 2-3).

What is the remedy for the church? "Be watchful" (v. 2).
Sardis fell twice through carelessness. As the enemies conquered the city, they climbed up that perpendicular wall
through a weakness in their defense system.

Even a child could have guarded against that onslaught. It
required no strength, but diligence and vigilance. Carelessness
doomed the city and carelessness has doomed many a church.

The things of eternal value God has given to us must not be
taken for granted. We never drift anywhere worth going. We
always drift *away* from God into sin and rebellion. We never
drift *into* obedience and Christlikeness. It requires care and
diligence for us to be what God wants us to be. God cannot
use the careless, the casual. Be watchful! Wake up! Be more
alert!

"Strengthen the things which remain" (v. 2). What remains?
The only thing that remains is the ritual: praying, preaching,
teaching, witnessing. In other words, do not abandon those
things. Strengthen those things.

How do we strengthen them? One translation says, "establish them" (ASV). We put meaning into them. Just because
some pray without any commitment to God, does not mean
that we should abandon prayer. But we put meaning into the
prayer; we put life into those forms.

We do not abandon the forms; we breathe life into them.
We do not cease worship and ritual, but we make them expressions of love for Christ and for God. Those are the things
"ready to die" (v. 2).

Ceremony, ritual, and form without the heart that God
intended for them will die, and the people will die within them.
Put life into them. God will bless it.

"For I have not found thy works perfect before God" (v. 2).
Do we dare look into the face of God and ask if our works are
perfect before him, or do we just have a name without the
reality, a reputation with no heart to live for him? Is our
worship perfect before him? Do we dare bring our hearts, our
service, our minds before him? Are they fulfilled perfectly
before him?

It is always just one small step from formalism to rationalism.

If external things lack internal force, they will decay and
crumble. If what we do in the name of God does not come
from a heart in love with God, it will decay and crumble. Are
our works fulfilled before God?

"Remember therefore how thou hast received and heard"
(v. 3). They had received forgiveness. They once had lived in
darkness; now they were in the glorious light of eternity. They
once had lived in heresy and falsehood and now they knew the
truth.

"Remember," Jesus said. Every church was born in revival.
In some special moving of the Holy Spirit, every church was
born. That is how churches begin.

It is only when the first movings of God in our lives are
forgotten that the church becomes institutionalized; the movement becomes a monument and loses its heart.

The Sardians had forgotten why they were a church, their
heavenly calling and holy character. So Jesus said, "Remember . . . hold fast, and repent. If therefore thou shalt not watch, I
will come on thee as a thief, and thou shalt not know what
hour I will come upon thee" (v. 3). That is a stern warning.

He was speaking to an apostate church—where within the
membership there were many people who were not saved.
They had the outward evidence and expression; and everyone, by observing, would think them fine, religious persons,
but inwardly they were dead.

The second coming is a time of joy, of rejoiceful anticipation.

But not for the lost. To those who have the name and not the reality, Jesus says, "Beware. If you don't repent and turn and watch, I will come as a thief upon you." It is a tremendous reminder to us to live and move in the presence, spirit, and power of God.

Remnant

Thou hast a few names even in Sardis which have not defiled their garments; and they shall walk with me in white: for they are worthy. He that overcometh, the same shall be clothed in white raiment; and I will not blot out his name out of the book of life, but I will confess his name before my Father, and before his angels. He that hath an ear, let him hear what the Spirit saith unto the churches (vv. 4-6).

There was a bright spot, even in Sardis, even among the ungodly and disinterested. A remnant of righteous persons remained faithful, and Jesus was pleased. Though the church was dead, and no remedy was offered it, Jesus had a few he could be proud of. We can be faithful among the faithless, sincere among the hypocrites, and humble among the proud. We can be separated from the worldly. Even if we live or work in an ungodly place where it is difficult to be a Christian, God can keep us even there.

Even in Sardis, God had kept a few. He will stand by us. He can be the strength we need to stand for him. He can be the courage we need to be his instrument in that place. He, who kept a few in Sardis, will keep us.

"But," we say, "there are so few of us." It has always been that way. Jesus said, "Broad is the way, that leadeth to destruction, and many there be which go in thereat: Because strait is the gate, and narrow is the way, which leadeth unto life, and few there be that find it" (Matt. 7:13-14).

There will never be a time when the majority of people in this world will turn to God. It is possible to capture a city, a town, an area for Jesus. In this part of the world it may be possible for Jesus to be the predominant force in our society, but in the world at large, there will always be only a few, a minority—the Master's majority.

But God plus one is a majority anywhere. God plus one carries the battle for the battle is not ours but the Lord's. Our call is to stand in the truth, and in obedience to Jesus where we are.

Jesus said he would give us a white robe and not blot out our names from the book of life. Some people worry about that. They think it is a hidden or veiled threat of a loss of salvation.

The book of life is the book in which all the names of all the people who have ever lived are written. Those who enter the second death at the great white throne judgment will have their names removed from the book of life. But from the Lamb's book of life there will be no such removal.

This is a message of security. Those who overcome (who believe in Jesus) have the promise of their names remaining in the book of life. By trusting him, we overcome. It is synonymous with being born again. It is the promise of his provision for our lives.

"I will confess his name before my Father, and before his angels" (v. 5). That is one of the most beautiful expressions we could imagine. When we stand in heaven Jesus will take us by the hand, usher us past the pillars of the gate, past the angels and heavenly messengers, past the waiting throngs, and take us to the very throne of God.

There he will confess us before the Father; that our names are synonymous with his. What a wonderful promise God makes to us!

God promises that no experience, sadness, sorrow, despair, or discouragement is a match for his grace. Every situation becomes a victory in him. Our mission is to be obedient, to stay true to him.

8

Philadelphia:
Church of the Open Door
3:7-13

The church at Philadelphia was a very special church. It was one of the two churches in the seven for which there was no condemnation, no criticism. Jesus affixed no blame to the church; it was very, very precious.

In fact, unashamedly, Jesus said that the day will come when all will know that "I have loved thee" (v. 9). That is a tender expression. This was a favorite church of our Lord. Jesus loved this church, and he spoke tenderly of his love for it. What a beautiful love!

He came to the church, first of all, to establish who he is. In the introduction, he described himself in four ways. When we see these four ways, we see a new dimension to the Son of God.

A church under pressure, in trial and tribulation, buffeted by temptation, is going to know when the divine Son of God speaks.

He described himself, first of all, as "he that is holy" (v. 7). Holiness is an essential characteristic of Christ. It tells us what he is: a holy, complete, righteous Being. Because he is holy, he tells us what he does; "he that is true" speaks of the rightness in his conduct.

That is not surprising because being comes before doing. Jesus is holy, so because of that he will do what is right. He described himself as one who in his essential nature is holy, and in his regular conduct he is true.

"He . . . hath the key of David" (v. 7). That is a beautiful expression. There have been those who have tried to tie this to the keys to the Kingdom that Jesus spoke about in Matthew 16, but I do not believe that is what he is referring to here.

He is simply saying that he is the rightful heir to the throne of David. The one who has David's key has rightful access to the throne. It is his by legal right, by inheritance, by lineage. He is the sole heir to the throne of David.

Then he speaks of his omnipotence. "He . . . openeth, and no man shutteth; and shutteth, and no man openeth" (v. 7). That simply means, in plain language, that we had better listen to God. When he opens the door, we cannot shut it; and when he shuts it, we cannot open it.

Can we not see why it is so important to get on God's time schedule? When God opens a door for us, we had better go through it. It is vital to respond as God gives opportunity.

This was a church in revival; it was an unusual church that had stood the test, had been tried and found true. The Philadelphia church had an evangelistic revival for it had a vision of reaching the world for Christ.

It had an ecclesiastical revival, for it had tested all the heresies, looked at all the doctrines; found those that were right, and rejected those that were wrong.

It had an eschatological revival because its watchword was the blessed return of our Lord. It was a church that Jesus loved and addressed in terms of his special love and concern for them.

Door

I know thy works: behold, I have set before thee an open door, and no man can shut it: for thou hast a little strength, and hast kept my word, and hast not denied my name (v. 8).

There are some most interesting terms in this verse. "I have set before thee an open door" is a strong expression. It does not just mean that he has opened the door. Literally, he is saying, "I have given you a door which I myself have opened for you. It is a door that is my gift to you, a privilege for you."

This opportunity of the open door was a special gift and privilege bestowed on the church. What is the door? Some have suggested that Jesus himself is the door. It means that and much more.

"For a great door and effectual is opened unto me, and there are many adversaries" (1 Cor. 16:9). "When I came to Troas to preach Christ's gospel and a door was opened unto me of the Lord" (2 Cor. 2:12). "Withal praying also for us, that God would open unto us a door of utterance, to speak the mystery of Christ" (Col. 4:3).

If we will check carefully the reference to the "door" and the "open door" in the New Testament, we will discover that the open door that Jesus spoke of to the church at Philadelphia was the right to preach the gospel, the right to evangelize the world.

Many people believe that these seven churches in Revelation represent seven great dispensations in history. There is a great deal of truth in that. The Philadelphian church represents the present age. It is the age we call the age of grace, the age of the open door, the age when we can preach the gospel, and the last age of the church.

The last age in the history of the church will be the Laodicean age—an age of indifference and unconcern where doors are shut, and opportunity is abandoned. But now, Jesus said, the door is open.

The perfect tense in the Greek language indicates the door is opened and remains opened. It is still open. It is open until God shuts it. The doors of opportunity to preach the gospel are controlled by Jesus Christ, and when he opens a door for us, we must go through it.

The days are fast coming when the open door will be closed. We are in the last hours of the age of the open door. We are in an age where we can preach the gospel, but doors are closing around the world. The age of the open door is coming to an end.

Jesus said to this church, "I, myself, have set before you the open door." There are many doors open to us today, but many of us are blinded by greed, selfishness, love for comfort and pleasure, and we often fail even to see the doors that are open.

How much we need to see the opportunities of the day in which we live! There is no way we can give too much money to the cause of Christ. There is no way we can devote too many hours to the ministry and the service of the gospel. There is no way we can tell the story of Christ too much. There is no way we can do too much for Christ. The door is open. God save us from the enemies that would keep us from seeing the opportunities before us.

"Thou hast a little strength" (v. 8). That seems like strange reasoning. The door is open because you are weak; you do not have much strength. The members of the church at Philadelphia did not have much wealth. In fact, they probably did not have any wealth, and there were not very many of them. They were a minority, just like the Christians at Sardis.

So Jesus praised them not for their strength but for their weakness. He praised them because they have just a little strength. He did not praise them because they were strong and energetic and able to do great things in the community. He praised them because they were weak; they knew it and were faithful to the opportunity they had.

That is the test of a church. It is not how strong we are and how we use our strength but how weak we are and how we bring our weakness to God. The apostle Paul said, "Therefore I take pleasure in infirmities, in reproaches, in necessities, in persecutions, in distresses for Christ's sake: for when I am weak, then am I strong" (2 Cor. 12:10).

It is in the weakness of the church in Philadelphia that Jesus Christ, the Savior, was glorified and magnified. It was in the weakness of that church that Jesus was able to move in power through it. Because the Philadelphian Christians recognized their weakness and went through the door that was opened, he was able to use them.

There is great similarity between the church at Smyrna and the church at Philadelphia. Both of them received no criticism from the Savior, no blame, no condemnation. Both of them were weak and had no outside reputation, no great well-known members of the church.

Both were under tremendous pressure and persecution. They were both under great opposition from the Jews. They had a little strength, and he praised both of these churches. The last things we ever ought to boast about are our wealth and our numbers.

The things we ought to boast about are our holiness, the vigor of our spiritual life, and our hunger for God. And these must be "boasted about" with great humility of heart. These are the things we must cling to.

The church in Philadelphia was a weak, small church, but it had a big faith, and it had a faithful commitment to the things of God. They were faithful to the things God had called them to do.

"Thou . . . hast kept my word" (v. 8). The church that is to please God needs to be a church that will be loyal to the Scriptures, the Word of God. Satan corrupts the Word of God. Critics subtract from it and others add to it.

Liberal-minded people supplant the Word of God with their own ideas. Many people neglect it, and the world rejects it. But the true Christian ought to love the Word of God, obey it, study it, and live by it. The church at Philadelphia was true to the Word.

"Thou . . . hast not denied my name" (v. 8). That is not surprising. When we keep the Word of God, we will not deny his name. But if we deny the Word and do not keep it, we will deny his name. That is the end result of skepticism. Here we see loyalty to Christ and to the Scriptures, the Word of God.

Deliverance

> Behold, I will make them of the synagogue of Satan, which say they are Jews, and are not, but do lie; behold, I will make them to come and worship before thy feet, and to know that I have loved thee.
>
> Because thou hast kept the word of my patience, I also will keep thee from the hour of temptation, which shall come upon all the world, to try them that dwell upon the earth (vv. 9-10).

Apparently, the church at Philadelphia and the church at Smyrna both were under heavy attack from the Jewish community. Jesus said they were people who claimed to be Jews, but they were not even good Jews. Jesus was making no assault upon the Jewish community. He just said they were not Jews.

They assaulted the character of the Christians, lied about them. Many times the property of early Christians was seized. They lost their jobs; were robbed of everything most of us say it takes to make us happy.

Their names were condemned. Lies and slander were spread about them that destroyed their reputations.

Jesus said, "I am going to make those who are the synagogue of Satan, those who say they are Jews but are not, to come and worship before your feet and to know that I have loved you." God will vindicate his people without fail! "Vengeance is mine, I will repay, saith the Lord" (Rom. 12:19).

It may be a long time coming and it may not be on our time schedule. It may not even be in our lifetimes, but the time will come when God will vindicate his own. He who has "made us kings and priests unto God and his Father" (Rev. 1:6) will come and rule and we will be vindicated.

"I also will keep thee from the hour of temptation" (v. 10). This hour of temptation is that sequence of cataclysmic events preceding the establishment of the millennial kingdom of Christ upon this earth.

"Which shall come upon all the world, to try them that dwell upon the earth" (v. 10). There has not been a testing, a time of tribulation, that has encompassed all the world. It has not happened yet historically.

So this refers to the great tribulation spoken of in the Book of Revelation. The church is going to be saved out of that tribulation. The church will be raptured out of this earth before the tribulation time.

We cannot prove it by this verse because the verse can be interpreted two ways. Some people interpret keep you "from the hour of temptation" to mean that he will keep us by taking us out of it. It could be interpreted like that. Others say it means that he will keep us "through" the time of temptation.

This is a strong possibility because in John 17:15, Jesus prayed concerning the saints, "I pray not that thou shouldest take them out of the world, but that thou shouldest keep them from the evil one."

This viewpoint holds that whatever tribulation comes, Jesus will walk through it with us, sustain us, and keep Satan from being unleashed upon us and will see that we are provided for in that time.

Whichever way we choose to interpret it, it is a beautiful promise of the provision that Christ has made for us. There will never come a time when Jesus will abandon or forsake us. He will keep us and deliver us out of that time of trial.

Descent

Behold, I come quickly: hold that fast which thou hast,
that no man take thy crown. Him that overcometh will I
make a pillar in the temple of my God, and he shall go no
more out: and I will write upon him the name of my God,
and the name of the city of my God, which is new Jerusalem, which cometh down out of heaven from my God:
and I will write upon him my new name. He that hath an ear,
let him hear what the Spirit saith unto the churches
(vv. 11-13).

Now he is speaking to the church to remind these saints of
the wonderful promise of his return, his descent back from
heaven. The church that is going to be moving on for God is
the one that is looking for the return of the Lord.

We do not know when he is coming back, but it could be
anytime. It could be in this generation. It could be tomorrow
. . . or today. The church must always live in a sense of the
soon-to-be returning Lord.

This crown is not our salvation. It does not mean that
someone can take our salvation away. Our crown is our reward
and we get that reward by our works. We are saved by faith but
we are rewarded by works. The service that is rendered
through us will accrue for us rewards that we will bring and
present to the Savior.

They are for him, not for us. Every Christian has the
opportunity through his faithful, diligent service for God to
gain crowns. Our Lord declared, "Don't let anybody steal your
crown." There are so many enemies who are trying to rob us of
our crowns. There are so many things that would steal the
crowns God wants to give us: cold hearts, worldliness, prayer-
lessness, discouragement, heresy, friends, sometimes even our
families.

Success or failure will seek to take our crowns. There are
always enemies striving to defeat us in our personal commit-

ments to Christ, to keep us from our crowns.

Jesus said, "Hold fast what you have, and do not let anybody take your crown." That is good counsel for us. Hold fast to your profession of faith, your trust in Christ, your relationship to him. Hold it fast so that no one or thing will take your crown.

When Jesus comes, this is what he is going to do: "Him that overcometh will I make a pillar in the temple of my God, and he shall go no more out" (v. 12). There will be a stability, an intimacy, a fellowship, a security in our relationship with him.

"And I will write upon him the name of my God, . . . and I will write upon him my new name" (v. 12). Later in this blessed book John wrote, "And there shall be no more curse: but the throne of God and of the Lamb shall be in it; and his servants shall serve him; And they shall see his face; and his name shall be in their foreheads" (Rev. 22:3-4).

When he comes, we shall receive the name of Christ. That name entitles us to entrance into the city of God. It entitles us to service and worship of our eternal God. It is our stamp of citizenship, our security of eternity—in the name of Jesus Christ.

The church at Philadelphia was not praised for its wealth or numbers but for its faithfulness to the purposes of God. That was the strength of the church.

9
Laodicea:
Apathy and Lethargy
3:14-22

The letter to the Laodiceans is the last of the letters of our Lord to the churches in Asia Minor. They were seven actual churches in seven literal cities. Historically, they coexisted at the same period of time.

In a sense, that which is said in each letter applies to all churches in all times. Certainly we have been able to see how portions of each letter have specific application to us.

There is also a sense in which these letters represent great stages in the history of the church, the history of the world, and the drama of redemption. As we move toward that inevitable time of the return of our Lord, these seven letters represent seven great ages or dispensations.

When we come to the churches at Philadelphia and Laodicea, we are in the end times. The church in Philadelphia is the church of the open door, a true, genuine church on fire for God and seizing the opportunities God gives it.

But in the same period, as we come toward the end of that Philadelphian age, there is the spirit of Laodicea, the spirit of indifference, apathy, and unconcern. When we look at this passage, we doubtless will see much we already know to be true about ourselves and the contemporary world.

Reading this letter is like looking into a mirror and seeing our own face—our own time. Already we have moved into the spirit of the Laodicean age. The word *Laodicea* means "the rule of the people" or "the rights of the people." It speaks of a time when the church will become enamored with its own strength, its own power, the rights of the people, and the democratizing of the church. It is a time when the authority of God and the authority of the Word of God are ignored and the rights of the individual are magnified. The church establishes itself as its own guideline. We are seeing much of that happen today.

Jesus has nothing good to say about this church. Do not look for a commendation; it is not there. Even when he speaks of those whom he loves, the word *love* is not *agape*; it is *fileo*. *Agape* is that godly, self-giving kind of love.

This church had been so rebellious against God that his rebuke and his message are given out of a love that means an affection with a less than intense love than *agape* would speak of.

In speaking to the church, he first identified himself as "the Amen." Amen is the last word one can say. When everything else has been said, the only thing left to say is Amen. It is a word of finality, certainty, and authority. Jesus establishes God's promises. He is the final word, the absolute truth from God.

Then Jesus called himself the "faithful and true witness" (v. 14). That means that he keeps his word. He means what he says. He promises to save, and he does. He promises to walk with us through life, through all the valleys and mountains, and he does. He keeps his word.

He is the "beginning of the creation of God." That means he is the King of creation. Everything in creation indelibly bears his mark upon it. His is the beginning of all creation.

Indifference

I know thy works, that thou art neither cold nor hot: I would thou wert cold or hot. So then because thou art luke-

warm, and neither cold nor hot, I will spue thee out of my
mouth (vv. 15-16).

Lukewarm is the worst possible condition anyone could be
in. It is the condition of apathy or indifference. In examining it
more closely, we find that lukewarm means "without enthusiasm." It means criticism without compassion.

That is typical of the indifferent. They are more concerned
for their own comfort and ideas. From such persons criticism
flows freely without compassion. It describes one who is without conviction of sin.

They can hear sermon after sermon and attend worship
service after worship service, and there is no sense of sin—no
conviction of their need of God in their hearts. They were self-
centered, self-occupied, self-satisfied, self-sufficient, and self-
confident. They were proud and boastful.

They had no zeal for the Word of God, but they would not
repudiate it. In a word, they completely compromised the
things of God.

I think there is probably more hope for the atheist than there
is for the spoiled, halfhearted, conceited, self-deceived reli-
gionist. These people were largely lost people to whom Jesus
was speaking. They were people who gave lip service to the
things of God but had no heart in their worship. They were
lukewarm.

The people in Laodicea would understand this very clearly.
There were mineral springs in Laodicea where people would
come to bathe for health purposes. Those springs had the taste
of mineral content and they were not hot or cold; but if one
tried to drink the water, it was nauseating.

That is how Jesus described these people. They were
nauseating to God. A lukewarm Christian is a contradiction of
terms. It is like saying dry water, cold heat, clean dirt. It just
does not make sense.

They did not deny the gospel; they were just indifferent to it.
They knew that sinners were lost; they just made no attempt to
win them to Christ.

Isn't that like us today? What makes us think we have a right
to know the gospel and not share it? The Christians at Laodicea did not deny the gospel; they just had no enthusiasm for
it, no interest in spiritual things. They were indifferent and
apathetic. Church and religion was just so much formality to
them. Although they gave mental assent to the truth, they put
none of it into their lives.

"I will spue you out of my mouth" (v. 16) clearly tells us that
Jesus cannot stand that condition. It is an intolerable condition.
He is not talking about revoking an individual's relationship to
Christ. He means he will take the candlestick away from the
church, remove the opportunity for the church to be a light-
bearer.

How sad for any church to be in that position!

Independence

> Because thou sayest, I am rich, and increased with goods,
> and have need of nothing; and knowest not that thou art
> wretched, and miserable, and poor, and blind, and naked
> (v. 17).

This church was independent and arrogant. Laodicea was
known for its wealth. It was a silk-stocking town, a real life
success story, famous for its wool industry and materially
wealthy. It was the epitome of wealth.

That was Laodicea. The whole attitude of Laodicea was that
they had everything they needed. They did not need anything
or anybody, including God. Isn't that the attitude of America
today? We do not need God. We have it made.

When was the last time we read about someone starving to
death in America? We are an affluent people. We do not need

anything. Oh, we would like to have more so we can squander it on our selfishness, but we do not need anything—until a crisis comes.

America responds to a crisis two ways. Either we fall on our faces and begin to pray to God, or we begin to curse God. We make demands of God. That was the spirit of Laodicea.

Wherever we find a church that feels it does not need revival, that is the very one that needs it. Wherever we find a Christian that does not feel the need of God, that Christian really needs God. They did not understand their true condition: "knowest not that thou art wretched, and miserable, and poor, and blind, and naked" (v. 17).

The word *wretched* means "pressed with a burden." It is not the burden of poverty but the burden of wealth. The greatest burden that Christians will ever carry is the burden of wealth. We do not know how to handle it. We think our creativity—our genius—has produced it.

Here was a church that was wretched not because it was poor, but because it was wealthy. The real question today is not whether the church can survive persecution, but whether it can survive prosperity. We think wealth is a blessing, but God says it is a curse. Few people learn how to hold their wealth. Most are held by their wealth and dominated by it.

The word *miserable* means "pitiable." The word *poor* means "pauper," "beggar." And *blind* could better be translated "nearsighted." They could not see beyond themselves; their vision was opaque. They lacked light and vision. Then he says they were "naked." A church should be adorned with the glory and beauty of God.

Here was a church that had nothing. It possessed none of the things the bride of Christ should possess. Other churches had white raiment. This church had nothing. There is infinitely greater chance for someone cold to be reached with the gospel than someone lukewarm.

It is always that way. I believe there is more hope for the man outside the church than for the man within the church who is near enough to its warmth not to appreciate it and yet far enough away from its burning heat to be useless to God and to man. Wretched, miserable, poor, blind, and naked was this church.

Instruction

> I counsel thee to buy of me gold tried in the fire, that thou mayest be rich; and white raiment, that thou mayest be clothed, and that the shame of thy nakedness do not appear; and anoint thine eyes with eye-salve, that thou mayest see. As many as I love, I rebuke and chasten: be zealous there- fore, and repent (vv. 18-19).

Now he gives them instructions. Eternal riches cannot be purchased with a bank account. How can a poor church buy anything? "Ho, every one that thirsteth, come ye to the waters, and he that hath no money; come ye, buy, and eat; yea, come, buy wine and milk without money and without price" (Isa. 55:1).

If we admit our poverty, the riches of God are at our disposal. We do not buy from God through our goodness, determination, or anything we have, but through confession of our poverty.

"White raiment, [buy from me] that thou mayest be clothed" (v. 18). If we are conscious of our nakedness, he has clothing for us. White raiment speaks of the righteousness required to enter God's presence. If we are ever to walk into the presence of God, we will need to be clothed in his righteousness.

"I will greatly rejoice in the Lord, my soul shall be joyful in my God; for he hath clothed me with the garments of salva- tion, he hath covered me with the robe of righteousness" (Isa.

61:10). When we recognize our nakedness, God clothes us.

"Anoint thine eyes with eye-salve, that thou mayest see" (v. 18). If we are conscious of our blindness, God has a cure: spiritual illumination and understanding.

"As many as I love, I rebuke and chasten" (v. 19). If he had not loved this church (even though with a love of lesser depth) he would not have rebuked them. It was his love that was the reason for the rebuke. "Be zealous therefore, and repent."

Literally, he was saying, "Be boiling and repent. Get set on fire for God." If my arm is numb and has no feeling, that is bad because pain is a friend. It tells me what the problem is. When I go to a doctor, the first thing he asks is: "Where does it hurt?" A numb limb feels no pain at all.

Indifference feels no need. When we are indifferent, we have no concern for God. Our consciences have been drugged, our wills have been paralyzed. We have no consciousness of need. Jesus says, "Be boiling and repent."

Invitation

Behold, I stand at the door, and knock: if any man hear my voice, and open the door, I will come in to him, and will sup with him, and he with me. To him that overcometh will I grant to sit with me in my throne, even as I also overcame, and am set down with my Father in his throne (vv. 20-21).

Here he gives an invitation. We quote this verse as a beautiful desire of God to enter our lives, and it is, but it is a sad, sad, verse.

When we started these seven letters, Jesus was seen walking among the churches. He was among his people, in fellowship with them and they with him. When we come to the end, he is on the outside. He has been excluded. He is outside the church, knocking. He is the excluded Christ. They do not need him anymore. They are rich and increased with goods and have need of nothing. The last picture of Jesus is a picture of him standing on the outside, knocking and calling. These verbs are in the continuous, present tense. It means he is always standing and always knocking. See how much he longs to be in the heart of his people, how much he wants a place in us and among us.

He knocks in many ways. He knocks through his Word, through his Holy Spirit, and through his people. He knocks through providence, those things he allows to come into our lives. Every experience is designed by God to reveal a fresh facet of his character and his nature to us.

He did not say he was going to wait for the church to vote in business meeting whether or not they wanted him to come in. He did not say he was waiting for all the deacons to get together to decide if they wanted him to come in.

But he did say if anyone will hear his voice—just one—he will come in. Do you see the pathos in the call of Christ? Do you see the love in the call of Christ? He who looks at a church in its deadness, lethargy, and indifference, calls and knocks. And if anyone opens the door, he will come in.

There is no doubt about it. There is no negotiating. All that is required is to hear his voice and open the door, and he will come in. Sins and problems cannot be handled before opening the door. If we could, we would not need Jesus. All we need do is open the door.

We do not need understanding or special wisdom. All we need is to determine that more than anything else, we want Jesus in our lives. The only cure for lukewarmness is the readmission of the excluded Christ. Let him in again.

"To him that overcometh will I grant to sit with me in my throne, even as I also overcame, and am set down with my Father in his throne" (v. 21). This is the promise he started with in 1:5. We are going to be kings and princes and rule and reign with him. If we walk with him we will be associated with him in his Kingdom.

The worst form of blasphemy is lukewarmness. It is more blasphemous for us to hear the gospel and not be zealous for it, to hear the message of Christ and not be thrilled by it, than for us to curse God and shake our fists in his face.

Indifference and lukewarmness are the worst forms of blasphemy. We stand condemned by this passage. Are we indifferent to the eternal message of God who sent his Son to die for our sins? Do we teach and preach mechanically and indifferently? We stand condemned by our Lord's message to the church at Laodicea. "Be boiling and repent" is God's word to us.

10
The Heavenly Throne
4:1-11

When we come to chapter 4, we turn a corner. The scene has shifted, and John is beckoned to come into glory to be shown the "things which shall be hereafter" (1:19). The focus is turned from the church. Now through chapter 18, there are no further references to the church.

The extensive use of Old Testament symbols and the language used indicates that it is Israel God is dealing with at this time and the tribulation period involves Israel and not the church. There are 485 specific references to the Old Testament in the Book of Revelation.

The tribulation is a time of Jacob's trouble, according to the Old Testament. It is Daniel's seventieth week. It refers to the dealing of God with Israel. There are many reasons for believing that but I simply believe that the church will not be on the earth during the tribulation. The church will be taken away before the tribulation begins.

The first verse of chapter 4 could be a form of the rapture itself. We are looking at the things which must be hereafter. It is at this point that we come to that which is future, that which is prophetic in the truest sense.

We can debate all the facets of eschatology, but if we do we will miss the message God has for us. The simple focus is on a throne. Twelve times in this chapter, the throne is mentioned.

The throne is a place of authority, the center of God's rulership for the activities of heaven. It is the place where his government is carried out. This throne is the central focus of this chapter, but more especially attention is focused on the One who sits on this throne.

If we are to understand Revelation, we need to remember that its purpose is to magnify our Lord Jesus Christ. The one who sits on the throne is Jesus Christ. When we get to heaven, I believe the only God we will ever see is Jesus. God is spirit, and the Bible makes very clear that we cannot see the Spirit of God. God sent Jesus so we could have a God to see and touch. This book is all about Jesus Christ.

That should not come as a surprise because he started with that direction. In the first chapter, it is made very clear that Jesus is the focal point of the book. Verses 13 through 18 are a beautiful, specific description of the majesty, holiness, and righteousness of Jesus Christ.

That is why John said, "And when I saw him, I fell at his feet as dead" (1:17). When John saw Jesus he realized his own nothingness and fell as dead in awe of his majesty at his feet. Revelation tries to bring us to the feet of Jesus on his throne.

The fourth chapter is strange to us. It is unfamiliar to us because we have no point of reference. Thrones, elders with crowns, white raiment, lightnings and thunders coming out of the throne are foreign to us. It is like being in a foreign country. There is enough similarity with one's native country that we make some sense out of it, but there is enough difference that it makes us uneasy.

It is rather like that when we come into this sacred place in the fourth chapter and stand before the throne. How can we grasp it? How can we explain it? How can we understand it?

Maybe it would be best to remind ourselves again that this picture of Jesus in Revelation is not so much something to wrap our minds around as it is our hearts.

Presence

> And immediately I was in the spirit; and, behold, a throne
> was set in heaven, and one sat on the throne. And he that
> sat was to look upon like a jasper and a sardine stone: and
> there was a rainbow round about the throne, in sight like
> unto an emerald (vv. 2-3).

Here a divine presence is revealed. We are introduced
immediately to that One who sits upon the throne, and he
is described with the brilliance of jewels. He is likened to a
jasper.

A jasper is equivalent to our diamond. In the twenty-first
chapter, the jasper stone is called "clear as crystal" (v. 11). A
jasper in ancient times was not clear; it was opaque. This is a
clear jasper and must be something like our diamond. It speaks
of the light that is shone on our hearts and lives. A diamond is
also the hardest stone to be found. It underscores the firmness
of God's judgment. It is a reminder that the moral and spiritual
laws of God are just as inflexible as his physical laws.

The physical laws are set and fixed. That is why we can
function in this world and probe outer space. His spiritual laws
and moral laws are likewise fixed. He who sits on the throne is
one who represents the light of God and the firmness of his
judgment.

The sardine is elsewhere called the sardius stone. It is a
flashing, fiery-red stone. It reminds us of the sacrifice of Jesus
Christ and his shed blood upon the cross. It speaks of the love
of God and is a reminder of the holiness of God in his judgment and his government.

We see the one upon the throne as one of principle as well
as one of passion. He is firm, but loving. The piercing colors of
these stones are like the glory of his righteous government.

The rainbow, a perfect circle, speaks of perfection. God's
promises will be fulfilled. As that circle is unbroken, so there

will be a promise and a hope from Christ himself consistent with the very nature of God.

It also means the storm is over. This emerald rainbow means for God's children the storm is past.

Prestige

> And round about the throne were four and twenty seats: and upon the seats I saw four and twenty elders sitting, clothed in white raiment; and they had on their heads crowns of gold (v. 4).

Who are the twenty-four elders? If we understand something of the history of Israel, we can grasp the meaning of the twenty-four elders. In 1 Chronicles 24, King David appointed twenty-four elders to represent the levitical priesthood before his throne. These twenty-four elders around the throne of our Lord are a symbol of the entire heavenly priesthood.

They are representative of all the redeemed. There are no absentees. Their attire speaks of perfect righteousness and perfect dignity for they are clothed in white raiment. They are the victors and now reign with their Lord. The crowns on their heads are not crowns of royalty but of victory.

This is the throne of judgment. Today the Lord is on the throne of grace. He is giving opportunity for us to respond. But history is moving toward a time when he who sits upon the throne of grace will sit upon the throne of judgment. All of the redeemed, he has already declared, will rule and reign with him (1:6).

Pronouncements

> And out of the throne proceeded lightnings and thunderings and voices: and there were seven lamps of fire burning before the throne, which are the seven Spirits of God. And before the throne there was a sea of glass like unto crystal:

and in the midst of the throne, and round about the throne, were four beasts full of eyes before and behind. And the first beast was like a lion, and the second beast like a calf, and the third beast had a face as a man, and the fourth beast was like a flying eagle (vv. 5-7).

In verse 5, lightnings, thunderings, and voices proceed out of the throne. It means exactly what it means today. When we see the lightning and hear the thunder, we know a storm is brewing. This lightning and thundering is a prelude to God's judgment.

We see the warning that judgment is imminent. "There were seven lamps of fire burning before the throne, which are the seven Spirits of God" (v. 5). Fire is a representative of judgment. The precious Spirit of God that woos our hearts and invites us to trust Jesus will in that day be the Holy Spirit of fire. He will be the spirit of judgment.

Over and again, the refrain runs through this book that if we do not respond to the wooings of his Spirit and respond to his offer of grace, there will come a time when we shall face his judgment.

There are not seven different spirits. Seven simply means completeness and fullness. In this instance because we are dealing with judgment, *seven* refers to the all-knowing Spirit of God. He has full and complete knowledge of every thought, every word, every deed.

Everything will be shown against those who have rejected him. There will be no false evidence. It will all be genuine. The full, perfect spirit of God will reveal the whole truth.

"And before the throne there was a sea of glass like unto crystal: and in the midst of the throne, and round about the throne, were four beasts full of eyes before and behind" (v. 6).

The "sea of glass" is not like the Pacific Ocean. In the Old Testament Temple of Solomon there was a laver where one washed his hands before he entered into the presence of God.

It was sometimes called a "sea" (1 Kings 7:23).

When the apostle John beheld the inside of the laver he saw that it was no longer liquid, no longer capable of change. It was a sea of glass, fixed because the cleansing was complete. Cleansing was no longer necessary.

Jesus Christ has perfectly cleansed us in his blood, and those who are there will no longer wash in the water of the sea or laver before the throne. We will stand upon it as transparent glass claiming the eternal purposes and promises of God. The cleansing does not have to be repeated.

Everytime we come to worship, we have to confess to God. But when we stand at the throne we will be perfect as he is perfect and there will be no need for further cleansing.

Now enter the four beasts. It is unfortunate that the seventeenth-century King James translators used the word *beasts*. In the thirteenth chapter, we are introduced to a real beast, a real *thaleon*. That is the beast; this is *zoan*, living creature.

It is not a beast that is fearful or horrible. These are living beings. They are angelic beings, seraphim or cherabim. They are what Isaiah described in Isaiah 6:1-3. Whatever else they mean, they do whatever the Judge tells them to do.

They primarily worship and praise God. But they have other duties, too. They are full of eyes, before and behind. That simply means they can see everything in the future and in the past. They have full knowledge, complete spiritual perception, and understanding. They are described as a lion, a calf, a man, and a flying eagle. These are their various functions for the Judge. The lion has great strength and majesty to enact the purposes of God with strength and majestic dignity.

The ox is an animal of service, so these angelic beings are servants of God and render service to him.

A man is a being of intelligence and, hopefully, compassion. These angelic beings have the intelligence and the understanding of man.

The flying eagle is one of the fastest things in the animal kingdom. So they have the swiftness of a flying eagle.

Whatever their description, their main purpose is to praise God. They have perfect wisdom, and render unceasing worship and service for the Heavenly Father.

Praise

And the four beasts had each of them six wings about him; and they were full of eyes within: and they rest not day and night, saying, Holy, holy, holy, Lord God Almighty, which was, and is, and is to come. And when those beasts give glory and honour and thanks to him that sat on the throne, who liveth for ever and ever, The four and twenty elders fall down before him that sat on the throne, and worship him that liveth for ever and ever, and cast their crowns before the throne, saying, Thou art worthy, O Lord, to receive glory and honour and power: for thou hast created all things, and for thy pleasure they are and were created (vv. 8-11).

Jesus Christ is the object of the worship of heaven. That is the picture. These angelic beings are leading the praises of God. They are what Adrian Rogers calls "God's cheerleaders." They are up there singing his praises, his glory, his majesty.

One may lead, praising God for his love and compassion. Another may praise God for his holiness and righteousness. Another may thank God for his sacrifice on the cross. They are God's cheerleaders of praise, and they render devotion and praise to Jesus.

Why? Jesus did what they could not do! They could not redeem men from sin. They could not forgive sins. They could do many things. They are strong and mighty creations of God, but they could not save humanity. Jesus did. He alone is worthy of their eternal praise—and ours.

In verse 9 when they began to give glory and honor, the four and twenty elders fell down before Jesus and worshiped him for ever and ever. That is enough reason to believe it is Jesus on the throne—he is the one who lives for ever and ever!

Another reason to believe it is Jesus on the throne is found in verse 11. "For thou hast created all things, and for thy pleasure they are and were created." In the Book of John we find, "In the beginning was the Word, and the Word was with God and the Word was God. The same was in the beginning with God. All things were made by him; and without him was not any thing made that was made" (John 1:1-3).

And in Colossians 1:16: "For by him were all things created, that are in heaven, and that are in earth, visible and invisible, whether they be thrones, or dominions, or principalities, or powers: all things were created by him, and for him."

That is another reason to believe Jesus is on the throne. One thing for sure, there are no songs of evolution in heaven. Praise God who created all things. Eternal praise is given to the Creator God.

If we do not enjoy praising Jesus, I believe we will not enjoy heaven. Do not think that your heart will be changed in heaven. Our bodies will be changed but not our hearts.

If we find we do not love Jesus, do not praise Jesus, do not want to obey and live for Jesus, God is not going to change that in the resurrection. In my opinion, the purpose of the resurrection will be to change the body. We will have more understanding, but God will not suddenly make one who does not love Jesus love him in the resurrection.

If we do not love praising Jesus, we will not like heaven. Of course, if we do not love praising Jesus, we will not have a chance to do so. If the name of Jesus does not thrill us now, we will not delight in it in heaven because in heaven the object of worship is Jesus Christ.

"The four and twenty elders . . . cast their crowns before the throne" (v. 10). Our first impulse will be to lay at Jesus' feet every crown we are ever going to get. That crown of righteous-ness, the soul-winners crown, the incorruptible crown we will lay at his feet.

Do not waste your life on trivialities or things that are transient. The things we give ourselves to are so fleeting. The ways we spend our time, the things we get upset about are so trivial, so meaningless.

Jesus will save you, cleanse you, give you new life; and will give you a heart full of praise and thanksgiving toward the Lord.

We do not know much about that. Our prayers do not reveal much adoration. Somehow that is a missing ingredient in the prayers of man. The ingredients of adoration, reverence, and worship of the holiness and majesty of God are missing.

For most of us, God is like a magic wand. He is the one who gives us things that make us "feel good." That is modern man's idea of God. But the biblical picture shows God's people casting themselves before Jesus crying, "Holy, holy, holy, Lord God Almighty."

11
Worthy Is the Lamb
5:1-14

We now come to the beginning of the pouring out of the wrath of God in judgment upon the earth. That judgment does not begin here but the door is opened for it.

This chapter shows us the fulfillment of Daniel 12:8-9 where Daniel said, "O my Lord, what shall be the end of these things? And he said, Go thy way, Daniel: for the words are closed up and sealed till the time of the end."

God did not unveil the end of time to Daniel but told him it was sealed up until then. Here in Revelation is the scroll and the seals to be broken so the things of the end can come to pass.

"And I saw in the right hand of him that sat on the throne a book written within and on the backside, sealed with seven seals" (Rev. 5:1). The word *book* could better be translated "scroll." In the times of the writing of the Bible, they did not have books as we know them; they had scrolls. There is a scroll written within and sealed with seven seals. It is also spoken of in Ezekiel 2.

What is inside the scroll and why is it so significant? Very simply, the scroll represents the title deed to the earth, the right to rule upon this earth.

When Adam sinned and Satan was loosed among humanity, Satan became a usurper. He became the one who rules and governs the affairs of the earth. He is the evil presence that opposes and attacks. He promotes sadness, sorrow, and death.

The scroll represents that right to rule. When the scroll is opened and the seals are broken, God will reveal his divine program for the end of time. He will see his perfect purposes fulfilled and Satan bound and cast into hell itself.

The exciting thing in this chapter is when the Lamb emerges on center stage. He had been hidden until now. But now the Lamb steps into the spotlight. We see him in the midst of the throne, in the midst of the twenty-four elders, and the four living creatures. From this point on, he is the central figure of the end time drama.

Weep

> And I saw a strong angel proclaiming with a loud voice, Who is worthy to open the book, and to loose the seals thereof? And no man in heaven, nor in earth, neither under the earth, was able to open the book, neither to look thereon. And I wept much, because no man was found worthy to open and to read the book, neither to look thereon (vv. 2-4).

God will release his judgment upon the earth and vindicate his saints. He will punish evil. Right will prevail, and a rule of perfect justice will be established. Who is worthy to open up the judgments of God and to loose the will of God in this earth?

John said, "I wept much, because no man was found worthy to open and to read the book, neither to look thereon" (v. 4). Who *is* worthy to open the book? Who has paid the price of redemption? Who is the rightful heir, the one who deserves to open the book?

The seal had to be opened by someone with the lawful right to do so. It was a legal seal and only the rightful heir could break it. When the question was asked, there was silence in heaven. No one spoke up. "No man in heaven, nor in earth, neither under the earth, was able to open the book, neither to look thereon" (v. 3).

Man cannot rescue himself. There have been many people who have claimed they would rule the world. But they have died and their dreams have died with them.

Can we imagine it? Here they are in heaven, and the question has been asked, "Who is worthy?" Not Abraham, not Moses, not Joshua, not David, not Solomon, not Jeremiah— none of these who are there could open it.

Not even John the Baptist could. Jesus said of him that there had never been a greater man born of woman. But John the Baptist did not step forth to break the seal. No man is able to break it.

When will we learn that this earth does not belong to us? The subtle heresy of secular humanism today is that man is center stage, that man can govern himself and make a perfect world. It will never happen. The title deed of this sin-scarred earth has never been transferred to man. No man is able. So John wept.

Think about it for a moment. If the scroll is not taken from the hand of him who sits upon the throne, opened, then the unopened scroll means that the inheritance of God's people is unredeemed. It had to be opened for God to vindicate the righteous, for God to set right all of the terrible wrongs of this world.

We talk about being on the winning side, but the seal has to be broken and the scroll opened before we can win. When John saw no one was able to open it, he wept. Promises to the redeemed could not be fulfilled.

John wept because he did not have the right perspective. It seemed futile to him. It looked as if the purposes of God would be thwarted. But he had not yet seen the lion of the tribe of

Judah—the Lamb slain—come forward and take the book. Because he did not have the perfect understanding of God, he wept.

Are we not like that? Do not we often weep in despair and sometimes wonder why tragedy happens and sadness occurs, why death comes and disappointments pervade, why discouragement surrounds us and depression sets in. We wonder why God has left us.

But we do not have God's perspective. In God's time, in his way, all that will be set right and climaxed in the proper way. God's purposes will not be thwarted by man nor by Satan. But the book had to be opened and John's perspective caused him to weep.

Weep Not

And out of the throne proceeded lightnings and thunderings and voices: and there were seven lamps of fire burning before the throne, which are the seven Spirits of God. And before the throne there was a sea of glass like unto crystal: and in the midst of the throne, and round about the throne, were four beasts full of eyes before and behind.

And the first beast was like a lion, and the second beast like a calf, and the third beast had a face as a man, and the fourth beast was like a flying eagle (4:5-7).

Weep not! God never leaves himself without a man to do the job and he will not in the end times. The man Christ Jesus, the eternal Son of God, King of kings, steps to center stage.

The "Lion" speaks of the kingly character of God, of Jesus Christ and the strength and might of Christ. He is the one who has been born of David's seed. The Lion and the Root of Jesse have prevailed.

He has won! He has conquered! He is worthy! Whatever demand is made to open the book, Jesus Christ has prevailed:

"to open the book and to loose the seven seals thereof." Weep not!

"And I beheld, and lo, in the midst of the throne and of the four beasts, and in the midst of the elders, stood a Lamb as it had been slain" (vv. 6). Isn't that just like God? Against all the forces of evil, all of the marshaled armies of hell, he sends a Lamb to do battle.

There are some interesting things about this Lamb. First we see that he is in the midst of the throne. How had John missed him? He had been there all the time, in the midst of the throne, in the midst of the elders, and the living creatures. John had not seen him, but he was there in the midst.

Many times in our lives, amid circumstances that confuse, if we look carefully, we will see Jesus in the midst. He is always there. In the midst of that despair, sorrow, and disappointment, he is always there. John missed him, but he was there.

The Lamb who had been slain was standing. That means that he had conquered death. He suffered for our sins. But this is a living, risen Savior! The Lamb that was slain is standing in victory and conquest.

This Lamb is not weak. He is an unusual Lamb. He has "seven horns and seven eyes, which are the seven Spirits of God sent forth into all the earth" (v. 6). The "seven horns" mean "perfect horns," complete, fulfilled.

The horns represent authority and power. This Lamb has strength and might, authority and power. He is the Lion of the tribe of Judah. He is a powerful Lamb, with seven horns.

The seven eyes mean perfect understanding, perfect knowledge. Nothing we have ever done will escape his eyes. Nothing that has ever happened in the world will be a mystery to him. He will have perfect knowledge, perfect understanding.

It is wonderful to know that our Savior, Jesus Christ, knows everything about us; he understands all. He has perfect knowledge. These are the seven Spirits of God, the fullness of the Spirit of God. Everything God is rests upon this Lamb who stands in the midst of the throne holding the book.

"And he came and took the book out of the right hand of him that sat upon the throne" (v. 7). He took the book because the world is his. It belongs to Jesus Christ. The world is his by creation. It is his by redemption. He purchased it. He bought it with his own blood.

There are some who will not accept the creation or the redemption of God. It is as though Jesus Christ said, "For those of you who will not accept me as Creator and those of you who will not accept me as Redeemer, I am going to war, and I will win." It is his by conquest. He will prevail in the great battle of the final days.

It will be a great war. Millions of people will marshal themselves against God's people. They will get ready to fight, and Jesus will come. It will all be over. With a word it will all be done.

When he took the scroll, it showed he was the only one who had a right to have it. It belongs to him. No one questioned him. No one asked for his credentials. The world is his.

Worship

And when he had taken the book, the four beasts and four and twenty elders fell down before the Lamb, having every one of them harps, and golden vials full of odours, which are the prayers of saints.

And they sung a new song, saying, Thou art worthy to take the book, and to open the seals thereof: for thou wast slain, and hast redeemed us to God by thy blood out of every kindred, and tongue, and people, and nation; And hast made us unto our God kings and priests: and we shall reign on the earth.

And I beheld, and I heard the voice of many angels round about the throne and the beasts and the elders: and the

number of them was ten thousand times ten thousand, and
thousands of thousands; Saying with a loud voice, Worthy is
the Lamb that was slain to receive power, and riches, and
wisdom, and strength, and honour, and glory, and blessing.
And every creature which is in heaven, and on the earth,
and under the earth, and such as are in the sea, and all that
are in them, heard I saying, Blessing, and honour, and glory,
and power, be unto him that sitteth upon the throne, and
unto the Lamb for ever and ever.

And the four beasts said, Amen. And the four and twenty
elders fell down and worshiped him that liveth for ever and
ever (vv. 8-14).

The last portion of this passage is described as "worship."
Look at what happens. When we see Jesus Christ as the Lamb
slain, that it was for our sins he was nailed to the cross, we will
do the same.

"And when he had taken the book, the four beasts and four
and twenty elders fell down before the Lamb" (v. 8). When we
see Jesus, who he is, what he is, and what he has done, our
first response is to fall at his feet. In chapter 4, those who fell at
his feet laid their crowns at his feet. This is worship.

Notice how they worshiped, each with a harp. There is going
to be music in heaven. Some of the greatest sounds on earth
are heavenly music.

The harp was a sign of thanksgiving, the signal for the
celebration of victory. When these fell before him, it was in
thanksgiving and praise for the victory that he had purchased
for them.

"And golden vials full of odours, which are the prayers of the
saints" (v. 8). In real worship, there are music and intercession.
There are several things we can deduce from this phrase. It
tells us that many prayers that we think are unanswered are
really going to be answered.

But it speaks specifically of the millions of people who have prayed as Jesus taught us to pray: "Thy kingdom come, thy will be done on earth as it is in heaven" (Matt. 6:10). That prayer has never been answered. Prayers are stored up. When the Lamb stands, takes the scroll, breaks the seal and God's judgment falls upon the earth, the prayers of the saints will be right at the heart of what is happening. They will be answered. God will bring splendid victory to his people.

This tells us that no prayer is ever lost. The prayers of the saints are precious, and always reach the heart of God. When we lift our prayers of intercession to God, he stores them and in his time, the answer comes.

"And they sung a new song, saying, Thou art worthy to take the book, and to open the seals thereof: for thou wast slain, and hast redeemed us to God by thy blood out of every kindred, and tongue, and people, and nation" (v. 9).

He created us, yes, but he died for us. By his blood we are redeemed. This is redemption's song, and it is a beautiful song.

"And hast made us unto our God kings and priests: and we shall reign on the earth" (v. 10). That song had three stanzas. The first stanza was redemption. "Thou was slain and hast redeemed us unto God." The second stanza was royalty. He has made us kings of a kingdom. And the third stanza is consecration. He has made us to be priests. Whatever else a priest does, he offers sacrifice to God; he consecrates to God.

When that happened, the Lamb went and took the scroll out of the right hand of him that sat upon the throne. The redeemed of all ages broke forth with their harps and voices in a new song.

And John said, "I beheld, and I heard the voice of many angels round about the throne and the beasts and the elders: and the number of them was ten thousand times ten thousand, and thousands of thousands" (v. 11).

The angels were not singing in the first song. Angels only know redemption by observation. They do not know it by experience. But now they start singing. And there were so many they could not be counted: "ten thousand times ten thousand, and thousands of thousands."

"Saying with a loud voice, Worthy is the Lamb that was slain to receive power, and riches, and wisdom, and strength, and honour, and glory, and blessing" (v. 12). Everything we can give him, he is worthy of. All the angels of heaven and the redeemed cry, "Worthy is the Lamb!"

"And every creature which is in heaven, and on earth, and under the earth, and such as are in the sea, and all that are in them, heard I saying, "Blessing, and honour, and glory, and power, be unto him that sitteth upon the throne, and unto the Lamb for ever and ever" (v. 13).

Paul wrote to the Philippians: "Wherefore God also hath highly exalted him, and given him a name which is above every name: That at the name of Jesus every knee should bow, of things in heaven, and things in earth, and things under the earth; And that every tongue should confess that Jesus Christ is Lord, to the glory of God the Father" (Phil. 2:9-11).

God has created man to choose Jesus as Savior. Everyone has a choice. We can either reject or accept Jesus. But man does not have a choice about whether to crown him as Lord.

We may never bow our knees in this life to Jesus Christ, and our tongues may never pray in prayer to him in this life, but when Jesus comes as the Lamb slain standing with the scroll in his hand, every creature in the earth, under the earth, in the sea, in the universe is going to bow before him and proclaim that he is Lord.

We ought to proclaim his lordship now. We are going to do it someday. Every knee is going to bow to Jesus one day. And every tongue is going to declare his Lordship.

Everywhere, John said, "I heard them saying Blessing, and honour, and glory, and power, be unto him that sitteth upon the throne, and unto the Lamb for ever and ever" (v. 13).

"And the four beasts said, Amen. And the four and twenty elders fell down and worshiped him that liveth for ever and ever" (v. 14).

What a glorious Savior we have! What a wonderful Christ! No man is worthy, but he is. The Lion of the tribe of Judah, the Lamb slain, in perfect power and perfect knowledge stepped forward, and he was in control.

History is moving inevitably, irretrievably toward that climax!

12

The Great Tribulation

6:1-17

The chapter before us is a portion of that time we call the seven years of tribulation. The intensity of the tribulation, however, does not come until chapter 8. Then following chapter 9 there are amplifications, enlargements of what we shall see in these chapters.

When we come to chapter 6, we are faced with something that is repugnant to modern man—that God will ever punish sin. The modern mind does not want to believe that God would ever be a God of judgment. People want to believe in a God who is only love, compassion, grace, and mercy.

All these things are true but the modern mind wants to perceive only one facet of the character of God. We will simply not allow ourselves to accept the fact that a God of love is also a God of judgment. There is a point beyond which it would be sinful itself for a Holy God not to judge the rebellious heart of humanity.

This chapter is the beginning of the judgments of God. This passage is a solemn word and warning of the inevitable judgment that lies ahead by Jesus Christ.

If you are not saved, I plead with you to give your heart to Jesus. You do not know what lies ahead. You cannot mock God. A time is coming when God will move against those who have consciously rejected Jesus Christ, who have turned their backs on him. We do not have to encounter this kind of judgment. But God is going to judge sin.

The Riders

And I saw when the Lamb opened one of the seals, and I heard, as it were the noise of thunder, one of the four beasts saying, Come and see. And I saw, and behold a white horse: and he that sat on him had a bow; and a crown was given unto him: and he went forth conquering, and to conquer.

And when he had opened the second seal, I heard the second beast say, Come and see. And there went out another horse that was red: and power was given to him that sat thereon to take peace from the earth, and that they should kill one another: and there was given unto him a great sword.

And when he had opened the third seal, I heard the third beast say, Come and see. And I beheld, and lo a black horse; and he that sat on him had a pair of balances in his hand. And I heard a voice in the midst of the four beasts say, A measure of wheat for a penny, and three measures of barley for a penny; and see thou hurt not the oil and the wine.

And when he had opened the fourth seal, I heard the voice of the fourth beast say, Come and see. And I looked, and behold a pale horse: and his name that sat on him was Death, and Hell followed with him. And power was given unto them over the fourth part of the earth, to kill with sword, and with hunger, and with death, and with the beasts of the earth (vv. 1-8).

"The noise of thunder" (v. 1) is a warning of an impending storm: judgment. The four beasts are living creatures, not to be confused with the beasts that we will see in the thirteenth chapter.

These are living creatures. They cry continually of the holiness of God and lead the cheers for the praise of God in

heaven. One of those living creatures said, "Come and see."
He is speaking to the horsemen that are about to arrive on the
scene.

These four horsemen are not individual personalities but
world conditions. They are man's inhumanity to man. Without
Jesus Christ as Lord, man is in control ruling the world. When
man rules the world, nothing but sadness, sorrow, disappointment, and despair will be the experience of humanity.

The four horsemen represent man in control causing suffering with false hopes of peace, followed by wars and famine
and death. The cry goes out to the horsemen, for they are
prepared to ride.

In chapters 4 and 5, everything was in heaven. We were
viewing the glory of God and the majesty of God. We are now
back on this earth in this chapter, commencing with the
judgments of God. This is where Daniel's seventieth week
begins (Dan. 9).

The first rider to come is seen in verse 2: "And I saw, and
behold a white horse." The white horse always represents
victory. Here is a conquering, victorious rider. There are some
who would say this is Jesus but that cannot be so because this
rider is only one of four. Jesus is not just one of anything! He is
everything!

Jesus will be seen in chapter 19 as King of kings and Lord of
lords. He is not one of four of anything. Others say it is the
Antichrist. It certainly represents the spirit of the Antichrist, a
bloodless victory, peaceful victory (he has a bow but not an
arrow). He threatens and intimidates. He negotiates and wins
without war.

The spirit of Antichrist that comes in the end times will
persuade men he is the savior of the human race and that he is
the one who can bring the world together. He will be a messiah
figure in the last times.

This rider on the white horse is symbolic of the spirit of

Antichrist and antichristian ideologies which prepare men's hearts for the devil's gospel. He is going to be so persuasive, he will convince the world that wrong is right and right is wrong. He will come riding on that white horse, but not with a sword. He is in a cold war to win without violence.

The second rider comes on a red horse. Red is the spirit of violence, the symbol of bloodshed on a worldwide scale—a bloody, global war. Remember we are talking about the judgment of God on the people who have endlessly forsaken and rebelled against him.

This rider on the red horse brings strife, violence, and war. He does not have a bow anymore but a great sword. One-third of the people of the earth will be killed in a cataclysmic global war.

A third horse comes, this one black. It is famine. War is not a time for sowing seed. There will be a worldwide war. People will be engaged in the bloodiest and most brutal of all wars. There will be no time to plant crops. The natural consequence of war is famine. The rider on the black horse has a pair of balances which is for the purpose of measuring grain. That is symbolic of the dreaded famine.

We see his shadow today. We have not seen the rider on the black horse yet, but we have seen how it could be, for there are millions of people starving to death all over the world today.

If those who talk to us about nutrition and ecology are right, if there is a significant change in the ecological balance in the world, we are only a few years away from worldwide famine. Famine shall ride.

We read about a measure of wheat for a penny, three measures of barley for a penny. Back then, a penny was a day's labor. In other words, the time will come when a man will have to work all day just for barely enough food to survive. Then he will have to share it with his wife and children. It will be a time of unprecedented famine.

Then the fourth horse comes—the pale horse. This horse is a morbid, tragic figure. It is the color of a corpse; the picture of death itself. Under this seal, Death and Hell incorporate some of the terrors that have already been loosed.

All of the judgments predicted by Ezekiel 14:21 are unleashed in this seal. Listen to what Ezekiel said: "For thus saith the Lord God; How much more when I send my four sore judgments upon Jerusalem, the sword, and the famine, and the noisome beast, and the pestilence, to cut off from it man and beast."

Those four judgments of God predicted by Ezekiel are now to be unleashed upon the earth. One of the horrors of the tribulation will be a ghastly trail of death: War, famines, persecutions, pestilences, earthquakes.

The sight of the pale horse and its rider will be an all too common sight as the shadows of final judgment gather around a condemned world. Disease will run wild in this judgment of the pale horse.

We are seeing some of that now. Our bodies are building up immunities to many prescription drugs. The time could well come when our own bodies will not resist the diseases that sweep the world. A global epidemic could result.

What do wild beasts have to do with death and hell in this judgment of the fourth seal? Some think it represents the spirit of Antichrist, the beastly spirit that longs to destroy. It could represent that.

Some think it means all the wild beasts of the world. This is a different word for beast than the word used earlier in this chapter. The earlier word should be translated "living creature."

Here is another possibility. Maybe it does not mean wild beasts like lions, tigers, etc. What about rats? Rats live where we live. If we exterminate 95 percent of them in any given area, they will replenish themselves in one year. They destroy;

they carry germs and diseases that have spread plagues; they devour and contaminate food.

It could be that all of the beasts, large and small, are unleashed during this judgment of the pale horse. Our imagination cannot be as bad as the reality will be when God summons the pale horse and the one who rides upon it is called Death, and Hell follows him.

The Redeemed

> And when he had opened the fifth seal, I saw under the altar the souls of them that were slain for the word of God, and for the testimony which they held: and they cried with a loud voice, saying, How long, O Lord, holy and true, dost thou not judge and avenge our blood on them that dwell on the earth?
>
> And white robes were given unto every one of them; and it was said unto them, that they should rest yet for a little season, until their fellow-servants also and their brethren, that should be killed as they were, should be fulfilled (vv. 9-11).

The tribulation saints will be the souls of those who have been slain for the word of God and for their testimony. They will have been saved during the tribulation. It cannot be the church because the church has already been identified with the twenty-four elders around the throne. The church will already be in heaven.

So these will be newly redeemed saints who have been saved during the tribulation. Now they will cry out for vindication. That they plead for God to judge their murderers on earth indicates their murderers will still be living. Those who had slain them will still be on the earth and the saints will cry for God to avenge them.

Who of us has not asked God why he waits so long to bring vindication? God's answer is very interesting. It provides a glimpse into the complicated problem of why God allows evil to reign. They were to "rest yet for a little season, until your fellow-servants and brethren who should be killed as you were, should be fulfilled."

God simply allows it for his own purposes which are best seen from his viewpoint, though it is difficult for us to understand from our own. The Old Testament told us centuries before that God's ways are higher than our ways. His thoughts are higher than our thoughts.

He operates on a different level than we do; though we cannot understand the problem of suffering and evil and do not know why God waits, he does so because it is a part of his plan. The day is coming when his plan will have been fulfilled, and he will move in judgment and vindication upon evil.

That is the message of this chapter. In the meantime, he will give these saints white robes and instruct them to sit down and rest a while.

The Retribution

And I beheld when he had opened the sixth seal, and, lo, there was a great earthquake; and the sun became black as sackcloth of hair, and the moon became as blood; And the stars of heaven fell unto the earth, even as a fig tree casteth her untimely figs, when she is shaken of a mighty wind. And the heaven departed as a scroll when it is rolled together; and every mountain and island were moved out of their places.

And the kings of the earth, and the great men, and the rich men, and the chief captains, and the mighty men, and every bondman, and every free man, hid themselves in the dens and in the rocks of the mountains; And said to the mountains and rocks, Fall on us, and hide us from the face of him that sitteth on the throne, and from the wrath of the Lamb: For the great day of his wrath is come; and who shall be able to stand? (vv. 12-17).

We looked first at the riders, then we saw the redeemed, and now we see the retribution. There will be absolute chaos upon this earth—total collapse of human society. Every authority, everything we have counted on will collapse.

It will be the total destruction of the present world order. All of the authority of this world, whether it be of worldwide magnitude or the smallest element, will be dominated by Satan. Then God will move in judgment.

This is the forerunner of the great tribulation that will soon begin: the total disintegration of human society. The truth is, if we leave God out of our lives, everything about us is going to collapse and disintegrate.

That is why I think it is absolutely appalling that we would adopt the godless doctrine of humanism. Humanity has never built a lasting society that is equitable or peaceful. And we will not start to in our time. This is the conclusion of human reason—total chaos, total collapse, total disintegration.

Every element in society, every class of society from the lowest to the most prominent, will be affected. In that setting, all people will lose hope. They will know it is judgment, but they will not turn to God.

They will be so rebellious in their hearts they will hide in the rocks and the dens of earth. They will know it is God's judgment upon them and there is no place to hide.

They will pray but not to God! They will pray to the mountains to fall on them and hide them from the face of the Judge who sits on the throne.

The rebellious, sinful heart of humanity, carried to its logical conclusion, will be in such a state of degradation and decay by then that they will simply pray to the mountains but not to God! At that hour, there will be only one refuge—the Rock of ages. But he will offer no protection then for the unrepentant, for the day of grace will be gone. It will be too late to repent!

This will be the wrath of the Lamb. These verses are a

prelude to the great tribulation and to the horrors that have just begun. Everything we have seen is only a foretaste of when the seventh seal will be opened.

The church has known persecution through all the ages. There have always been times when people have persecuted Christians. But there are two characteristics that make this Great Tribulation period different from other times of persecution.

First, this trouble and persecution will be worldwide. No one will be free from it. Secondly, people will not only know that the end of the world is near, but they will truly act like it is the end. Today, people know the end is near but they do not make preparation for it.

When the Great Tribulation comes, they will know the end is near and act accordingly. No more buying and selling, no more comfort and leisure, saving or planning for the future! People will dig holes and cry for death.

This is what Jesus described in Matthew 24: "For then shall be great tribulation, such as was not since the beginning of the world to this time, no, nor ever shall be. And except those days should be shortened, there should no flesh be saved: but for the elect's sake those days shall be shortened" (Matt. 24:21-22). Such a terrible time of persecution and tribulation will follow that if God did not intervene none would survive.

These seals are opened one right after the other. We do not know how long it will take, but I am persuaded that it all will happen very quickly. In the first chapter we read that these things "must shortly come to pass." When it starts, it will move speedily.

In Revelation, there are seven seals, seven trumpets, and seven vials. How do they relate? The seven seals are God's comprehensive program. The whole picture is in the seven seals. Out of the seventh seal, we have the amplification of that judgment in the seven trumpets and the seven vials.

We shall see that as we proceed through this blessed book. But there is a question asked at the very last which needs to be pressed to our hearts. Who shall be able to stand? The answer is obvious: only those who are in Christ will be able to stand.

No *flesh* shall stand. No one is smart enough, wealthy enough, or strong enough to stand unaided.

When God unveils his terrible suffering and judgment on this earth, there is always that penetrating searching of the Holy Spirit to draw us to him. We cannot stand except in Christ. We have no hope for life eternal apart from Jesus Christ.

When we have done the best we can do and achieved all we can, it is empty and shallow. When we have flown as high as we can with all artificial stimuli, we must come down. There is no hope unless we find it in Jesus Christ. That is the message of this passage of God's Word.

13
World's Greatest Revival
7:1-17

In Daniel's prophecy which was divided into three sections, the last period was one week and is referred to as Daniel's seventieth week. That seventieth week is the primary concern of the Book of Revelation. Starting with the sixth chapter Revelation deals with the seventieth week of Daniel. It is called the tribulation period, sometimes the great tribulation.

Let me remind you that God does not have to conform to our eschatology. We are not studying this book in order to set dates, chart a course, etc. The truth is that we cannot go very far into Revelation until we have many diverse interpretations.

However, since God gave it to us it is important to study this book. God gives us nothing that is superfluous.

There are two basic reasons why we study the Book of Revelation. First, we need an overall picture of where God is headed. We need to be reminded that God is still in control, and moving toward a specific goal. Nothing in this universe can deter God from his purposes.

In fact, the very forces of hell including Satan himself are going to do exactly what God wants them to do to bring in the climax of the ages! Even Satan becomes an instrument in the hand of God!

A second reason we study Revelation is to learn about the character of God. What is God like? Does God really love us?

What has he done for us? What does he want us to do in response? We study the Book of Revelation to get a glimpse into the very nature of God.

In the seventh chapter, we come to a parenthesis. The sixth chapter was a stormy chapter where our Lord broke six of the seals and his wrath came down on the earth.

Here in chapter 7, there is a lull in the storm. The winds of judgment cease to blow. God stops long enough to show mercy to those who will accept him.

This is the great revival: millions of people responding to Christ. It is the answer to the prophet Habakkuk's prayer: "O Lord, I have heard thy speech, and was afraid: O Lord, revive thy work in the midst of the years, in the midst of the years make known; in wrath remember mercy" (Hab. 3:2).

This chapter is a parenthesis of grace, an interlude of mercy. It reminds us that God's greatest desire for everyone is salvation, not judgment. This chapter shows that there will be souls saved during the tribulation period. They will be saved by the millions.

But I give one word of warning: There is no evidence of any man who rejects Christ in this age having another chance later. Such a person will be without hope in the coming age. We are without excuse because we have heard the gospel. In the messages we have heard, the songs we sing, we are confronted by the claims of God on our lives.

No one who rejects Christ now will have a chance to be saved in the coming age. There will be millions who have never had that opportunity, and we see in this chapter the great ingathering of souls that God will accomplish.

There are four angels that come into view in verse 1. They are seen from four directions: the four directions on the compass. This is a familiar biblical phrase. Isaiah 11:12 refers to the four corners of the earth. Revelation 20:8 speaks of the four quarters of the earth.

In a word, these angelic beings will be commanded to hold back the four winds, to stop the judgment. The terrible movement of judgment upon the earth will stop until God accomplishes his purposes.

Verses 2 and 3 tell us that purpose. The word *till* means a limited time. The restraint will be temporary. The judgment will be stopped, but it will come again.

Preservation

> And I heard the number of them which were sealed: and there were sealed an hundred and forty and four thousand of all the tribes of the children of Israel (v. 4).

There will be twelve thousand from each of the twelve tribes. In my opinion, these will be literal Israelites, actual Jewish people who will be saved, through the testimony of the two witnesses that we read about in the eleventh chapter. After the church is raptured away to heaven, God is going to send two witnesses who will preach the gospel. From their preaching, a great multitude of souls from the nation of Israel will be saved, 144,000 of them. They will be protected: sealed.

All the forces of hell will not be able to kill these 144,000 preachers. The 144,000 will go all over the world preaching. Nothing will be able to stop them. They are sealed with the seal of the living God. This seal is a mark of divine possession and protection.

The word *seal* is very important for us. It forms the basis of our own salvation. Ephesians 1:13 says that on believing, we were sealed with the Holy Spirit. That is the same word—*seal*—that we find here. It is a marking, a permanent identification, a transaction completed.

In the tribulation time God will seal 144,000 preserved through it all. That is a beautiful symbol. When we are saved, we are sealed with the Holy Spirit and we are kept until the Lord comes for us.

The reason for the sealing of the 144,000 is obvious. The Antichrist will be in control of the world at this time. When an individual commits his heart to Jesus he immediately rejects the Antichrist. Most of the people who are saved during this time will be killed immediately. This 144,000 will be preserved from all the forces of evil operating during this terrible time.

Position

> After this I beheld, and, lo, a great multitude, which no man could number, of all nations, and kindreds, and people, and tongues, stood before the throne, and before the Lamb, clothed with white robes, and palms in their hands;. And cried with a loud voice, saying, Salvation to our God which sitteth upon the throne, and unto the Lamb (vv. 9-10).

We are confronted now with a vast multitude of Gentile people of every nation and race. This is so great a number of people that no one could count them. It will include additional Jews. Here we see worldwide revival. People from every part of the earth give their hearts to Christ.

Notice the position of these saints. They stand before the throne of God. What a tremendous privilege to stand accepted before the throne of God! They are not on their faces begging mercy from him, not trying to hide from him, but standing before God accepted and approved!

They will be clothed with white robes. They have washed their robes and made them white in the blood of the Lamb (v. 14). They are now clothed in the righteousness of Christ, in the robes of holiness and salvation.

It is thrilling to realize that the blood will never lose its power. The blood that had power to save and redeem in the first century will be just as powerful in the coming age. Until the very end of time, the blood of Christ will be able to cleanse and to wash white as snow. The very last soul to trust Jesus Christ has just as much standing before God as the first one.

They will have palm branches in their hands. Remember that these saints will have come through a time of great persecution. They will have been oppressed, tormented, tortured, and killed. We have already heard their prayers for God's vengeance upon those who have murdered them.

But here they stand with palms in their hands. The palm is a symbol of deliverance, the joy of being no longer shackled by sin, no longer oppressed by Satan, no longer depressed by evil. They will cry with a loud voice of praise and thanksgiving. There will be no cool dignity about their worship. They have been delivered, set free, and with a loud voice they will cry in gratitude to God.

Privilege

And all the angels stood round about the throne, and about the elders and the four beasts, and fell before the throne on their faces, and worshipped God, Saying, Amen: Blessing, and glory, and wisdom, and thanksgiving, and honour, and power, and might, be unto our God for ever and ever. Amen. And one of the elders answered, saying unto me, What are these which are arrayed in white robes? and whence came they? And I said unto him, Sir, thou knowest.

And he said to me, These are they which came out of great tribulation, and have washed their robes, and made them white in the blood of the Lamb. Therefore are they before the throne of God, and serve him day and night in his temple: and he that sitteth on the throne shall dwell among them.

They shall hunger no more, neither thirst any more; neither shall the sun light on them, nor any heart. For the

> Lamb which is in the midst of the throne shall feed them, and shall lead them unto living fountains of waters: and God shall wipe away all tears from their eyes (vv. 11-17).

This is a list of the privileges of these saints. First is praise. They praise God and the Lamb on the throne for their salvation.

Sometimes we forget what it was like to be lost. We do not spend much time praising God for our salvation yet it was a great miracle of grace.

We were not saved because we deserved to be, but because we *needed* to be. We ought to ever praise God for the salvation he has given to us.

Salvation means a total change in life: "If any man be in Christ, he is a new creature: old things are passed away; behold, all things are become new" (2 Cor. 5:17).

Put that beside the average church member in America and it has a hollow ring to it. The average church member does not go to church. Sixty-five percent of this country's people say they are church members. Yet never more than 15 percent of them attend church.

That is not real worship and certainly not real commitment. I can understand how some of them could think one could lose his salvation. If we can be saved and not be changed, we could lose salvation and never miss it!

I believe that many church members have no encounter— no experience—with God, no living relationship with him. They have no understanding that they were saved from their sins. Church is not intended to be only a religious exercise we go through once a week. It is adoration and praise to our God for what he has done for us.

He has purchased us. When we were sealed we were sold to him, and now we belong to him. Be sure you understand that you cannot lose your salvation. However, salvation will always produce a change. No change equals no salvation! These saints who came through the tribulation will be praising God. What a privilege!

They will also be serving God. They "serve him day and night in his temple" (v. 15). This means ceaseless, unending service. They forever serve God. The concept of sitting on a cloud in heaven and playing a harp is a false picture. We will serve God day and night, endlessly, forever.

We try to serve God now. Our hearts desire to please him and in our imperfect way we feel there are certain things we can do in serving God. But then we will have perfect, genuine service of God. We will be as these tribulation saints, engaged in one glorious, unbroken, glad, perfect service.

Many of us think of heaven like a great football stadium. We imagine that the really sharp, spiritual person will have 50-yard-line seats, close to the front. The less spiritual will be in the less favorable seats. And if we just barely make it, we will be in the end zone.

But this verse reveals that "he that sitteth on the throne shall dwell among them" (v. 15). We are limited in our physical forms and can only be in one place. But in heaven, everyone has a front row seat! Everyone has intimate fellowship with God.

It is as though no one is there but God and the believer. What a beautiful realization: in heaven we will all be close to the Lord. He will be among us, next to us, in us. And we shall serve him.

What a delight that will be! We can serve only when we know of needs and without closeness we cannot know. In heaven we will be eternally close to our Lord and he to us.

Then we can render spontaneous, unceasing service. That is why we serve and worship God now, pointing to that time when we will serve next to the Father with the saints of all ages.

Then a fantastic thing happened. They had been through

great tribulation. They had been unable to buy food without the identifying mark of the beast.

Some of these tribulation saints had starved to death. Many of them had no water and no warmth. Many were in barren, frozen wastelands; yet here they will not hunger or thirst any more. They will not need the sun to warm them anymore. They are warmed by the presence of the Father.

Look closely at verse 17. The Lamb now becomes our shepherd. What a beautiful picture! "And God shall wipe away all tears from their eyes." Tears had been a way of life for them. They had known nothing but a trail of tears, nothing but physical pain and heartache. They had been oppressed and persecuted. They had seen loved ones and friends die. Many of them had been tortured and killed.

Tears were a way of life for them. Now, however, God himself—not an angel—but God himself shall wipe away the tears! God will not allow an angel to minister to them at that time. An angel may stay the hand of God's judgment, an angel may administer God's judgment, but God himself will wipe away these tears.

Sorrow will not always have the upper hand. Everyone of us has walked through the vale of sorrow. We have seen someone we love hurt or die. We have seen separation, have watched misunderstanding and confusion fracture relationships. We have known grief, but it will not always be that way. Until then, we can know that God in his providence will keep, shield, and protect us. Whatever God allows to come into our lives is meant for our good. God will be blessed and praised and we shall be eternally benefited, for God will bring us to that glorious day when he himself shall wipe away every tear. This chapter is the blessed interlude of grace.

14

The Trumpet Judgments
8 and 9

These two chapters form a unit and need to be viewed together. We come now to the opening of the seventh seal. The opening of the seals extend over the entire tribulation period. Within the seventh seal are the trumpets. There are difficulties in knowing the exact times and orders of the trumpets and vials, but whatever the sequence, they describe a time of unbelievable horror.

This is a picture that must be viewed like a diamond. The Book of Revelation takes the awful judgment of God, turns it like a precious stone and allows us to view each terrible facet.

At the opening of the seventh seal we find the introduction of seven angels who sound seven trumpets. The seventh seal includes the seven trumpets. In Jewish tradition, the trumpet was used for many things. It was used to call soldiers to battle, call worshipers to worship, gather a convocation, announce a festival or feast.

It held a very prominent place in the life of Israel. In this case, the sounding of each trumpet announces specific judgments of God on earth.

The devil's messiah is presented to the world in this chapter. Here is Satan's man. The seals have been broken, the cries have rung out, the riders on those horses have appeared, the conditions of the world have grown steadily worse and humanity has become horrified.

At the end of chapter 6 it was assumed that the great day of God's wrath had come. But the worst is yet to come. What has come before is but a prelude. It is minor compared to what is about to come.

Now we see worldwide wars worse than anything recorded in history, accompanied by plagues, pestilence, and destruction unimaginable. When the seventh seal is opened, there is silence in heaven for about the space of half an hour.

There is no explanation for the silence, and there is nothing more terrifying. To know that something is about to happen but to hear only silence is devastating. The great hosts of heaven watched the Lamb of God open the seals one by one. Each one grew more terrifying than the last.

When he came to the seventh seal there was only silence. Nothing! Absolute, abject, terrifying, foreboding silence! Silence is more eloquent than noise and more terrifying in its anticipation.

After the silence, seven angels appeared with seven trumpets. The seven trumpets tell us of the great, final intervention of God in judgment. The first six verses of chapter 8 are preparatory to the seven trumpets. Here the prayers of the saints arise to God.

It is as though their prayers had been concentrated. They may have been given over a period of time, but they had been concentrated, and the angel of God anointed those prayers so that they were brought in a potent way before the throne of God. As soon as the prayers of the saints who have been martyred ascend to the throne, the judgment of God will descend upon the earth.

Some people think God does not answer our prayers. A day is coming when the prayers of the saints that have been bottled up over the years will rise in a great final offering of incense, and the judgment of God will descend on the earth. That is what we have in these two chapters.

The trumpet judgments occur just before the second coming of Christ when he returns to the earth to establish his kingdom. For, when the seventh trumpet sounds, the mystery of God will be finished (Rev. 10:7). When the seventh trumpet is sounded, it is the sign of the coming of the Lord.

This giddy, pleasure-mad age has little knowledge of the trouble it is fast approaching. We are living in a world that is headed for destruction and does not know it. We assume everything is going to be all right. We are not serious about much.

If anything should make us serious, it is the economic condition of our society and world. We are in so much debt as a nation that there is no way we will ever pay it back. One would think that we would apply principles of economics to cause us, as a nation, to turn the tide economically.

But no, we want someone else to sacrifice. We go on believing everything is going to be alright. If anything ought to distress us, it is the tremendous rise of violence and the utter disregard of authority today.

We ought to be concerned about these problems but we are not. We just keep going our way, putting into our lives the garbage of a rebellious spirit. The world does not understand, and God's people seem to be of virtually no help in teaching it. So finally the trumpet of God's judgment is going to sound.

The trumpets are divided into two groups. The first four trumpets deal with natural catastrophes or calamities. The last three deal with specific judgments directly upon the people of this earth.

The First Trumpet

The first angel sounded, and there followed hail and fire mingled with blood, and they were cast upon the earth: and the third part of trees was burnt up, and all green grass was burnt up (8:7).

What a bleak picture of the desolation that comes by the hail and the fire from heaven with this judgment.

The Second Trumpet

The second angel sounded, and as it were a great mountain burning with fire was cast into the sea: and the third part of the sea became blood; And the third part of the creatures which were in the sea, and had life, died; and the third part of the ships were destroyed (vv. 8-9).

The second trumpet will cause a great meteorite or asteroid to be cast down to earth. It will look like a mountain was cast into the sea. The sea will actually turn to blood. One third part of the creatures of the sea will die and one third of the ships in the sea will be destroyed.

The Third Trumpet

And the third angel sounded, and there fell a great star from heaven, burning as it were a lamp, and it fell upon the third part of the rivers, and upon the fountains of waters; And the name of the star is called Wormwood; and the third part of the waters became wormwood; and many men died of the waters, because they were made bitter (vv. 10-11).

Wormwood is the bitterest of all the shrubs known to the human race. Normally, it would make one sick but not to death. But this wormwood will be so bitter that many people will die because it poisoned the water.

There are many natural events that parallel this. For instance, on March 23, 1823, a volcanic eruption in the Aleutian Islands caused all of the water in that particular area to become bitter and unfit for any human use.

In the science section of *Time* magazine scientists projected what would happen if an asteroid one mile in diameter hit the middle of the Atlantic 2,000 miles from shore. The impact would be the equivalent of a 500 million megaton bomb blast.

The splash it would make would displace 1,000 cubic miles of sea water and would form a crater fifteen miles across on the floor of the ocean. It would produce tidal waves up to 100 feet in height and earthquakes 100 times worse than any ever recorded, according to Dr. Paul Sandorf of the Massachusetts Institute of Technology.

We can see how something similar could cause the death of the creatures in the sea and the destruction of ships.

Scientific American tells us what did happen when an asteroid, one mile in diameter, hit the earth. They found the crater and deducted scientifically that an asteroid with the equivalent force of a 1.5 million megaton bomb (one megaton is one million tons of TNT!) hit the earth. We already know that our own atmosphere and the universe in general are filled with meteorites and asteroids that could easily do exactly what God says is going to happen.

The Fourth Trumpet

And the fourth angel sounded, and the third part of the sun was smitten, and the third part of the moon, and the third part of the stars; so as the third part of them was darkened, and the day shone not for a third part of it, and the night likewise. And I beheld, and heard an angel flying through the midst of heaven, saying with a loud voice, Woe, woe, woe, to the inhabiters of the earth by reason of the other voices of the trumpet of the three angels, which are yet to sound (vv. 12-13).

God will withdraw the light. For one third of the twenty-four hour period there will be no sun, no moon, no stars.

Scientists tell us that if we diminish the light upon this earth by one third, when it does shine it will not be as bright as when it shone all the time.

It is easy to understand what would happen if that took place. It would unbalance all of nature. Plant life alone gives enough insight for us to understand the importance of light in the balance of nature.

The worst is yet to come. Verse 13 speaks of the inhabitants of the earth, the people who have totally disregarded God. Those who have lived for this life and world only, who have had no time for God, are being warned about what is going to happen. This message is to earthbound people.

God's people are not earthbound. Satan's are. These woes will fall on earthbound people. In the ninth chapter, the plagues that will come are specifically instructed to strike those who do not have the seal of God. Those who are sealed with the seal do not suffer that judgment.

Notice the progression of these trumpet judgments: first, one-third of the trees and the green grass, one-third of the marine life and shipping, one-third of the water and then one-third of the heavenly lights will be destroyed. In other words, the food is destroyed first, then the distribution of food is crippled, the water supply is limited and production is hampered.

We can see what will happen. The first four trumpet judgments deal with the physical aspects of this world that we take for granted. When war erupts, the first thing that goes is the water supply. It only takes one well-placed bomb and we have no water. The second thing to go is food. Then, medical supplies, facilities, and personnel are unavailable. That is the picture of what takes place in these trumpet judgments. They are God's final judgments on a rebellious world.

The Fifth Trumpet

> And the fifth angel sounded, and I saw a star fall from heaven unto the earth: and to him was given the key of the bottomless pit. And he opened the bottomless pit; and there arose a smoke out of the pit, as the smoke of a great furnace; and the sun and the air were darkened by reason of the smoke of the pit (9:1-2).

The star that will fall from heaven will be Satan himself. It is obviously a personage for it says "to him was given the key." Isaiah 14 talks about Lucifer falling from heaven in his rebellion against God. Jesus said, "I beheld Satan as lightning fall from heaven" (Luke 10:18). We now have Satan intervening personally in the tribulation time.

The day is coming when all hell will be loosed on this earth. The bottomless pit, which is the dwelling place of all the demonic, evil, hellish things in this universe, is going to be opened. A cloud of awesome blackness and obnoxious smoke will be emitted. A strange darkness will blot out the sun, and demonic terrors will be loosed on the earth.

> And there came out of the smoke locusts upon the earth: and unto them was given power, as the scorpions of the earth have power. And it was commanded them that they should not hurt the grass of the earth, neither any green thing, neither any tree; but only those men which have not the seal of God in their foreheads (vv. 3-4).

These locusts come to attack directly unbelieving, rebellious, ungodly men. "And to them it was given that they should not kill them, but that they should be tormented five months" (v. 5).

The period of time is very specific. We do not know why five months. It does not matter. It is a long time to be tormented. It is going to be so bad that people will "seek death, and shall not find it; and shall desire to die, and death shall flee from them"

(v. 6). The victims of this plague, the judgment of God, will be inflicted with such excruciating pain that they will long to die but will not find death. In this life, we do everything we can to avoid death. But they will be seeking death and will not die. God will not let them. What a judgment on evil and sin!

When we read the Gospels concerning the death of Jesus Christ on the cross, we will realize the extent to which the judgment of God will be poured out on the earth.

The locusts are described as horses and look like nothing we have ever seen. They have a king over them, the angel of the bottomless pit, whose name in the Hebrew tongue means destruction. In the Greek, his name means destroyer.

That is a description of Satan. Satan is a destroyer. He hates us and wants to destroy everything in our lives. If we think we are going to find something good, satisfying, or fulfilling by following the devices of Satan, forget it! He wants to destroy us. He will take our Lves, twist, warp, and destroy them.

Christ came to save but in this judgment, Satan will come to destroy. These locusts, shaped like horses, will afflict men for five months led by their king, Satan himself.

The Sixth Trumpet

And the sixth angel sounded, and I heard a voice from the four horns of the golden altar which is before God, Saying to the sixth angel which had the trumpet, Loose the four angels which are bound in the great river Euphrates. And the four angels were loosed, which were prepared for an hour, and a day, and a month, and a year, for to slay the third part of men.

And the number of the army of the horsemen were two hundred thousand thousand: and I heard the number of them. And thus I saw the horses in the vision, and them that sat on them, having breastplates of fire, and of jacinth, and brimstone: and the heads of the horses were as the heads of lions; and out of their mouths issued fire and smoke and brimstone.

By these three was the third part of men killed, by the fire, and by the smoke, and by the brimstone, which issued out of their mouths. For their power is in their mouth, and in their tails: for their tails were like unto serpents, and had heads, and with them they do hurt.

And the rest of the men which were not killed by these plagues yet repented not of the works of their hands, that they should not worship devils, and idols of gold, and silver, and brass, and stone, and of wood: which neither can see, nor hear, nor walk: Neither repented they of their murders, nor of their sorceries, nor of their fornication, nor of their thefts (vv. 13-21).

This is the same altar from which the prayers of the saints ascended. The horns of the altar have always been a place of mercy. It has always been a place where sacrifice for sinners is welcome. If we wanted to be saved, needed mercy and forgiveness, we could always come to the horns of the altar. But now, there is no more mercy, no more sacrifice upon that altar. The altar of divine mercy will one day put forth divine judgment.

Paul put it another way. He said, "Be not deceived; God is not mocked: for whatsoever a man soweth, that shall he also reap" (Gal. 6:7).

We never make a fool out of God. Sometimes we think God does not see or know what we are doing or thinking. But God knows and we reap what we sow. We are not going to get away with our rebellion against God.

At the horns of the altar a voice commands the sixth angel to release the four bound angels (v. 14). These are four different angels because the other four angels have not been bound. These are obviously evil angels, because they have had to be restrained. If they are turned loose, they will bring havoc upon the earth.

All of this is under divine control. God will use Satan's own hosts to bring the powers of evil to naught. God is still in control. He uses even Satan himself to accomplish his purpose. And these four angels are prepared to slay one third of the people of the earth. At today's population, that would be about 1.5 billion.

Under the fourth seal, one fourth of the earth was killed. When we add just these two judgments together, we have a loss of one-half of the population, more than 2.4 billion people. When we consider that millions of others died from the other plagues, we begin to see the devastation of the people of this earth.

It will happen at an exact time known only to God. When Jesus Christ came into this world, the Scripture says that he came in the fullness of time. That means he came exactly when God planned it.

God did not plan for Jesus to be born in Nazareth with Caesar Augustus throwing God a curve and Jesus instead being born in Bethlehem. God had it all planned out and Caesar's evil decree worked out the purposes and plan of God. He came at the right time, at the exact moment—not one day too soon or one day too late.

At the precise moment, Jesus Christ was born. And the precise moment of this judgment is already scheduled in the plan of God. It will be carried out on schedule!

Then will appear an immense army of 200 million horsemen. They will be like nothing we have ever seen on the earth and will represent the combined power of Satan and rebellious humanity. But again they will unknowingly carry out the judicial purposes of God.

Everything will seem to be under satanic control but God

will really be behind the scene. No power on earth will be able to restrain these hellish horsemen. Their weapons will be fire, smoke, and brimstone (v. 17). Those are the weapons of hell but they are emblems of God's judgment. What a ghastly place earth will become when hell is turned loose.

A great portion of these evil people will be spared, not because they deserve it, but because in wrath, God remembers mercy. God never delights in the punishment or death of the wicked. In the midst of the severest judgment the earth has ever seen, God delights to be gracious even to the guilty.

Yet an amazing thing happens. "And the rest of the men which were not killed by these plagues yet repented not of the works of their hands" (v. 20).

There is not one thing we can do to force a man to repent. We cannot punish a man severely enough, make life miserable enough, intimidate him enough to make him repent. We may shackle him but we cannot make him repent.

The worse judgment ever to come on the earth will not soften the hard hearts of people. They will not repent. In fact, they will go the other way. Verse 20 says there will be a revival of idolatry.

They "repented not of the works of their hands, that they should not worship devils, and idols of gold, and silver, and brass, and stone, and of wood: which neither can see, nor hear, nor walk."

Then there follows a list of their evil practices: "Neither repented they of their murders, nor of their sorceries, nor their fornication, nor of their thefts" (v. 20).

Murder is a common crime. Approximately one out of every twenty-five deaths in a major city is homicide. It will be rampant in the last days when people with hardened hearts return to idol worship.

Sorcery in the original language speaks of impure practices with toxic drugs. It especially refers to tampering with personal health with drugs, potions, intoxications, and magical acts and incantations invoking demonic spirits.

The drug culture is going to deepen. We already know that one step leads to another and always deeper into dependence. At this time it will deepen and deepen until sorcery and the abuse of poisonous drugs will run rampant.

Fornication means the flagrant disregard for marriage. Today there is a limited restraint on the violation of marriage vows. But in this day of judgment all restraint will be gone and human passion will break loose.

Nor did they repent of their thefts. Honesty will evaporate. There will be no regard for anyone's property. It will be the law of the jungle. Whoever is strong enough to take what one has will get it. There will be no integrity or character evident in that day.

Why does God paint such a picture? This is all in the future. The solemn words of God through this revelation ought to cause sinners to repent. Anyone who has never given his heart to Jesus should not wait another moment to do so.

Every child of God should determine to dedicate and consecrate his life totally to Jesus Christ, to be used by the Holy Spirit in these days of grace. We are living in wonderful days when we can preach the gospel freely and tell others about Jesus. These are days when the Holy Spirit of God is dealing with hearts and drawing men to God.

This is a day God has given to us before these terrible, tragic days of the tribulation time. Today we can serve God joyfully, gladly, and praise God openly. What a day for us to be alive, but what a responsibility!

We cannot play church. We cannot go on with business as usual. We cannot simply be content to open the doors of the church and "let" people come. We cannot be content to compare ourselves with other religious people.

Christians who truly know God must live for him in these

days of grace. Perhaps then our hearts will catch fire and join others until a great band of the saints has marched to the ends of the earth with the good news of the gospel before the four angels are loosed with the bad news of judgment.

15

The Angel and the Scroll
10:1-11

Chapter 10 is another interlude in the judgment of God. Here is a scene that is not a part of the ongoing judgments of God. This interlude begins with the first verse of the tenth chapter and continues through the fourteenth verse of the eleventh chapter.

The Mighty Angel Comes

And I saw another mighty angel come down from heaven, clothed with a cloud: and a rainbow was upon his head, and his face was as it were the sun, and his feet as pillars of fire: And he had in his hand a little book open: and he set his right foot upon the sea, and his left foot on the earth. And cried with a loud voice, as when a lion roareth:

and when he had cried, seven thunders uttered their voices. And when the seven thunders had uttered their voices, I was about to write: and I heard a voice from heaven saying unto me, Seal up those things which the seven thunders uttered, and write them not (vv. 1-4).

Now we see a great and mighty angel. What an appealing individual he is. This is a very powerful being. Many commentators and scholars believe this is a description of Jesus Christ, that the cloud draped about him is a sign of the glory and power of God, and his face shining as the sun is a reminder of the mount of transfiguration. They feel the rainbow upon his head is a sign of the covenant that God has made with the human race. However, I do not agree.

We need to understand the power of angels. This angel, as all angels do, has many Godlike characteristics. He is powerful and has a divine nature.

But never in the Book of Revelation is Jesus called an angel. The angels are created beings of an unusually high order and they have a prominent place in Revelation. More than sixty-six times in this book, we have references to angels.

But every time we see an angel—and it is true in this tenth chapter—that angel is in a position of service. He does not create but administers the will of God in human affairs. This angel is not worshiped. If it were Christ, he would be worshiped as he appeared.

While angels are very powerful beings and fulfill a responsible, needed service in the economy of God, never is Jesus Christ in Revelation referred to as an angel.

This is one of the most practical passages found anywhere in the Book of Revelation, and perhaps the most significant passage in the book. The angel descends to the realm of earth. The cloud signifies the glory of God. He is on a divine mission. The rainbow about his head is a sign of God's covenant relationship. Every rainbow we see is a reminder of God's covenant. The angel comes with such a visual reminder. Fire always represents judgment and wrath, so the description of his feet as pillars of fire show him to be one who will also be declaring the judgment of God.

Notice the destination of his descent. He descends to the earth with one foot placed on dry land and the other one on the sea. It is a very obvious reference to the fact that "the earth is the Lord's and the fullness thereof."

The angel who comes in the glory and power of God with a

reminder of his covenant is claiming the earth for God. Jesus Christ will establish his kingdom on the earth, and the earth belongs to him. The destination of the angel is the earth itself. He stakes God's claim to it.

Notice the determination of this angel. "And cried with a loud voice, as when a lion roareth: and when he had cried, seven thunders uttered their voices. And when the seven thunders had uttered their voices, I was about to write: and I heard a voice from heaven saying unto me, Seal up those things which the seven thunders uttered, and write them not" (vv. 3-4).

Do not try to speculate about what the seven thunders said. God said we are not supposed to know. (That is one of the interesting things about some religious groups who believe that God told their leader what the seven thunders said. The Bible very plainly says, "Don't write them, seal them. They are not to be revealed." It is not good speculation or good Bible study to try to determine what the seven thunders may have said.)

A lion roars just before he is about to complete whatever he is doing. Whatever his victim, when the lion roars, he is ready to complete his kill. It is a determined cry. When this lion roars, God expresses his right to rule the earth.

Satan says, "I want to rule the earth." God says, "No, you cannot. I shall rule this earth." When the determined voice of the mighty angel cries, all the trumpets of heaven will sound. The number seven is the number for completeness and finality. It means the complete and final judgment of God is at hand.

The Mighty Angel Speaks

And the angel which I saw stand upon the sea and upon the earth lifted up his hand to heaven, And sware by him that liveth for ever and ever, who created heaven, and the things that therein are, and the earth, and the things that therein are, and the sea, and the things which are therein, that there should be time no longer: But in the days of the voice of the seventh angel, when he shall begin to sound, the mystery of God should be finished, as he hath declared to his servants the prophets (vv. 5-7).

He speaks with great authority. This is no ordinary angel. He will have an authoritative word, shown by the lifting of his hand to heaven. Always, the lifted hand is a sign of authority. Men have claimed the lifted hand as a sign of earthly authority. But when the mighty angel of God lifts his hand, it is a sign of the eternal authority of God himself.

Then he will take an oath by him that lives for ever and ever. This is one of the reasons not to believe that this angel is Jesus because he would be taking an oath on himself if he were.

This angel will swear by a power greater than himself. When God allows an oath to be taken by the very character and nature of himself, it is a sign of authority.

In verse 6 this angel declares time should be no longer. Literally, there will be no more delay. He is not saying that time will cease to be but there will be no more delay in what God is going to do. The declaration of the mighty angel means God is about to move; judgment is about to come.

Today we are in a time when the judgment of God upon the earth is delayed. But at this point, the mighty angel declared there will be no more delay. Evil will be judged speedily, quickly.

In verse 7 he declares that the mystery of God is finished. There are many ideas about what that means, but most scholars agree that the mystery of God refers to the martyrdom and suffering of God's people.

Have you ever asked, "Why do bad people seem to do so well and good people seem to have such problems? Why does evil seem to prevail and good seem to be defeated?"

In the tribulation time, there will be millions of saved persons who will be murdered. God has heard their prayers for revenge, yet he will be silent. The mystery is silence of God in the face of the apparent victory of evil.

Why does God not answer our prayers? When we hurt, our hearts are broken; when difficulties surround us and evil overwhelms us why does God not do and/or say something?

The silence of God is one of the most difficult things we have to deal with. When this mighty angel makes his declaration, he will be saying the mystery is finished.

Get ready: God will answer all questions. God is going to clarify the dilemma. Every covenant promise God has ever given to us will be completed and consummated. God's purposes are moving toward the completion and fulfillment of his purposes.

Satan is not in control of this world. It appears that he is and God's silence remains a mystery. But we can know that God is using even Satan and the forces of evil to achieve his purposes.

When this seventh trumpet sounds (11:15), it will not be a mystery anymore. The kingdom will have been established. Then the mystery of God will be finished and time for judgment will no longer be delayed.

The Mighty Angel Obeys

And the voice which I heard from heaven spake unto me again and said, Go and take the little book which is open in the hand of the angel which standeth upon the sea and upon the earth. And I went unto the angel, and said unto him, Give me the little book. And he said unto me. Take it, and eat it up; and it shall make thy belly bitter, but it shall be in thy mouth sweet as honey.

And I took the little book out of the angel's hand, and ate it up; and it was in my mouth sweet as honey: and as soon

as I had eaten it, my belly was bitter. And he said unto me,
Thou must prophesy again before many peoples, and
nations, and tongues and kings (vv. 8-11).

John is ordered to eat the little book containing the revelation of God, the Word of God. Many times in Scripture, the
Word of God is compared to food. It is not an uncommon
reference (Matt. 4:4; Jer. 15:16; Ps. 119:131; 1 Pet. 2:2). Verses
10 and 11 tell of the obedience of this mighty angel. It is at this
point we have some tremendous practical application to our
own lives. Here is a tremendous teaching in prompt obedience.

The first obvious lesson is that whatever God tells us to do
we should do it. We never make a mistake to promptly obey
God. Obedience brings blessing and fulfillment. We may not
understand the reason, but we must do it. It is in obedience to
God that God is able to bless us and give satisfaction and
fulfillment.

There is another practical lesson. The Word of God has to be
received, digested, and absorbed into our being before we can
effectively share with other people. Second-hand truth is never
very convincing. To repeat someone else's words is never very
satisfying and it does not convince others of the truth of the
Word of God.

Here is the picture of the man who is going to prophesy, who
is given the assignment to go back and teach and preach,
having to digest it for himself.

Teaching the Word of God is the most important thing we do
apart from worship. We must do it with great deliberation,
dedication and diligence. Nothing is more significant than
digesting of the Word of God. When we have studied his
Word, we have something to share.

The interesting description of this meal is that it tasted sweet
in his mouth but gave him indigestion. We have all eaten things
that tasted great but, afterwards, made us sick. Why is it that

the Word of God is sweet to the taste and bitter to the stomach?

The Word of God to John was sweet because it was a word of promise, a word of praise and a word of grace and love. It was a wonderful word from God of the victory of his purposes: the covenant fulfilled. That was a sweet word.

But it was also bitter because it told of divine judgment yet to be poured out on the earth. The destruction of the wicked is never an attractive thing to God. It must not be to us. It ought to grieve us.

If we feel that wicked men "have it coming," we do not have the mind of God. It grieves God when men have to be judged and punished. He longs for them to know him. The Word is sweet in the promise of fulfillment, grace and love. It is bitter in the judgment to come. That is why it is called elsewhere "sharper than any two-edged sword" (Heb. 4:12).

The Gospel itself is like that: sweet to those who respond and bitter to those who do not respond. The same gospel that guarantees salvation to those who receive it guarantees judgment and damnation to those who reject it.

This is also true of the Christian. The Word of God is sweet if we obey; bitter if we disobey. Chastisement is never sweet. Its results may be sweet in a closer walk with God, but it is not pleasant to be chastised.

God does not tell us to do something to make life miserable for us. He tells us in order to make life sweet for us. If we do not do it, life is bitter.

Our bitterness is not because God planned some misery for us. It is a misery God knew was coming, and he wanted us to avoid it. The Word of God is sweet to those who hear and obey it and bitter to those who reject it.

The testimony that John gave by eating the Word of God was his responsibility for telling others. He was told he must prophesy again to other peoples, nations, tongues and kings.

John was called to faithfully deliver the Word of God as it was delivered to him.

That is what we are to do. Every Christian who has received the Word of God needs to ask, "Where do I fit into God's plans?" One thing is for sure. What we have received from God, we are responsible to give away.

16

The Two Witnesses
11:1-14

We are in an interlude. We will get confused if we think that Revelation is chronological in order. It is not an attempt to place events in a time order. At this point, we are between the sounding of the sixth and seventh trumpets. We are somewhere in the first three and one-half years of the tribulation period.

The period called the Great Tribulation is the last three and one-half years when the great judgment, turmoil, and disaster come. We are seeing what takes place in the first half of Daniel's seventieth week.

It is obvious that God is not finished with the Jews. In this chapter, Jews revert to an Old Testament form of worship. A magnificent temple is built. It does not specify where, but a system of priesthood and a system of sacrifices are set up in the midst of an ordered system of worship.

This seems to be necessary because in both Daniel 9:2 and Matthew 24:15, Jesus tells of the "abomination of desolation," which speaks of the desecration of the Temple. It would be difficult to desecrate something that was not there. There must come a time when the Temple is rebuilt.

In 2 Thessalonians 2 concerning the man of sin, the Antichrist, it says, "Who opposeth and exalteth himself above all that is called God, or that is worshiped; so that he as God sitteth in the temple of God, shewing himself that he is God" (2 Thess. 2:4).

The Antichrist will actually claim to be God from a temple that is called his temple, erected to his worship. Thus the temple must be rebuilt. The religious system of the Antichrist is to be connected with this worship.

It is amazing that the world at large will still reject Jesus Christ, even though there are 144,000 Jewish evangelists. In this chapter we meet the two witnesses who have fire that proceeds out of their mouths and kills anyone who tries to keep them from preaching.

That is a dramatic witness, but in spite of it the world does not listen. We now see the absolute degradation, the absolute wickedness of human hearts. In the face of incredible and spectacular witness for Christ, people still say no. The heart of the human race is desperately wicked.

Rod

> And there was given me a reed like unto a rod: and the angel stood, saying, Rise, and measure the temple of God, and the altar, and them that worship therein. But the court which is without the temple leave out, and measure it not; for it is given unto the Gentiles: and the holy city shall they tread under foot forty and two months (11:1-2).

In Revelation 2, 12, and 19, the rod is an instrument of God's chastisement of Israel. It is laid on Israel by the Gentiles for forty-two months or three and one-half years. That is the first half of Daniel's seventieth week. John is told to measure that which belongs to God, the Temple, the altar, and the people who worship therein. The people refer to God's believing children, his dwelling place.

Do you suppose that worship is a two-way process where we adore and worship God but God also measures us? God measures and evaluates his people. I pray that when God measures us, we would measure up to what he desires.

But the godless Gentiles are not to be measured. God is dealing with the apostate part of the Gentile world and he is about through with it. Their time is almost over. When we come to this point, we are approaching the last half of Daniel's seventieth week.

Revelation

> And I will give power unto my two witnesses, and they shall prophesy a thousand two hundred and threescore days, clothed in sackcloth. These are the two olive trees, and the two candlesticks standing before the God of the earth. And if any man will hurt them, fire proceedeth out of their mouth, and devoureth their enemies: and if any man will hurt them, he must in this manner be killed.
>
> These have power to shut heaven, that it rain not in the days of their prophecy: and have power over waters to turn them to blood, and to smite the earth with all plagues, as often as they will (vv. 3-6).

We are now introduced to two magnificent witnesses. God never leaves himself without a witness. Here in the midst of tribulation time, God sends two witnesses. We do not know who they are, but there is much speculation.

Some say they are Elijah and Moses because Elijah is the one who prophesied that it would not rain, and it did not rain. Moses is the one who turned the water into blood during the plague in Egypt. Some say Enoch is one of them.

Scholars are particularly intrigued with the Elijah and Enoch idea because neither one of them died, but were taken up to be with the Lord. Others think Elisha and still others, John the Baptist. It does not matter who they are, and God does not give us a clear indication.

We do know they are going to prophesy and declare the truth of God. They are going to confront the wickedness of this world in the tribulation age. These two witnesses are going to absolutely distress the world. The world will be angry at these two witnesses. They will need all the power they have to keep from getting killed. They incur the wicked wrath of the world.

They will be clothed in sackcloth. Sackcloth is what a prophet wore when he called a nation to repentance. They will call for repentance from the people.

The two olive trees and the two candlesticks refer to the fruitfulness, the living nature of their witness and the light they give. That is really all we know about these two witnesses except their power.

They have great power. Verse 5 tells us they slay with fire that comes from their mouths. They have power to shut up heaven so that it does not rain and turn the water to blood. They have the power to smite the earth with plagues. They have the weapons of drought, death, and disease.

They repeat the miracles that Moses and Elijah performed against slavery and apostasy. And they are invincible. They cannot be killed until God gets through with them.

The Word of God, whenever and wherever it is preached, makes folks very uncomfortable. The Word of God, faithfully preached, makes people unhappy. Here in Revelation it will make the people so angry that they will try to kill the two witnesses.

Revolt

And when they shall have finished their testimony, the beast that ascendeth out of the bottomless pit shall make war against them, and shall overcome them, and kill them. And their dead bodies shall lie in the street of the great city, which spiritually is called Sodom and Egypt, where also our Lord was crucified.

> And they of the people and kindreds and tongues and
> nations shall see their dead bodies three days and an half,
> and shall not suffer their dead bodies to be put in graves.
> And they that dwell upon the earth shall rejoice over them,
> and make merry, and shall send gifts one to another;
> because these two prophets tormented them that dwelt on
> the earth (vv. 7-10).

We are now introduced to the Antichrist himself. The beast
that ascends out of the bottomless pit comes in a revolt against
these two witnesses and he overcomes them and kills them.
The first part of verse 7 says, "And when they shall have
finished their testimony."

All the forces of hell will not be able to stop them until God
gets through with them. Nothing can stop or hinder a man who
walks in the power of the spirit of God from doing what God
has set for him to do.

Jesus was only thirty-three when he finished his work on
earth. The death of Jesus was not a tragic accident. Just as he
was born in the fullness of time, he died in the fullness of time.
Here we have a graphic illustration of the fact that God's
people who walk in his will and power cannot be stopped until
he is finished with them.

It matters not how old we are; when God is finished, the call
will come. Not before. Not old age, not disease, not decay—
nothing can stop the man who proclaims the message of God
until God gets through with him. The end for him will be in the
frameword of the purposes of God.

Then the Antichrist will come and two witnesses will meet a
violent death. "And their dead bodies shall lie in the street of
the great city, which spiritually is called Sodom and Egypt,
where also our Lord was crucified" (v. 8).

Sodom is a symbol of wickedness, and Egypt is the nation
that oppressed the people of God. These are two symbols of
oppression and slavery, and the verse says that Jerusalem will

become so spiritually corrupt that it will be like Sodom and Egypt.

"And they of the people and kindreds and tongues and nations shall see their dead bodies three days and an half, and shall not suffer their dead bodies to be put in graves. And they that dwell upon the earth shall rejoice over them, and make merry, and shall send gifts one to another; because these two prophets tormented them that dwelt on the earth" (vv. 8-10).

This is one of the most tragic passages anywhere. Here is a real revelation of the wickedness of the human heart. The bodies of these two dead witnesses are not even buried. They leave them on the streets of Jerusalem and everyone rejoices in their death.

Within the heart of every man every conceivable wickedness resides. There is nothing man will not do. Wickedness is rampant in his soul. It is written into the fiber of his flesh. And we see here the extreme to which man's rebellion against God can go.

Man in his flesh is a rebel against God. "All have sinned and come short of the glory of God" (Rom. 3:23). There is nothing but exceeding wickedness in the heart apart from God. A world apart from God is a world bound to bring hell on earth.

In this picture of the two witnesses we see the extreme to which man will go. Can we imagine joining hands and dancing around two corpses, laughing and rejoicing? It is a picture of the utter decay of the human heart.

Resurrection

And after three days and an half the Spirit of life from God entered into them, and they stood upon their feet; and great fear fell upon them which saw them. And they heard a great voice from heaven saying unto them, Come up hither. And they ascended up to heaven in a cloud; and their enemies beheld them (vv. 11-12).

Imagine the picture. They have been watching these two corpses decay for three and one-half days. Then all of a sudden the ashen gray of death gives away to the rosy color of life and they stand up in the street. The resurrection of these two witnesses demonstrates the awesome power of God.

Imagine the consternation and the dismay in the hearts of the peoples of the world: "and their enemies beheld them." When Jesus ascended into heaven his faithful few watched him, not his enemies. When Elijah was taken off in a chariot, only the faithful Elisha saw it.

But here, these two prophets are taken away in the full view of their enemies. Even in the light of that, the world does not turn to Christ!

Jesus told the story of a rich man who died and went to hell. He saw Abraham across a great gulf and they began to carry on a conversation. He asked Abraham just to dip his finger in water and come put a drop on his tongue to ease the torment of the flames.

When Abraham told him that it was impossible, the man in hell asked Abraham to send someone back to his brothers and tell them about God. Abraham replied, "They have Moses and the prophets. If they won't believe them, they won't believe even though one came back from the dead" (see Luke 16:19-31).

If we rebel and reject the spirit of God, we shall come to a time just as evil and wicked as this future time when the world will rejoice over the death of two witnesses and then, seeing their resurrection and ascension, still not give their hearts to God.

Remnant

And the same hour was there a great earthquake, and the tenth part of the city fell, and in the earthquake were slain of

men seven thousand: and the remnant were affrighted, and
gave glory to the God of heaven. The second woe is past;
and, behold, the third woe cometh quickly (vv. 13-14).

Remnant means only a few. Most of the people will not pay
much attention. Most of the people, in the face of this
resurrection and ascension and in the face of an earthquake
where 10 percent of the people are killed, will have no interest
at all.

The point is that there will be sweeping ingathering of souls
even in the face of such a divine and a supernatural moving of
God.

The passage is a sobering passage because it shows us
where we will go if we stay away from God. It shows us how
hardened our hearts will get if we continually reject God. It
shows us the natural tendencies of our hearts.

Apart from God there is nothing we will not do. There is no
sin, no crime, no deed we will not do apart from God. We are
dependent upon God's grace, God's power, God's life in us.

In this interlude between the sixth and seventh trumpets is a
call for us to commit our lives to God and a warning of the
desperate extremes the wicked human heart will go in its
rebellion against God.

17

The Seventh Trumpet
11:15-19

It seems too early in the Book of Revelation to come to the climax, but this passage is the conclusion of the Book of Revelation. The first eleven chapters take us from the beginning to the end and climaxes with these verses.

Beginning with chapter 12, John repeated everything again in more detail, giving us a more comprehensive view. This trumpet announces the establishment of the kingdom of Christ on the earth. The kingdom is not actually established until the nineteenth chapter, but here we have a preview.

These verses summarize everything in the Book of Revelation. The kingdom of Christ consumes the earth, accompanied by the worship and praise of all God's people. God's name is revered and glorified throughout all the earth. His power is demonstrated and brings an angry response of the nations to Christ's coming.

This ultimately results in the battle of Armageddon.

We see the judgment of the dead who shall stand at the great white throne; the unbelievers who will be cast into hell. We behold the judgment of the saved: God's children receive their crowns. We are shown a picture of the perfect Temple in heaven open for us. The last verse details the confusion and terror upon the earth during the tribulation time. This is a synopsis of everything in the Book of Revelation.

The Announcement

> And the seventh angel sounded; and there were great
> voices in heaven, saying, The kingdoms of this world are
> become the kingdoms of our Lord, and of his Christ; and he
> shall reign for ever and ever (v. 15).

When we read these verses, we do not find anything being
initiated on earth. This scene is in heaven. It introduces the
next series of judgments to come.

This is the continuing story of the King of kings and Lord of
lords. It is the proclamation of the event that heaven has long
awaited: the establishment of the kingdom of Christ on earth.
The sounding of the seventh trumpet is the official proclamation of the coming coronation of our Lord Jesus Christ.

We cannot read this without being deeply moved if our
hearts long for the coming of Christ and for the restitution of
righteousness, the retribution of God against evil, and the
triumph of God's purposes on earth.

If we long to be free from those things that destroy, depress
and bring despair to our hearts, this verse is exciting and
precious. We can scarcely read it without tears of joy and
anticipation. "The kingdoms of this world have become the
kingdoms of our Lord and of his Christ; And he shall reign
forever and ever."

The whole question of sovereignty will now be settled. Who
controls the universe: God or Satan? The issue has raged in
the minds of people throughout all ages.

Now the issue is settled.

Jesus Christ, our sovereign Lord, comes to establish his
kingdom on this earth and the whole question is settled. At
Jesus' temptation, Satan carried him to a high place and
showed him the kingdoms of the world. "Fall down and
worship me and all of these kingdoms will be yours."

Jesus did not deny Satan's ability to deliver those kingdoms (see Matt. 4:1-11). We are living in a time when Satan seems to be in control of this world. God is allowing Satan to exercise his dominion.

But even during the apparent dominion of Satan, God is working out his purposes.

Everything Satan has done, every evil scheme he has conceived in his heart, everything he has propagated on people that he thought would work against God, has in fact been working together to bring the kingdom of Christ into fruition on this earth.

"The kingdoms of this world are become the kingdoms of our Lord, and of his Christ" (v. 15). In the original text, "kingdoms" is singular. The kingdom of Satan, the kingdom of Antichrist, will become the kingdom of our Lord. When God looks at this world now, he sees endless desperation, cemeteries, graves by the millions, tragedies unnumbered.

We cannot open a newspaper without being confronted with a disaster or some difficulty. God sees a world full of sin, evil and disappointment; full of fear, death, disease, and decay. But it will not be that way forever.

Christ's kingdom will consume the kingdom of this world. It will be one universal kingdom. Philippians 2:9-11 will be fulfilled: "Wherefore God also hath highly exalted him, and given him a name which is above every name: That at the name of Jesus every knee should bow, of things in heaven, and things in earth, and things under the earth; And that every tongue should confess that Jesus Christ is Lord, to the glory of God the Father."

John described that day. He announced the coronation of Christ, the coming of the King. The government of Christ will be a righteous government. Man's laws, man's religion, and man's wisdom will never produce a righteous government. But Christ's government will be righteous and perfect.

"For ever and ever" is the strongest possible phrase in the

original language. It literally says, "It is for ages and ages." It means that once Jesus Christ comes to this earth and establishes his kingdom, there will be no interruption of it. Not even the battle of Armageddon will interrupt it. The enemies of Christ will amass themselves against him and come with all their weapons and armor, but Jesus will simply step out and with a single breath put an end to it.

Once our Lord sets his foot on the earth, there will be no change in his kingdom. That is the announcement. The kingdom of this world will become the kingdom of our Lord. And he shall reign for ever and ever.

This announcement is made as though it had already taken place. The verb tense in the original language says it is already history.

That is the way of prophecy. It is history God has written down before it happens. It is an established fact that cannot be changed. The kingdom of Christ has now consumed the kingdom of this world and we await the fulfillment of that prophetic, historic truth.

The Adoration

> And the four and twenty elders, which sat before God on their seats, fell upon their faces, and worshipped God, Saying, We give thee thanks, O Lord God Almighty, which art, and wast, and art to come; because thou hast taken to thee thy great power, and hast reigned (vv. 16-17).

When the announcement is made, there is an instantaneous adoration, worship and praise of Christ. As soon as the announcement of the coming King is made the elders, or the saints, fall on their faces and worship God.

That ought to happen now. When we realize the purposes of God are moving inevitably toward a climax where Christ will be declared King of kings and Lord of lords of a kingdom that shall be for ever and ever, our response ought to be praise, worship, and obedience to God.

It will be an instantaneous response to the Word of God. They will hear the Word and respond immediately. We should respond to the Word of God that way. Never just consider it. When we hear the Word, we should do it. That ought to be our response.

For us to be happy and growing Christians, the Word of God must be more than an item on our menu. It must be nourishment for our souls, to be consumed and made part of us. That is the way to happiness. Hearing the word and acting upon the word ought to go together.

Notice the names or titles they gave to Jesus: "Saying, We give thee thanks, O Lord God Almighty, which art, and wast, and art to come; because thou hast taken to thee thy great power, and hast reigned" (v. 17). He is the eternal God. He is Lord which means he is in absolute control. He is the Owner, Creator and Sustainer of all things. He is God; almighty and all powerful.

What a glorious name. Our praying and worship would take on a new dimension if we would learn to praise the Lord God Almighty. How long has it been since we got on our knees and praised him for his name, his power, his wisdom, his might, his sustenance, all that he has done?

That is what will happen at the announcement of the coronation. His power is described as "great power." Power ought to be sufficient in itself. But in God, it is "great power."

The Anger

And the nations were angry, and thy wrath is come, and the time of the dead, that they should be judged, and that thou shouldest give reward unto thy servants the prophets, and to the saints, and them that fear thy name, small and great; and shouldest destroy them which destroy the earth (v. 18).

It is interesting that the things which cause rejoicing in heaven cause anger on earth. That's how it is. This world will never understand the things of God. When Christ's coming is announced, there will be rejoicing in heaven but anger on earth.

That should not surprise us. If we interpret the plan and pursuits of any person today who has comfort and wealth as goals, we arouse their anger. Anything that calls for sacrifice, for a putting aside of the pursuits and selfishness of people, arouses their hostility.

Psalm 2 is a description of the raging of the nations against the things of God. People in general will never welcome Christ. One of the lessons of the Book of Revelation: regardless of the circumstances, people apart from Jesus Christ will not welcome God.

Put them in a perfect millennium with the perfect, righteous rule of Christ and at the end of that time, they will still marshal an army against Christ. Apart from God, people will never welcome Christ. They will never receive him because heaven and earth have nothing in common.

Earth dwellers are bound to time, material things, and self-centered pursuits. Heaven dwellers worship and adore the Lord God Almighty. The two have nothing in common.

When the end time comes and earth dwellers have to relinquish everything they have to the Creator, they will be very unhappy about it. But Christ will take only what is his. "The earth is the Lord's and the fulness thereof" (Ps. 24:1).

We do not own anything. Our possessions are only ours to hold for a season. When we die, they will go to someone else.

Everything that we call ours really belongs to God. We came into the world without anything and what we now hold is ours to hold only for a season. Christ will come one day and claim what is his.

"Thy wrath is come" (v. 18) refers to the judgment of God.

"The time of the dead" refers to the great white throne when unbelievers will stand in judgment before God at the end of the millennium. "That thou shouldest give reward" speaks of the judgment of the Christian's works at the judgment seat of Christ.

We will never see justice meted out in this world. We will never see things as they ought to be in this life. There are inequities and discrepancies between what is and what ought to be. We will never find satisfaction in the justice of humanity.

But when Christ returns, perfect justice will be administered. This life is not all. It is only a small capsule in eternity, a small piece of time. In eternity, God will mete out perfect justice.

The prophets he is going to reward are the ones who received the revelation of God and proclaimed it, many times amidst great stress and persecution.

Hebrews 11 speaks about these prophets:

> Who through faith subdued kingdoms, wrought righteousness, obtained promises, stopped the mouths of lions, quenched the violence of fire, escaped the edge of the sword, out of weakness were made strong, waxed valiant in fight, turned to flight the armies of the aliens. Women received their dead raised to life again: and others were tortured, not accepting deliverance; that they might obtain a better resurrection. And others had trial of cruel mockings and scourgings, yea, moreover of bonds and imprisonment: They were stoned, they were sawn asunder, were tempted, were slain with the sword: they wandered about in sheepskins and goatskins; being destitute, afflicted, tormented; . . . and these all, having obtained a good report through faith, received not the promise: God having provided some better thing for us, that they without us should not be made perfect (Heb. 11:33-40).

These prophets will be rewarded. He is going to reward his saints, all those who have committed themselves to the work of the kingdom of God. Faithfulness is going to be rewarded.

Sometimes we think nobody sees; nobody cares what we do. We may think it all goes unnoticed. But when Jesus Christ comes to be crowned King of kings upon this earth, he will reward his saints.

He will "destroy them which destroy the earth" (v. 18). This refers to the Antichrist and the false prophet who will be cast into the lake of fire. Judgment is going to come upon this earth. The anger of men will be matched with the perfect anger of God.

The Ark

> And the temple of God was opened in heaven, and there was seen in his temple the ark of his testament: and there were lightnings, and voices, and thunderings, and an earthquake, and great hail (v. 19).

In this verse, we have a picture of the ark. Heaven is opened and as John looks up, he sees the Temple. In Exodus 25:40 we are told that Moses designed the Temple after a pattern that had been given to him. In Hebrews 9:23-24, again the inspired writer speaks of the fact that the earthly Temple was a pattern of the heavenly Temple.

The Temple here on earth is a facsimile of the one in heaven. This is one of the reasons we can believe that God has a special place for Israel in prophetic times because the church has no Temple.

The Temple was opened, and John saw the ark of God's testament. It is the only object seen. The ark was the most precious thing in the nation of Israel. It represented their faith, their heritage.

The ark had five names in the Old Testament. The most prominent name was the ark of the covenant because it contained the tables upon which were written the covenant requirements of God with his people (Num. 10:33).

It was also called the ark of testimony (Ex. 25:22) because it was a testimony of God's mercy toward sinning Israel. There at the mercy seat on the ark, the people could find forgiveness. It was called the ark of God (1 Sam. 3:3) because it was the only visible throne of God upon this earth.

It was called the holy ark (2 Chron. 35:3) because it was a place where holy God met with his people. It was called the ark of God's strength (Ps. 132:8) because everywhere the ark went, great and mighty miracles occurred and significant things surrounded its presence.

What is the significance of John's seeing the ark? The ark was located in the holy of holies. Nobody saw it but the high priest and he saw it only once a year.

In that day, the ark will be opened for all to see as a reminder that God's glory and innermost secrets will be revealed to his people. Everyone who knows God shall know the mind of God. Seeing the ark will also remind us that God is a covenant God and does not forget his covenant or his people.

"There were lightnings, and voices, and thunderings, and an earthquake, and great hail" (v. 19). The scene now shifts from heaven to earth. These catastrophic events tell of rising confusion and terror that shall come to the earth during the last half of the tribulation period.

As we look at this beautiful synopsis of God's purpose as revealed in the Book of Revelation, it ought to move everyone to show praise, gratitude, and thanksgiving to God, just as those elders fell prostrate before God, praising him, thanking him.

I believe everyone should turn to Jesus Christ to escape that terrible period of tribulation that lies ahead.

18
War in Heaven
12:1-17

Beginning with this chapter, there is a review of all the events of the tribulation period in the last days of human history. There is an amplification and explanation giving us keen insights into our own day as well as some anticipation of what is to come.

There will be war in heaven, against God himself and against his people. When those wars fail there is at the end of the chapter war against a remnant of God's people, probably the 144,000 who were sealed.

This war started at the dawn of history, at the very beginning of man's experience on earth. God declared this war against Satan in the garden of Eden. God said, "I will put enmity between thee and the woman; . . . it shall bruise thy head and thou shalt bruise his heel" (Gen. 3:15).

That was a declaration of war. All of the wars, battles, and conflicts on earth from that day until this are just a continuation of that great spiritual war between God and Satan.

Toward the end of this chapter, we find the answer to one of the most puzzling questions the world has ever seen: anti-Semitism.

Why is the Jew so hated? Jewish people are—genealogically speaking—the purest race in the world. Yet they have been haunted, hunted, and outcast throughout the earth. Why? According to this chapter, anti-Semitism—hatred for the Jewish people—is instigated by Satan himself.

As terrible as the persecution of the Jews has been, as terrible as Hitler's holocaust was, there is going to be an even worse time of persecution of the Jews in the last half of the tribulation period.

The Wonders

And there appeared a great wonder in heaven; a woman clothed with the sun, and the moon under her feet, and upon her head a crown of twelve stars: And she being with child cried, travailing in birth, and pained to be delivered. And there appeared another wonder in heaven; and behold a great red dragon, having seven heads and ten horns, and seven crowns upon his heads.

And his tail drew the third part of the stars of heaven, and did cast them to the earth: and the dragon stood before the woman which was ready to be delivered, for to devour her child as soon as it was born. And she brought forth a man child, who was to rule all nations with a rod of iron: and her child was caught up unto God, and to his throne. And the woman fled into the wilderness, where she hath a place prepared of God, that they should feed her there a thousand two hundred and threescore days (vv. 1-6).

The word *wonder* is an interesting word. It is the Greek word *semeion*. It is found fifty-one times in the New Testament, and forty-eight times it is translated "sign."

Here it is translated "wonder." It is in fact a sign, representing something to come. It is a key to the puzzle of much that has happened in the world around us.

"And there appeared a great wonder"(v. 1). The word *appeared* is the past tense of "to see." It simply says, "and there was seen a great woman."

This does not fit into a chronological time slot. It spans the breadth of human history.

The woman represents the nation of Israel and all of God's people through time. She is magnificently attired: clothed with the sun, walking on the moon, with a crown of twelve stars on her head.

That reminds us that Israel and all God's people have always been the light-bearers. We have always been God's light-bearers to humanity.

She represents the people of Israel for she is the one who travailed in birth, who presented the Messiah to the world.

The second wonder is a red dragon, the one behind all of the bloodshed of the world. Every murder, every act of cruelty, every act of bloodshed the world has ever seen ultimately come from Satan. The dragon has seven heads, ten horns and seven crowns on his heads.

We could get bogged down examining all the symbolism here. The seven heads represent the completeness of wisdom. Seven is the number of perfection/completion. The head means wisdom.

Satan is a master strategist, a sly and cunning adversary. The ten horns could represent the ten-nation confederacy that is going to appear in the tribulation time. Certainly, it identifies Satan with the Antichrist.

The seven crowns upon his heads link Satan to Antichrist as described in chapter 13, and to the governments that are energized by the Antichrist in chapter 17.

"And his tail drew the third part of the stars" (v. 4) describes Satan's fall from heaven (Isa. 14:12). Jesus said that he beheld Satan falling as lightning from heaven (Luke 10:18).

This passage tells of Satan's descent into this world.

He came to devour the woman's child as soon as it was born. The whole war between sin and righteousness is a battle between Satan and Jesus Christ. Satan has from the very beginning opposed everything that Jesus Christ stands for.

He stood ready to devour the child, to thwart God's redemptive plan. All through the Bible runs the story of Satan seeking to detour the purposes of God, opposing him.

But God maneuvered and directed the path of history until his salvation of the human race was fulfilled through Christ. Satan tried to stop Jesus before he could accomplish human salvation.

He has been at war with Jesus Christ ever since Genesis 3:15. Satan hates Jesus Christ and his testimony. He will use any method to silence it.

Satan will use murder as he did with Cain. He will use slander, destroying the reputation of those who testify. He will use compromise and deception. He will do anything to stop the witness of Christ.

That is why the more serious our own commitments to God, the more we have a problem with Satan. Whenever we give our lives to Jesus Christ, we not only get a new Savior but a new enemy who is against everything and everyone who stands for Christ.

When we experience a great spiritual victory, very often the next day we will be down. Satan is no fool. When God begins to do something, Satan makes his move to oppose it.

When a church begins to sense the Spirit of God, we can count on difficulties arising to threaten the spirit of that church. When an individual begins growing and maturing in Christ, Satan will move in and attack.

It can be discouraging, for Satan does not bother us as long as we are going his way. But when we turn around and go God's way, we run head-on into Satan. That is the way it is.

But Satan is a defeated foe: a paper lion! He cannot defeat us or stop us. Victory is ours if we "put on the whole armor of God" (Eph. 6:11-17).

The woman brings forth a man child who is Jesus Christ: the

only one of whom it could be said, he "was to rule all nations with a rod of iron" (v. 5). Only Christ fits this description (Ps. 2:8-9).

In this verse we have a simple statement of the whole life and purpose of Jesus from the time he appeared on the earth as a child until the time when he will rule in his millennial kingdom on the earth.

In a word, Christ was born into the world, caught up to God and his throne, and will rule with a rod of iron.

The man child can also be a symbol of the church, for what happens to the head happens to the body. It is interesting that the words *caught up* is the exact same word that is used in 1 Thessalonians 4:17 concerning the rapture of the church.

Christians are hated in the world. Satan wants to destroy not only Christ but every vestige of his witness, his church. The man child has a secondary application to the church.

The War

> And there was war in heaven: Michael and his angels fought against the dragon; and the dragon fought and his angels, And prevailed not; neither was their place found any more in heaven. And the great dragon was cast out, that old serpent, called the Devil, and Satan, which deceiveth the whole world: he was cast out into the earth, and his angels were cast out with him (vv. 7-9).

This is not a sign. We have reached beyond the *semeion,* the sign, and now we see reality. This reality is war in heaven. There are two reasons for this conflict. The forces of God want to cast Satan down from heaven to earth. Ultimately, Satan will be cast into the lake of fire.

The first great character in this conflict is Michael the archangel and his angels. There are only two angels named in the Bible: Michael and Gabriel. Gabriel is the angel who proclaims; he is God's messenger. Michael seems to be the commanding general of the Lord's armies. He opposes Satan in heaven and on earth. Jude 9 talks about Michael contending with Satan for the body of Moses.

Here he contends with Satan in heaven. When God gives the order, Satan and all his hosts will be cast out of the heavens, down to earth. Michael is the principal in the drama.

The dragon who personifies Satan has five names in the ninth verse. He is called a dragon because of his fierce, destructive nature; a serpent because of his crafty cunning; the devil because he is a slanderer and an accuser; and Satan, which means adversary, because he is the enemy of God's people. And finally he is called a deceiver because he deceives the whole earth. That is a fitting description of Satan and what he does.

He is called the accuser of our brethren (v. 10). Many people think that Satan is in hell, but he is on earth and is opposing heaven! Someday he will be in hell. But we see very clearly here that Satan had access to the throne of God, where he accused the believers.

He accuses us. He tells God how reprobate we are. Satan's work today is to discredit the saints before the throne of God.

Satan not only accuses the brethren before the throne of God, he accuses the brethren before the brethren. We call it "gossip." He has many willing helpers.

The Bible calls gossip "evil speaking." Perhaps the greatest sin in the church today is gossip. What a tragedy!

H. A. Ironside said, "Satan is the accuser of the brethren. Let's leave the dirty work to him." It is unbecoming of a Christian to help Satan in his slanderous "dirty work."

At the signal of God, Satan was cast upon the earth. We cannot imagine the effect this is going to have. Satan maintained access to the throne of God but suddenly, halfway through the tribulation, he was cast down and confined to the earth.

That is why the last half of the tribulation is going to be such a terrible time. Satan will know no limits. His fury will know no end. It marks the end of Satan's rule in the air, his dominion. God will give him almost complete freedom here on earth.

The Witness

And I heard a loud voice saying in heaven, Now is come salvation, and strength, and the kingdom of our God, and the power of his Christ: for the accuser of our brethren is cast down, which accused them before our God day and night. And they overcame him by the blood of the Lamb, and by the word of their testimony; and they loved not their lives unto the death.

Therefore rejoice, ye heavens, and ye that dwell in them. Woe to the inhabiters of the earth and of the sea! for the devil is come down unto you, having great wrath, because he knoweth that he hath but a short time.

And when the dragon saw that he was cast unto the earth, he persecuted the woman which brought forth the man child. And to the woman were given two wings of a great eagle, that she might fly into the wilderness, into her place, where she is nourished for a time, and times, and half a time, from the face of the serpent.

And the serpent cast out of his mouth water as a flood after the woman, that he might cause her to be carried away of the flood. And the earth helped the woman, and the earth opened her mouth, and swallowed up the flood which the dragon cast out of his mouth. And the dragon was wroth with the woman, and went to make war with the remnant of her seed, which keep the commandments of God, and have the testimony of Jesus Christ (vv. 10-17).

When Satan is cast out of heaven, it will be a real blessing.

They will rejoice in a very great way (v. 12). Imagine the joy in heaven. Through the centuries, all the vices of the saints have been paraded before the throne of God and now their victories will be paraded before it.

With Satan gone, the saints will rejoice and tell each other the glories of the cleansing blood of Jesus Christ. They will tell how they overcame through the blood of Christ, of the glories of salvation, the strength of God and the power of Christ. There will be unbridled rejoicing and witnessing of their great salvation.

They overcame Satan through the shed blood of Jesus Christ. Satan accuses the saints before the throne of God, but Jesus' blood cleanses all. The blood is the answer: the rebuke of Satan. It is our fortress, our strength. How glorious! Victory is ours because Jesus shed his blood.

There is no sin too heinous, no rebellion too deep or great. The blood covers it all for those who will receive him. We do not overcome Satan by any resolve of our hearts but by the shed blood of Jesus Christ.

They overcame by "the word of their testimony" (v. 11). This is the outward act of telling of their faith in Christ. That testimony was used to help them overcome.

The same thing is true today. Show me a person who is always sharing what Jesus Christ has done in his life, and I will show you one who overcomes, who is victorious in his Christian life.

Show me someone who is timid and afraid to share that he belongs to Christ and I will show you a defeated Christian, one who does not walk in victory.

The word of their testimony can also apply to the Word of God because we have their testimony recorded in the Word of God. The Word of God is a mighty tool. It is the sword of the Spirit that we must use in overcoming.

"They loved not their lives unto the death" (v. 11). Every

child of God ought to have that attitude: a commitment even to the point of death. Their commitment to Christ was so strong they did not concern themselves with their own safety.

God is in control. Jesus Christ did not die until God said that it was time. If we love not our lives unto death, we are invincible until God gets through with us.

One's death is never an accident. We ought to have a reckless abandon to the things of Christ, living for God with all of our hearts.

When Satan is cast out of heaven and onto the earth, tremendous chaos will take place (v. 12). God will allow Satan almost unrestricted freedom on earth. In a fury that knows no bounds, Satan will run to and fro across this earth. It will be the time of the devil's wrath. He will know there is a limit to his time so he is going to wreak terrible havoc.

He is also going to persecute the nation of Israel. Verses 13-16 describe how Israel is going to flee into the wilderness for refuge. They will be "given two wings of a great eagle" (v. 14). Some have tried to interpret that as an airplane lift or some modern aviatorial accomplishment.

But God will miraculously provide a swift escape for these Jews who remain so they can find refuge in the desert. When the dragon sees that he cannot accomplish what he wanted to, he will persecute the woman—Israel—once again.

Satan hates the Jews because they are a reminder of God's purposes. They are a repository of God's Word. It was through the Jews that the Messiah was presented to this world. Satan hates the Jewish race and will intensify his efforts and make one last, great effort to destroy the nation of Israel.

He will send a flood against them. Some feel that the phrase "as a flood" is symbolic of a flood of opposition, perhaps propaganda. It could be, or it might be a real flood. Verse 16 says that the "earth helped the woman, and the earth opened up her mouth, and swallowed up the flood."

In Numbers 16:31-33 God was confronted with opposition from the people to his commandments and to Moses, and the Bible declares that the earth opened up her mouth and swallowed them.

God destroyed his enemies by opening the earth. He may do it again. Satan may send a flood and God may open up the earth to protect his chosen people. Many will attempt to destroy Israel, but God will protect her.

"And the dragon was wroth with the woman, and went to make war with the remnant of her seed, which keep the commandments of God, and have the testimony of Jesus Christ" (v. 17).

It is the nature of God's children to keep the commandments of God, to keep the testimony of Jesus Christ. Our testimony and our obedience is a vital part of our service to God. It is through that obedience and testimony that others are brought into the kingdom of God. This is what God expects of his people at all times.

As we approach the end of the age, we are approaching a time that will be characterized by lawlessness, hostility and opposition to Jesus Christ. We are already seeing a crescendo of opposition. In these days, Christians must be loyal to the Lord Jesus Christ and to his Word!

There is a battle raging today and no one can remain neutral. We are either for Jesus Christ or Satan. There is no middle ground. There must be a positive commitment to Christ or we have resigned ourselves to rebellion.

The battle is raging and God calls us to keep his commandments and his testimony. This is no day for compromise, immorality, impurity, heresy, or skepticism. This is a day for faith, trust and obedience.

Today is our greatest opportunity to stand on the Lord's side.

19
The Antichrist
13:1-10

Now we are introduced to the rise of Satan's superman: his incarnation. Just as Jesus is the incarnation of God, the Antichrist is the incarnation of Satan. Everything Jesus does, has done, and will do, Satan tries to imitate.

Satan is a counterfeiter, always trying to imitate what Christ has done. In tracing all Satan's attempts to establish his kingdom on earth, we find everything he has and is attempting to do is duplication of what Jesus Christ has already done. The Antichrist is Satan incarnate.

In this chapter, we see the rise of two beasts and the reign of terror and destruction that will accompany them.

The source of their power and authority is Satan himself. This is not too surprising because Jesus said, "I am come in my Father's name, and ye receive me not: if another shall come in his own name, him ye will receive" (John 5:43).

I believe that Jesus was thinking about that time when Satan's messiah will come and men who have rejected Christ will receive Satan himself. Satan conjures up a man who bears all the characteristics of Satan. He is the visible expression of the invisible devil. Every line of Satan's character is faithfully reproduced in the Antichrist.

This passage describes Satan's last all-out effort on earth. It is his last drive to defeat the program of God and to establish his own kingdom. The reason for Satan's urgency is that the Lamb holds the title deed to this earth and he is about to come and take possession.

Satan knows it and will make his last effort to throttle the divine plan. At this point, humanism will reach its height with a reign of terror and brutality.

This is the period prophesied by Paul:

> For the mystery of iniquity doth already work: only he who now letteth will let, until he be taken out of the way. And then shall that Wicked be revealed whom the Lord shall consume with the spirit of his mouth, and shall destroy with the brightness of his coming: Even him, whose coming is after the working of Satan with all power and signs and lying wonders. And with all deceivableness of unrighteousness in them that perish; because they received not the love of the truth, that they might be saved. And for this cause God shall send them strong delusion, that they should believe a lie (2 Thess. 2:7-11).

How could the Antichrist's appearance affect us?

In the Greek text the phrase "I stood upon the sand of the sea" belongs to the twelfth chapter. It literally says, "he stood upon the sand of the sea." If we look at the last verse of the twelfth chapter, it says, "The dragon was wroth with the woman, and went to make war with the remnant of her seed, which keep the commandments of God and have the testimony of Jesus Christ."

Thus it should also read, "And he stood." Satan, in the form of this great red dragon, stands upon the sands of the sea and calls out of the raging ocean a beast that is the Antichrist. Satan is the originator, the moving force behind the coming of the Antichrist.

The sea represents the masses of humanity, the nations of the world. Some people feel that this means the Antichrist will be a gentile, not a Jew. When another beast comes up out of the land, they believe that this means the land of Israel and thus the false prophet would be a Jew. That may or may not be true.

But one thing is clear: out of the raging sea described in Revelation 13, this beast came forth. That is not unusual. Historically, it has always been that way.

Out of the chaos and turmoil of the French Revolution, Napoleon was born and came to power. It was out of the chaos and turmoil of the masses during the revolution in Russia that Lenin came forth. Out of the chaos and turmoil Hitler was projected into power in Germany.

Many great world leaders have come to power out of the turmoil of revolution and rebellion. It will be so in the last days. Out of the raging sea, out of the chaos that exists in the world, this last great ruler will come.

His Person

> And I stood upon the sand of the sea, and saw a beast rise up out of the sea, having seven heads and ten horns, and upon his horns ten crowns, and upon his heads the name of blasphemy. And the beast which I saw was like unto a leopard, and his feet were as the feet of a bear, and his mouth as the mouth of a lion: and the dragon gave him his power, and his seat, and great authority (vv. 1-2).

The heads refer to his wisdom; the horns, as we see from Daniel's vision, refer to confederated power. He will rule many nations. The crowns represent his authority. This sounds like Daniel's description (Dan. 7).

Daniel described the beasts that he saw as a lion, as a bear, as a leopard, and the fourth beast he could not describe.

Here, John saw the same three. But they were in reverse order. Daniel was looking forward and he saw the kingdoms of the world as they were to be after him. John was looking back and he saw these kingdoms as they had been. It is all a matter of perspective. The little horn of Daniel 7:8 is now the first beast, the Antichrist in this thirteenth chapter.

His Power

> And I saw one of his heads as it were wounded to death; and his deadly wound was healed: and all the world wondered after the beast. And they worshipped the dragon which gave power unto the beast, saying, Who is like unto the beast? who is able to make war with him? And there was given unto him a mouth speaking great things and blasphemies; and power was given unto him to continue forty and two months (vv. 3-5).

The Antichrist is killed. Remember, Satan is going to counterfeit everything Jesus has done or will do. Christ was killed, but then resurrected.

Now an interesting thing will happen. This old world which has denied the resurrection of Jesus Christ is going to accept the resurrection of the Antichrist. This world would rather believe a lie than the truth.

That is one reason there is a whole system developed around atheistic evolution today. It does not even make sense and is certainly not scientific at all. But men would rather believe a lie than to believe that God can do something, including creation.

That is the way it will be in the end times. This world, having denied the resurrection of Jesus Christ, will believe a lie. That is exactly what Paul declared in 2 Thessalonians 2:11.

The Antichrist will be an attractive, fascinating personality. He will have exceptional qualities of wisdom, daring and leadership that will earn him the admiration of people all over the world. He will be admired for his military might and

strategy: "who is able to make war against him?" (v. 4). He will
be a magnificently talented individual.

Satan does not have the power now that he will have in the
tribulation period. The word *power* that is used throughout this
chapter means "unhindered power." He will have the ability to
do almost anything. He will have that authority in the last
portion of the tribulation through the Antichrist, but he does
not have that kind of power today.

We have that power today. To the believer God's power is
given. The power for victorious living, faithful witnessing, and
sharing the gospel is ours today.

It is absolutely amazing. We have the power and will not use
it. Satan does not have it, but he surely would use it if he did.
And when the end times come, he will have it and he will use it.

Unlimited power will be given to the Antichrist. The world
will go crazy, delirious with delight over this beast.

His Purposes

And he opened his mouth in blasphemy against God, to
blaspheme his name, and his tabernacle, and them that
dwell in heaven. And it was given unto him to make war with
the saints, and to overcome them: and power was given him
over all kindreds, and tongues, and nations. And all that
dwell upon the earth shall worship him, whose names are
not written in the book of life of the Lamb slain from the
foundation of the world. If any man have an ear, let him
hear. He that leadeth into captivity shall go into captivity: he
that killeth with the sword must be killed with the sword.
Here is the patience and the faith of the saints (vv. 6-10).

The Antichrist will have four things planned. First, he will
blaspheme and defy God. That is the very essence of Satan.
Both Isaiah 14 and 2 Thessalonians 2 reveal that Satan's desire
is to go to the very throne of God and sit on it. He wants to be

God. He is going to curse everything God stands for: his name, his tabernacle and his saints.

He is a blasphemous individual and his purpose will be to defy God. Everything related to God will come under his attack. As far as God is concerned Satan is now powerless. He is only a name-caller. He cannot do anything more than attack blasphemously the things of God.

But in that day he will have a vocabulary for vindictive vituperation never equaled on this earth. He will attack the purposes of God, the name of God. Every person who blasphemes today is in league with Satan! Blasphemous speech is not a little thing, it is a huge attack on God himself.

The name of God is the most powerful name in all the world. Christ declared, "Whatsoever ye shall ask in my name, that will I do" (John 14:13). No wonder Satan attacks the name of God. It is by the name of God—the name of Christ—that we are saved. It is by the name of Christ that we tap the resources of heaven. It is by his name that we live victoriously. No wonder Satan attacks his holy name.

Second, he will seek to destroy the saints: "it was given unto him to make war with the saints" (v. 7). These are the saints on earth who have been saved during this tribulation time. He cannot harm the glorified saints in heaven. But he can harm believers on earth. He will do this for forty-two months (v. 5). In that period of time, he will be permitted to use all of his power against the saints of God. This is the devil's last fling at the people of God. He will drink of blood and violence and be revealed for what he is: a monster with a quenchless thirst for blood.

Third, he will dominate the world. "Power was given him over all kindreds, and tongues, and nations" (v. 7). He is going to achieve his goal of unifying the nations against God. He will dazzle some, browbeat others, and solidify the whole world order with the cement of every evil passion and the mortar of a horrible, merciless, unrelenting persecution. We are moving in that direction today.

We are becoming philosophically prepared for a one-world government. That idea is propagated by Satan. God does not want a one-world government until Jesus Christ comes to establish his kingdom on earth.

The reason is simple: men will not usher in the millennium; God will. The things we dream about, work toward, and reach for—only God can make happen. The Antichrist will dominate the world and delude the masses of people.

He will deceive and delude the whole world except those who are saved (v. 8). He will come to blaspheme God, destroy the saints, control the world, and deceive the people of the world.

Scripture is not like the six o'clock news. It is to be used of God to make us the kind of persons he wants us to be. What does a beast rising out of the sea with seven heads and ten horns and seven crowns mean to us today? There are many applications.

First, all blasphemy and hostility toward God is from Satan. Anytime there is hostility or blasphemy in our hearts toward God, Satan is the originator. He is the source of all blasphemy. When we see the hostility of this world toward God, we have a foretaste of the tribulation.

When we are told on every side that God is to be kept out of the public schools and out of government, that is a warning. Society will not be happy until there is a hostility toward God. It is not a question of being neutral. Neither government nor the schools should be evangelistic enterprises for the church, but neither should they be used to destroy the faith of the church.

This is what we are seeing in the world today. All such blasphemy and opposition to God are of Satan.

Second, Satan counterfeits everything Christ has done, even our Christian experience. In the end times, there will be an incarnation and a resurrection—everything Jesus has done. Satan duplicates every valid religious experience that men and women can have.

Just because someone has a religious experience, it does not mean the experience is from God. We need to be careful that our hearts are tuned to him. We must measure our experiences by the Word of God. The value of our experience is not how we feel but what God says.

The Bible is not tested by our experience but our experience is tested by the Bible. God's Word determines if what we have is of God. Satan counterfeits everything Christ has done or will do.

Third, although the Antichrist will have power over most of the world, he will not deceive everybody. This is very important. There will be people during the reign of the Antichrist who will not believe him.

Even Satan's control in the world cannot keep men from receiving Christ as individuals. No one can keep us from Christ, not even the Antichrist. Not even a world controlled by Satan can keep people from being saved.

Fourth, men seek to worship what they can see. In the last days, Satan is going to provide a visible God with seemingly divine powers. Those who prefer a comfortable religion which does not demand righteous behavior will find exactly what they are looking for.

If they want a faith that does not require anything from them, does not demand anything, and that gives some ritual expression, they will find it the last days.

Satan is not opposed to religion. He loves it. He is opposed to real Christianity, to someone entering into a relationship with God through Jesus Christ. He is opposed to people on their knees before God, having a growing relationship with him. Satan does not mind us being religious as long as we do not get personally committed to Jesus Christ.

Fifth, we have power today for witnessing. Satan does not have the *dunamis*—power—of God, but we do. "I am not ashamed of the gospel of Christ: for it is the power of God unto salvation to everyone that believeth" (Rom. 1:16).

We ought to hunger to share our faith, witness for our Christ, and tell the world about Jesus. The promise of God's power behind us—within us—should thrust us into the world to win souls for our Lord.

Sixth, there is in this passage a confidence in the justice of God (v. 10). Everytime God tells us how bad it is going to be during tribulation, he always reminds us that he is going to act in judgment. He always tells us that justice will win.

Evil will not triumph; justice will. Satan will not win. Christ has already purchased the victory. We know that there will be a consummation in victory and we await that time. But we do not wait in defeat, we wait in victory.

We do not go out to win the war for Jesus; we go out to announce a victory. We do not fight toward victory, we fight from victory. It is a great comfort to know that the victory is already ours.

Seventh, we note the phrase in verse 8: " . . . whose names are not written in the book of life of the Lamb slain from the foundation of the world." Notice in Revelation 20:15: "whosoever was not found written in the book of life was cast into the lake of fire."

The book of life contains the names of all the living. When a person is born, his name is recorded in the book of life. If that person dies without receiving Jesus Christ as Savior, his name is blotted out.

"He that overcometh, . . . I will not blot out his name out of the book of life" (Rev. 3:5). When a person dies without experiencing the new birth in Jesus Christ, his name is blotted out of the book of life.

In eternity, the only people whose names remain in the book of life are those who receive Jesus Christ by faith.

The Lamb's book of life is something else. There are no erasures in the Lamb's book of life. Nobody's name is ever blotted out of it. It includes only those who have come to the Lamb for eternal life, who have received Christ as personal Savior.

A person's name is written in the Lamb's book of life because he asked God to put it there and because God chose him.

If we receive Christ and invite him into our hearts, the recording angel records our names in the Lamb's book of life, and those names can never be blotted out. That is what it means to be saved.

Here in the midst of a passage about the Antichrist and the terrible time of tribulation, we are reminded that God in mercy and grace has provided the Lamb as he promised. Jesus Christ, the Lamb slain from the foundation of the world, paid the price for our sins. When we receive him, our names are written in the Lamb's book of life.

What a wonderful truth! We who are in Christ have a written guarantee of eternal life.

20

The False Prophet
13:11-18

Now we behold another beast coming up out of the earth (v. 11). There are two words in the Greek language for "another." One means another of a different kind, and one means another of the same kind. This word means another one of the same kind.

This is another beast of the same origin. He also comes from Satan. This beast has the same disposition, the same characteristics, the same goals as the first beast.

There are some differences in these two beasts, however. The first beast will come up out of the sea; the second beast out of the land. In apocalyptic literature the sea always refers to the masses of humanity. According to chapter 12, the masses of humanity are in turmoil.

The beast out of the sea will be a product of social upheaval. There will be worldwide crises. Social turmoil and chaos will be developing everywhere. The first beast, the Antichrist, will be a world political leader who comes with the panacea for all the world's problems. He will appear to have the solution for world economic, political, and military chaos.

The land seems to represent people but with a more restricted view. Some believe the land symbolizes established order. In other words, he will come out of a very carefully planned process of human order and organization.

He will not come as a product of social upheaval but from social promotion and organization.

Some believe that it means he will come out of Israel; thus, he could be a Jew.

There is a more intriguing possibility. The church of the New Testament is heir to many of the promises of God as were the Jews in the Old Testament. It may well be that the second beast that will arise out of the land will be a religious leader, perhaps out of the Christian community.

He could profess to have the religious answers for the needs of the world. If that is true, he will come out of the religious community—not the conservative, Bible-believing community—but out of the Bible-disowning, God-dishonoring portion of the religious community.

The first beast will have secular power; the second beast, religious power. The first beast will have ten horns; the second beast, two horns. The first beast will have civil authority; the second beast, religious authority.

The first beast will head a vast military and political system; the second beast will rule Palestine with a religious system. The second beast will be subordinate to the first beast. The two are not identical by any means.

"He had two horns like a lamb" (v. 11). This is a mixed metaphor. There are no lambs with horns. It is a rather interesting combination. The horns mean strength, and the lamb signifies meekness or weakness. It certainly does not mean aggressiveness or power. That we have a lamb with two horns is confusing enough. But when he speaks, he speaks with the voice of a dragon!

This means this false prophet will speak with the authority of Satan, and for Satan. He will always promote the first beast. The second beast masquerades as a prophet, but he always calls attention to the first beast, the Antichrist. He never pushes himself. He is very persuasive and convincing.

This is not surprising. Jesus declared, "For there shall arise false Christs, and false prophets, and shall shew great signs and wonders; insomuch that, if it were possible, they shall deceive the very elect" (Matt. 24:24).

Later, in Revelation (19:20) we find out what will happen to this beast and false prophet: "And the beast was taken, and with him the false prophet that wrought miracles before him with which he deceived them that had received the mark of the beast, and them that worshiped his image. These both were cast alive into a lake of fire burning with brimstone."

That is the end of the story for the beast of the sea and the beast of the land, the Antichrist and the false prophet.

The Direction

And he exerciseth all the power of the first beast before him, and causeth the earth and them which dwell therein to worship the first beast, whose deadly wound was healed (v. 12).

The whole purpose of this second beast will be to get people to worship the Antichrist, to submit to the will and purposes of the Antichrist. The Antichrist will not be alone. He will have a partner, the false prophet. This false prophet will have the heart of a serpent and the voice of a dragon and by miraculous power he will coerce the whole earth into obeying the Antichrist.

Indeed the false prophet will be more dangerous than the Antichrist. Any man who commands the minds, wills, hearts and souls of men is extremely dangerous. He will have incredible authority over humanity.

There will be a softness about him, like a lamb. But his voice will betray him for who he really is: the voice of Satan himself. His whole task will be to make the new religion of the Antichrist appealing and palatable. He will combine political expertise

with religious passion; self-interest with benevolent philan-
thropy, and moral platitude with reckless self-indulgence.

He will control the communications media, and his great
appeal will be that what he says will sound so right. He really
will sound like he is telling the truth. He will make sense of this
new philosophy and religion of the Antichrist. The false
prophet will magnify the Antichrist, lead people away from
God, and mobilize them to support the work of the Antichrist.

The Demonstration

And he doeth great wonders, so that he maketh fire come
down from heaven on the earth in the sight of men, . . . And
he had power to give life unto the image of the beast, that
the image of the beast should speak, and cause that as many
as would not worship the image of the beast should be killed
(vv. 13-15).

The false prophet will demonstrate great authority and
power. Paul talked about this in 2 Thessalonians 2:9-10 when
he speaks of "lying wonders" and miracles. He will do great
and mighty works, many with religious significance. He will
appear to bring fire from heaven. (The Antichrist will seek to
imitate everything Christ does and the false prophet will speak
for the Antichrist.)

The Old Testament prophet Malachi said, "Behold, I will
send you Elijah the prophet before the coming of the great and
dreadful day of the Lord: And he shall turn the heart of the
fathers to the children, and the heart of the children to their
fathers, lest I come and smite the earth with a curse" (Mal.
4:5-6). The Old Testament prophets promised that Elijah the
prophet would come back before the Messiah came.

Elijah called fire down from heaven on Mount Carmel, a
miracle of God. In the end times, the prophet said that Elijah
would come back. That is why many people today believe that

Elijah will be one of the two witnesses of Revelation 11.

The Antichrist will try to convince the world that this false prophet is Elijah come back. He will call fire down from heaven. It is just another imitation of the real thing. The only thing Satan knows is to counterfeit.

Nothing Satan does is real, genuine, true, fulfilling, or satisfying. Everything he gives is empty, shallow, and hollow. He promises but never delivers.

This will be Satan's attempt to convince the world that Elijah the prophet has come back. It will convince many people to follow the religion of the Antichrist.

This false prophet will be vicious and mean. He will kill everyone who does not go along with him. That would be very persuasive! "As many as would not worship the image of the beast should be killed" (v. 15).

John also said, "I saw thrones, and they sat upon them, and judgment was given unto them: and I saw the souls of them that were beheaded for the witness of Jesus, and for the word of God, and which had not worshipped the beast, neither his image, neither had received his mark upon their foreheads, or in their hands" (Rev. 20:4).

Those who do not agree with the false prophet will be killed. Satan does not change his tactics. He tried the same thing with the three Hebrew friends of Daniel when King Nebuchadnezzar commanded them to bow down and worship his image or be thrown into the fiery furnace (Dan. 3).

He tried the same thing with Daniel, commanding him to worship the king's image or else! And here in the last days, he will attempt the same thing. He commands everyone to follow this new religion or be killed. That is the kind of power and authority he will have.

He will build a huge statue in the rebuilt temple. An image of the Antichrist will be erected there. "And he had power to give life unto the image of the beast" (v. 15). The word *life* is the Greek word that means "breath," "wind," or "spirit."

It will be another imitation. Genesis declares that God fashioned man out the dust of the earth and God breathed into him the breath of life and man became a living soul (Gen. 2:7). In the end times, the false prophet is going to take an inanimate object, an image, and somehow give "life" to it.

He probably will have it speak in some way, appearing to imitate the creative act of God. In that day of no restraints, it would be quite possible for an evil spirit or demon to come into the image and give every evidence of life.

We do not know exactly how he is going to do it, but he will give life to this statue. This will certainly be a very convincing and persuasive argument.

The real purpose of this great demonstration of his might and authority will be to prepare the minds of the people for what is said in verse 14. The whole purpose of his power and authority will be to get the people to worship the image of the Antichrist.

The Deception

And deceiveth them that dwell on the earth by the means of those miracles which he had power to do in the sight of the beast; saying to them that dwell on the earth, that they should make an image to the beast, which had the wound by a sword, and did live (v. 14).

The false prophet will deceive the whole population of the world. He will force people to worship the Antichrist's image in the temple. He will have a deceptive appearance. No one is afraid of a gentle, harmless, innocent lamb.

According to Scripture, the lamb is ceremonially clean and the false prophet will seem to be all of these things. He will have tremendous, dynamic appeal. Men are now prepared to fulfill Paul's prophecies that they will believe a lie (2 Thess. 2:11).

This is a very practical point for us today. Bible-rejecting theology ultimately leads us away from God. The end result of theological, religious liberalism is to do exactly what the false prophet does.

For instance, I believe that the "God-is-dead" idea arose out of theological liberalism. That did not lately come from the atheistic community, but out of a theological school. The ultimate end of extreme liberal theology is to deny God and to deny the supernatural. It is simply religious humanism with man at the center, and God as an incidental figurehead.

That is why it is so significant that we agree on certain basics of our faith. Everyone will not agree on every detail and interpretation, but let us agree on what we interpret: God's Word.

The church is the body of Christ, the expression of God himself. Let us agree on that. Let us agree that God calls us to holiness. When we come to Jesus, we give everything to him. Let us agree on that. If we disagree, let us disagree on the interpretation of the Word of God, not whether or not it is the Word of God.

The false prophet will lead people ultimately to deny God and to worship the Antichrist whom we shall soon see is only a man. Deception is the name of the game for this false prophet.

The Design

And he causeth all, both small and great, rich and poor, free and bond, to receive a mark in their right hand, or in their foreheads: And that no man might buy or sell, save he that had the mark, or the name of the beast, or the number of his name. Here is wisdom. Let him that hath understanding count the number of the beast: for it is the number of a man; and his number is Six hundred threescore and six (vv. 16-18).

I have heard that computer companies now have perfected an indelible marking system which can mark on a person's forehead (their words!) and on one's hands a number that can be read by a machine.

This system is already in use at the grocery store. Every item in many stores is marked in a way that it can be read by a sensing device. It is certainly conceivable that this system described in Revelation could become reality.

The banking industry is already working toward a cashless society. Before long, we will not have to carry cash. Instead, we will have a credit number. When we do business with someone we will give them the number, they will put it into their computer, the computer will check to see if we have any money. Then they will sell us whatever we want to buy, and the bank will automatically transfer funds from our account to the merchant's account.

The Social Security system has already given all of us a number.

This is an ingenious plan the false prophet will design and it is not as far-fetched as it sounds! He will give everybody an identifying number. We may have different numbers, or perhaps the same number. One thing is sure: without this mark, we will not be able to buy or sell anything.

"Here is wisdom" (v. 18) means "here is a mystery or a riddle" that is not possible to figure out. If anyone claims to know what the mark of the beast means, he does not know what he is talking about.

"Let him that hath understanding count the number of the beast: for it is the number of a man; and his number is Six hundred threescore and six" (v. 18). A time will come in the tribulation period when the false prophet has propagandized the world. He has really sold the world a bill of goods.

Most of the world will respond. Virtually everyone will worship the beast except for a remnant of godly people who like the disciples in the first century refused to burn incense on the altar and say "Caesar is lord."

Just like the Hebrew children would not bow their knee to say a simple prayer to an idol in that Old Testament scene, there will be people who will say, "I have given my heart to Jesus; I cannot worship another." After a while in an effort to destroy those who do not conform, the mark of the beast will come. The only way to receive the mark of the beast will be to blaspheme God and worship the Antichrist.

Some people will take the mark because they will be convinced it is the best thing to do. Some will just be careless. There will be others who have compromised all their lives and will go the most convenient way. Those who take the mark of the beast will in effect denounce Christ and confess that they have never committed their lives to him. What a tragedy that will be.

Do not look for some deep, mystical meaning to "666." Do not try to add up Hitler's initials or that of some contemporary man. This number is the number of a man. Seven is God's complete number.

Six is the number of humanity, an incomplete number. It comes short of seven. Six will never equal seven. Man will never equal God. Man can never do what God can.

Six means that it is just short of completeness. It is a reminder that the Antichrist will be a man. He will not be God, and he will come short of being what God is. Satan always does!

Nothing Satan gives us is complete or satisfying. Satan gives us that which creates a hunger that cannot be satisfied. God gives us that which does satisfy and keeps on satisfying and blessing. Nothing Satan offers is right, and despair ultimately comes from what he gives.

How many homes have been destroyed because Satan

convinced the husband or the wife of a lie that said, "If you just had another partner, you would be happy"? The truth is that another person is not what we need. We do not need just somebody; we need Jesus Christ to make the relationships we have meaningful and lasting.

Satan always gives that which lacks fulfillment. That is what 666 means: the Antichrist is a man. He is not God. He will never provide what God can provide. Even though it will mean death to refuse to wear the mark of the beast, it is better to be killed than to live with it.

Without the mark of the beast at this time, one will be considered a traitor to the government and will either be killed immediately or will be allowed to starve. Without the mark of the beast, people will not be able to buy anything. What a shrewd plan that is: very deceptive, very treacherous, and very effective.

Let us examine our hearts. Is Jesus Lord and Savior of our lives? Are we sold out to the things of the world? Are we trusting God or in man's ability to make the best of any situation?

The church will not be on earth during the tribulation time. But people will be saved during the tribulation and they will have to make a choice.

We have choices to make in our own day. We must choose to sell out for Jesus. We must choose to be his people in our homes and communities.

Someday, there may be a choice that will cost us employment and comfort or worse if we take a stand for Christ. What has our Christianity cost? What does it mean to us?

I pray that our confidence will be in Christ and our testimony will be that of the apostle Paul when he said:

> That I may know him, and the power of his resurrection, and the fellowship of his sufferings, being made conformable

unto his death; If by any means I might attain unto the resurrection of the dead. Not as though I had already attained, either were already perfect: but I follow after, if that I may apprehend that for which also I am apprehended of Christ Jesus. Brethren, I count not myself to have apprehended: but this one thing I do, forgetting those things which are behind, and reaching forth unto those things which are before, I press toward the mark for the prize of the high calling of God in Christ Jesus (Phil. 3:10-14).

21
The Beginning of the End
14:1-20

We have seen the darkness and desperation of a world ruled by Satan. Satan will be cast down from heaven and restricted to the earth, with virtually all limitations removed. We have seen just how vicious and terrible that time will be.

In chapter 14, we see a turning of the tide. From this point on, we see a world rescued by God. This is the beginning of the end. We need this blessed relief.

God never leaves us very long in the polluted atmosphere of the Antichrist's earth. He lifts us again and again above the mists of earth and lets us breathe the pure air of heaven. In this passage, we get a glimpse of what will be happening in heaven.

We are immediately confronted with a group of 144,000 redeemed. "And I looked, and, lo, a Lamb stood on the mount Sion, and with him an hundred forty and four thousand" (v. 1). We first met this great, illustrious company of the redeemed in chapter 7. There we were greeted by 12,000 from each of the tribes.

Chapter 7 tells us that these 144,000 were sealed by God for their protection. They had finished their testimony, and now we see them in heaven standing on Mount Zion with the Lord Jesus himself.

Not one of them is missing: there are still 144,000. The same word *sealed* is used in Ephesians 1:13. There it declares that when we believed, we were sealed by God. God does not lose anyone. God will take with him to glory everyone who is sealed! Everyone is accounted for with the Lamb.

The New Song

> And I looked, and, lo, a Lamb stood on the mount Sion, and with him an hundred forty and four thousand, having his Father's name written in their foreheads. And I heard a voice from heaven, as the voice of many waters, and as the voice of a great thunder: and I heard the voice of harpers harping with their harps: And they sung as it were a new song before the throne, and before the four beasts, and the elders:
>
> and no man could learn that song but the hundred and forty and four thousand, which were redeemed from the earth. These are they which were not defiled with women; for they are virgins. These are they which follow the Lamb whithersoever he goeth. These were redeemed from among men, being the firstfruits unto God and to the Lamb. And in their mouth was found no guile: for they are without fault before the throne of God (vv. 1-5).

This is redemption's song. It is exclusively and uniquely the song of the 144,000 redeemed. This is not a choir of angels, but a choir of the redeemed who have been saved by the blood of Jesus Christ. They now stand in heaven, and break into a new song.

Every person who has been saved has something to sing about. That is why music is so precious to the Christian faith. When God saves us, he puts a new song in our hearts.

The Book of Revelation—so full of sorrow, strife and sadness—is also filled with the song of redemption. When the Lamb comes into the picture a song breaks forth. The Lord has an amazing ability to make his people happy, to give them a song and put joy in their hearts.

No one can learn the song except the redeemed (v. 3). It is uniquely given to the 144,000. No age will ever produce a group like this: a veritable army of militant marchers for God who have been sealed, protected, and unscathed, though exposed to every form of danger.

It will be their task to defy the beast and expose the false prophet. Their calling will be to preach the gospel from the mountaintops in a day when just to mention the name of Jesus could be very dangerous. They will triumph gloriously on earth and then stand in heaven celebrating, singing a new song.

There is much about these folks that ought to challenge us. They will have a tremendous conduct (v. 4). The reference seems to be twofold. Morally and spiritually, they will be pure. Morally they will be pure but they will not compromise their faith, either. Their conduct will be of the highest ethical, moral, and spiritual order.

They will demonstrate wonderful consecration (v. 4). If we want happiness in life and success in our Christian experiences, we need only follow Jesus wherever he leads. The only questions that matter in our lives are what God wants us to do and where he wants us to go. Here are those whose consecration will say, "We will follow the Lamb wherever he goes."

They will have tremendous character (v. 5). When we look at this group of people and then remember that we, too, are a part of the family of God, we must consider what kind of people we ought to be.

A New Messenger

And I saw another angel fly in the midst of heaven, having the everlasting gospel to preach unto them that dwell on the earth, and to every nation, and kindred, and tongue, and

people, Saying with a loud voice, Fear God, and give glory
to him; for the hour of his judgment is come: and worship
him that made heaven and earth, and the sea, and the
fountains of waters (vv. 6-7).

This is the first time we find an angel preaching the gospel.
Always before, the gospel has been entrusted to us, the
redeemed on earth. There are several reasons why this angel
preaches.

He announces a message of the judgment of God and calls
for repentance. However, it is also called the gospel and that
means good news. Redemption is still possible. The angel will
preach so people can be saved. This gospel is everlasting and is
preached to every nation, tongue, kindred, and people.

God always gives adequate warning before he sends judgment. In the midst of the tribulation period, in the absence of
an adequate gospel witness, just before the greatest suffering
the world shall ever see, God makes an exception to his
normal pattern and sends an angel to preach the gospel. It is a
vivid reminder to us of how much God wants the lost to be
saved.

We see an amazing progression of man's blasphemous
response to God's judgment. Every time God's messenger
came, the majority rejected him and blasphemed God. The
more his judgment came, the more they blasphemed him.

If our hearts have a tendency toward rebellion against God,
it is a very dangerous direction to go. The more we rebel
against God, the further we go in our rebellion, the more
drastic and deep it will be.

In chapter 16 when God drops 135-pound hailstones, some
who survive will stick their heads out and curse God. Humanity's rebellious heart needs God. If one has started toward
rebellion against God, it may end in ultimate blasphemy
against God.

A New Destiny

And there followed another angel, saying, Babylon is
fallen, is fallen, that great city, because she made all nations
drink of the wine of the wrath of her fornication. And the
third angel followed them, saying with a loud voice, If any
man worship the beast and his image, and receive his mark
in his forehead, or in his hand, The same shall drink of the
wine of the wrath of God, which is poured out without
mixture into the cup of his indignation; and he shall be
tormented with fire and brimstone in the presence of the
holy angels, and in the presence of the Lamb: And the
smoke of their torment ascendeth up for ever and ever: and
they have no rest day nor night, who worship the beast and
his image, and whosoever receiveth the mark of his name
(vv. 8-11).

Babylon was where evil, pagan religion originated. Babylon
represents the origin of all anti-God philosophy and religion.
John declared that God is going to bring the enterprises of
Satan on this earth to an end.

At the end time, Babylon will fall. Those who worship the
beast are doomed. Those who reject Christ and follow Satan's
false Christ shall be consumed by the wrath of God. If anyone
does not take the wrath of God and his judgment seriously
ponder the above Scripture. These words are full of awe. We
may dislike the thought of coming judgment. We may think, as
some do in the Christian community today, that God just
would not do that. We may condemn such judgment, but here
it is.

It really does not matter what we think. God's judgment is
coming and those who are condemned will suffer endless
torment. All we can know about the wrath of God is what God
has written in his Word. Those who want to hear of the love of
God can find it in his Word.

Through a look at nature we can know there is a God, a powerful and intelligent God. But we cannot know God loves us except through his Word. And the same Word that tells us of the love of God also reveals that those who reject that love must come to judgment. God cannot condone sin.

The severity of this judgment is beyond imagination. "The smoke of their torment ascendeth up for ever and ever: and they have no rest day nor night" (v. 11). That is the destiny of those who reject God.

A New Blessing

> Here is the patience of the saints: here are they that keep the commandments of God, and the faith of Jesus. And I heard a voice from heaven saying unto me, Write, Blessed are the dead which die in the Lord from henceforth: Yea, saith the Spirit, that they may rest from their labours; and their works do follow them (vv. 12-13).

This minces no words. The alternatives are unmistakable: "Worship me or be doomed," cries the Antichrist; "Worship me or be damned," cries Jesus.

The choice is ours. Those who defy the beast in this tribulation time will face death in a thousand fiendish ways. Those who respond to the call of Christ will be put to death. But death will be instantly transformed by God into a blessing.

"I will make you suffer," cries the Antichrist. "You will make us saints," cry the overcomers. "I will persecute you to the grave," declares the beast. "You will promote us to glory," the overcomers say. "I will blast you," says Satan. "You will bless us," cry the Christians.

God says, "They who die will be blessed." The beast may have the power to kill believers, but God declares them blessed.

This blessing is shared by the saints of all ages who die in the

Lord. When we walk through the valley of the shadow of death, cross the raging tide of Jordan and are swept into the experience we call death, in the Lord we have blessed hope and joy.

Do not be afraid of death, unless you have rejected Christ. Then postpone it as long as you can because all of life you will ever know is what little you find here. "Blessed are the dead who die in the Lord." That puts a whole new perspective on death.

Saints will be martyred and killed and Satan may laugh and roar. But God says that they are blessed! He is the One who has conquered the grave. God declares that death to his children is a blessing.

His Word is consistent in that. The writer of Ecclesiastes declared that better is the day of one's "death than the day of one's birth" (Eccl. 7:1). The psalmist declared, "Precious in the sight of the Lord is the death of his saints" (Ps. 116:15). Paul declared, "For me to live is Christ, and to die is gain" (Phil. 1:21).

The consistent message of God's Word is that for his children death is a blessing. The world knows nothing of that kind of blessing. There is no such hope in the hearts of unbelievers. But in Christ there is a new blessing.

A New Day

And I looked, and behold a white cloud, and upon the cloud one sat like unto the Son of man, having on his head a golden crown, and in his hand a sharp sickle. And another angel came out of the temple, crying with a loud voice to him that sat on the cloud, Thrust in thy sickle, and reap: for the time is come for thee to reap; for the harvest of the earth is ripe.

And he that sat on the cloud thrust in his sickle on the earth; and the earth was reaped. And another angel came

out of the temple which is in heaven, he also having a sharp
sickle. And another angel came out from the altar, which
had power over fire; and cried with a loud cry to him that
had the sharp sickle, saying, Thrust in thy sharp sickle, and
gather the clusters of the vine of the earth; for her grapes are
fully ripe.

And the angel thrust in his sickle into the earth, and
gathered the vine of the earth, and cast it into the great
winepress of the wrath of God. And the winepress was
trodden without the city, and blood came out of the
winepress, even unto the horse bridles, by the space of a
thousand and six hundred furlongs (vv. 14-20).

Verse 14 shows that golden age which is soon to come and
the steps leading to the milennium period. But first there has to
be a harvest and here is a vivid description of that harvest. The
reaper is Christ himself. First comes a harvest of grain; the
second, a harvest of grapes.

Matthew 13 records the parable of the wheat and the tares
which explains the nature of this harvest. In the parable, a
sower went forth to sow seed. Jesus was the sower. Now he
will be the reaper. The harvest time will be ripe and he will reap
the earth.

This will be a religious harvest. The wheat and the tares are
going to grow side by side. That means that there will be saved
people and lost people in the church.

It is fair to say that perhaps the majority of the people in
churches today are not saved. The truly saved will truly love
the things of God: the church, the Bible, unsaved souls, prayer
and Bible reading, and service for God. If you do not enjoy
worshiping and adoring God, one of two things has happened:
either you have backslidden or you are not saved. There are
many people who are tares in the midst of wheat. There are
many who have accepted philosophically the truth but have

never been changed by the Spirit of God. If that describes you—if you have the same drives, impulses and tendencies as you had before you joined the church, I believe you are probably a tare.

This will be the harvest that separates the wheat from the tares. This is the time when the sickle of God is going to be thrust in, the tares cut and cast into the fire. I believe this will happen rapidly. Only a few swift strokes of the sickle and it will be done. It will not take God long to separate the wheat from the tares.

The magnificent worldly beauty of some church buildings may be sending more people to hell than all the efforts of the atheists in the world because of the false security such beauty gives. We are saved not by accepting a religion but by entering into a relationship.

It will be a sad harvest when the tares are separated from the wheat. The wheat shall be gathered safely but the tares shall be burned.

Beginning in verse 17, there is a harvest of grapes. It is an ugly scene. The blood shed covers about 175 miles and is four feet deep. That is the extent of the judgment of God on the world. God will step down into the arena of Armageddon and trample the beast and all who follow him. It will be the final conflict of the age.

Today we have a choice. We can either choose death and eternal suffering or life and eternal blessing. The choice is not whether or not we die. "It is appointed unto men once to die" (Heb. 9:27).

Our choice is what happens after death: either eternal blessing or eternal suffering.

Today is a day of grace. But God will ultimately judge all people. God's invitation to us is placed there by his Holy Spirit. We can choose eternal blessing today.

That is our hope. Death will come to all of us. We can choose eternal suffering or eternal blessing now. One of the most beautiful of all passages in the Old Testament declares, "I have set before you life and death, blessing and cursing: therefore choose life that both you and your seed may live" (Deut. 30:19).

22
The Seven Bowls of Wrath
15:1 to 16:21

Beginning with chapter 14, we see a world rescued by God, but one where judgment is meted out. We see the climax of the age old struggle between good and evil and the final establishment of the kingdom of God on earth.

The fifteenth and sixteenth chapters present the seven bowls of wrath. They will be very shallow bowls, not emptied slowly. The word *bowl* is significant because it tells us these judgments are going to be quick, in rapid succession.

There were seven seal judgments and seven trumpet judgments. But there is a break, an interlude between the sixth and seventh seal and trumpet, but not here. Even though there is a parenthesis in the last part of the sixteenth chapter, there is apparently no time lapse. These judgments follow each other very quickly.

Some people try to equate the bowl judgments with the seal and trumpet judgments. There are similarities in them but there are some big differences. They are separate, distinct judgments of God.

The word *sign* in the fifteenth chapter bothers some people. To them, a sign is something that is hidden and hard to understand.

Many have concluded that the Book of Revelation is obscure and difficult to understand because it has so much symbolism.

But if we examine the word *sign*, we discover that the opposite is true.

A sign is designed to help us understand, not to make comprehension more difficult. It is used many times in the New Testament: "This he said, signifying what death he should die" (John 12:33). This word *signify* is essentially the same word. Jesus was trying to explain his death, not obscure it.

"That the saying of Jesus might be fulfilled, which he spake, signifying what death he should die" (John 18:32). Here again Jesus used the same word, meaning an explanation of his death. And again he said, "This spake he, signifying by what death he should glorify God" (John 21:19). Jesus was telling Simon Peter how he would die. It is not obscure but a clarification.

A sign is not something hard to understand; it helps us understand. It is a sign of truth God wants to explain.

The same word is used again by Jesus in Matthew 12:38-41. The scribes and pharisees have approached Jesus saying, "Master, we would see a sign from thee. But he answered and said unto them, An evil and adulterous generation seeketh after a sign; but there shall no sign be given to it, but the sign of the prophet Jonas: For as Jonas was three days and three nights in the whale's belly; so shall the Son of man be three days and three nights in the heart of the earth."

Again, he was giving them this sign to help them understand his death, burial and resurrection. Do not let the word *sign* obscure the truth that is there. The essence of what God is saying to us is very clear.

Preparation for the Bowls of Wrath

And I saw another sign in heaven, great and marvellous, seven angels having the seven last plagues; for in them is filled up the wrath of God. And I saw as it were a sea of glass mingled with fire: and them that had gotten the victory over the beast, and over his image, and over his mark, and over the number of his name, stand on the sea of glass, having the harps of God.

And they sing the song of Moses the servant of God, and the song of the Lamb, saying, Great and marvellous are thy works, Lord God Almighty; just and true are thy ways, thou King of saints. Who shall not fear thee, O Lord, and glorify thy name? for thou only art holy: for all nations shall come and worship before thee; for thy judgments are made manifest.

And after that I looked, and, behold the temple of the tabernacle of the testimony in heaven was opened: And the seven angels came out of the temple, having the seven plagues, clothed in pure and white linen, and having their breasts girded with golden girdles.

And one of the four beasts gave unto the seven angels seven golden vials full of the wrath of God, who liveth for ever and ever. And the temple was filled with smoke from the glory of God, and from his power; and no man was able to enter into the temple, till the seven plagues of the seven angels were fulfilled (vv. 1-8).

As he looked into heaven, John saw a great host of the redeemed saints, victorious over the Antichrist. They are standing on a sea of glass mingled with fire. The fire represents the judgment and justice of God. The sea, which normally represents humanity, is hard, signifying their victory in Jesus Christ. They stand on the sea of glass singing the song of Moses.

The first thing John saw was people singing. The God who led Moses and the children out of the wilderness was Jesus because they were singing the song of Moses and the Lamb.

Apparently they were/will be the same song. The apostle

Paul had already said that the spiritual rock that followed them
through the wilderness providing water for them was Christ
(1 Cor. 10:4).

This will be spontaneous singing of the martyrs as they
praise the Lord who has made them victors over sorrow, pain,
and death. All their heartaches will be behind, all their
oppression over, all their pain and suffering past. Now they will
grasp what it will be like to spend eternity with the Father and
the Lamb. As they contemplate it, they will burst into the song
of Moses.

The song of Moses was the song of the children of Israel
when they were delivered from the Red Sea. God opened up a
path for them to walk through. With the armies of Pharoah
close on their heels the water closed up and destroyed their
enemies.

When the Israelites realized they had been saved from
overwhelming odds, in spontaneous gratitude to God they
lifted their hearts to God and sang a song of praise. These
saints will have had the same kind of experiences. They will
have just come through a terrible period. Now, safe in glory,
they will sing a song of deliverance.

Here is their song: "Great and marvellous are thy works,
Lord God Almighty; just and true are thy ways, thou King of
saints. Who shall not fear thee, O Lord, and glorify thy name?
for thou only art holy: for all nations shall come and worship
before thee; for thy judgments are made manifest" (15:3-4).
All of this will echo through the halls of heaven, in preparation
for the pouring out of the bowls of wrath.

Beginning with verse 5, John had a vision of the heavenly
tabernacle. A shocking change occurs in the character of the
heavenly sanctuary. Rather than a place of redemption where
people can find forgiveness for sins and salvation from God, it
will become the place from which the seven last plagues come.

It will become a place of judgment. The throne of mercy will here become the throne of judgment against those who have rejected God's plan.

The messengers will be clothed in white linen, with their breasts girded with gold. The white linen shows their divine righteousness. They do not act with impatience, independence, or by their own will, but in strict accordance to the will of God.

The judgments that are coming are God's alone. What they are about to do is terrible, but absolutely right. No stain nor spot of sin will be mingled with their action. They are actually characterized by divine restraint. The golden girdle about their breasts indicates that they are restrained by God himself.

There is no hot passion, no personal anger. They are calm and dispassionate in what they are about to do, methodical and businesslike.

A strange thing will happen. The Temple will be filled with smoke, not of earthly fire but of the glory of God. The *shekinah* glory of God will fill the place. No one will be able to enter the Temple until the seven plagues of the seven angels are fulfilled.

According to Jewish law, the high priest could enter once a year into the holy of holies. He would carry in a bowl of blood and there offer atonement for the sins of the people. When Jesus died on the cross, God opened a way into the holiest place for all who would come by faith in Jesus Christ. Because of the blood of Christ all who will may enter.

Now we come to a time when the door is shut. There will be no more redemption, no more forgiveness until the judgment of God is completed. Until then, no one may enter into the holy place.

The bright glory of God burns within the Temple filling it with smoke and guarding the door. There is no access. Once God starts these final seven judgments, the door to the tabernacle will stay closed until all of them are fulfilled.

Pouring Out of the Bowls of Wrath

And I heard a great voice out of the temple saying to the seven angels, Go your ways, and pour out the vials of the wrath of God upon the earth.

And the first went, and poured out his vial upon the earth; and there fell a noisome and grievous sore upon the men which had the mark of the beast, and upon them which worshipped his image.

And the second angel poured out his vial upon the sea; and it became as the blood of a dead man: and every living soul died in the sea.

And the third angel poured out his vial upon the rivers and fountains of waters; and they became blood. And I heard the angel of the waters say, Thou art righteous, O lord, which art, and wast, and shalt be, because thou hast judged thus. For they have shed the blood of saints and prophets, and thou hast given them blood to drink; for they are worthy. And I heard another out of the altar say, Even so, Lord God Almighty, true and righteous are thy judgments.

And the fourth angel poured out his vial upon the sun; and power was given unto him to scorch men with fire. And men were scorched with great heat, and blasphemed the name of God, which hath power over these plagues: and they repented not to give him glory.

And the fifth angel poured out his vial upon the seat of the beast; and his kingdom was full of darkness; and they gnawed their tongues for pain, And blasphemed the God of heaven because of their pains and their sores, and repented not of their deeds.

And the sixth angel poured out his vial upon the great river Euphrates; and the water thereof was dried up, that the way of the kings of the east might be prepared.

And the seventh angel poured out his vial into the air; and there came a great voice out of the temple of heaven, from the throne, saying, It is done. And there were voices, and thunders, and lightnings; and there was a great earthquake, such as was not since men were upon the earth, so mighty an earthquake, and so great.

And the great city was divided into three parts, and the cities of the nations fell: and great Babylon came in remembrance before God, to give unto her the cup of the wine of the fierceness of his wrath. And every island fled away and the mountains were not found. And there fell upon men a great hail out of heaven, every stone about the weight of a talent: and men blasphemed God because of the plague of the hail; for the plague thereof was exceeding great (16:1-12,17-21).

We will not discuss the seven plagues individually. They will be literal plagues, not symbols. These plagues will surely be something horrible.

There are some similarities between these judgments and the seals and trumpets, but the trumpet judgments fell on only one third of the earth.

These are universal judgments. In the trumpet judgments, God allowed Satan to do certain things but here God is acting alone.

We know that they are going to happen quickly because all seven angels get their instructions at the same time: "Go your ways, and pour out the vials of the wrath of God upon the earth" (v. 1). Then the plagues come.

One reason to believe they will be literal plagues is that four out of the seven occurred during the ten plagues in Egypt through Moses. It will be a repetition of some of the plagues of Egypt. Those were real plagues. No honest scholar can explain them away. There is no real reason to believe that these plagues are not literal, actual plagues.

The drying up of the Euphrates, which happens in the sixth bowl of wrath, also parallels the drying up of the Jordan River for the Israelites to cross. God can certainly do it again.

This is not one of those passages that is pleasant to read. The mere reading of chapter 16 causes us to shudder. It is a terrible time. The judgment is severe. It is one of the most awful, awesome times the world could imagine.

Why should the judgment be so severe? There must come a time when the judgment of God can no longer be delayed. Every judgment that God has ever given has been tempered with mercy. He has always given warning. He has always tried to spare some in the midst of judgment.

But when he finally comes to this point there will be no mercy. A time has arrived when the judgment of God will be fully expressed. From the smoke-filled Temple will come a great voice commanding the angels to proceed with the execution. It will be a fearful thing.

In spite of the severity and the universality of these plagues, some people will survive. And, unbelievably, they will blaspheme and curse God. That is incredible. Rather than turning to God for mercy, men will blaspheme God. Everything that the human race has built will crumble. The whole world will literally collapse. Islands will disappear into the sea, mountains will tumble down yet people will persist in thinking that they are their own masters without any need for God. And they will continue to blaspheme God.

Purpose of the Bowls of Wrath

And I saw three unclean spirits like frogs come out of the mouth of the dragon, and out of the mouth of the beast, and out of the mouth of the false prophet. For they are the spirits of devils, working miracles, which go forth unto the kings of the earth and of the whole world, to gather them to the battle of that great day of God Almighty. Behold, I come as a thief. Blessed is he that watcheth, and keepeth his garments, lest he walk naked, and they see his shame. And he gathered them together into a place called in the Hebrew tongue Armageddon (16:13-16).

When the bowls of wrath are poured out, the nations of the world will still rally in rebellion. They will gather against Israel. The evil trinity of the dragon, the beast and the false prophet will still rally forces against God.

The bowls of wrath will be to round up the nations. When those nations gather against Israel, then God's judgment will be perfected. This will settle, once and for all among every nation on earth, the absolute authority of Jesus Christ over this earth. People may laugh at him now. They may call another "Lord" now, but on that day the absolute lordship of Jesus Christ will be demonstrated for all to see.

When the seventh bowl is poured out, the personal return of Christ will follow. Then it will be accomplished: the perfecting of God's judgment, the consummation of his wrath, the final overthrow of all opposition.

With the exception of the hail and the lightning, man could produce these judgments now with our multimegaton bombs. Everything in these bowls are possible with nuclear explosions except the lightning, thunder and hail. The seventh angel will tip his bowl and there will be thunders, lightnings and hailstones weighing more than 100 pounds.

It will signal the final destruction of every religious, political and educational institution that humanity has built apart from God. Here is the final destruction of every institution, agency and organization man has ever built to eliminate God. This will mark the collapse of all manmade hopes and dreams. But with all of this, man will still refuse to submit to God's rule.

The picture of the Temple in the fifteenth chapter is very significant. Always before the sanctuary had been a place of mercy where expiation was made for sin, where forgiveness was asked from God. Now it will be a place of wrath and judgment.

God is never mocked; his judgment is sure. We may think that we have fooled God. We may have sins we think we have gotten away with. We excuse in ourselves what we condemn in others.

We are told by Satan that we will be exceptions. Just because no one knows does not mean we have put one over on God. This passage declares to us that God will surely bring us to a time of his wrath when judgment will be filled to the brim! His patience will wear out!

When it does wear out, judgment will come. There is no blasphemer who has ever lived who will get away with it. There will be a day when they will stand before God and receive judgment.

The temple indicates that judgment is coming. If anything ought to cause us to run to God, this should be it. The day is coming when that will not be possible, when the door to the heart of God will be closed and no man can enter into that place until the judgment is completed.

We see, also, the response of the people to the judgment of God. In tracing through the sixteenth chapter, we find blasphemy in response to the plague (vv. 8-11). Whenever people turn their hearts away from God, whenever people rebel against God, they start in a direction from which there may be no return. God's judgment will not bring them to repentance.

Even the fires of hell will not bring some people to repentance. The more God's justice reigns and the more his judgment is poured out, the more many people will curse God. In this tribulation time, when the obvious judgment of God will be poured out, still many will blaspheme and curse God.

The utter perversity of human nature rejects the sovereignty of God in the face of overwhelming evidence. People do not fail to believe in God because such a belief is not logical; they fail to believe in God because they refuse to believe. Logically, it is hard not to believe in God. Only a fool can look at the universe and say that its existence is just an accident. But many people would rather believe a lie than to acknowledge God.

Because of the perversity of the human heart many people will not respond to God. Even the lake of fire will not produce the necessary repentance in the people who have hardened their hearts.

This of course applies to the lost. But, dear Christian friend, there is a lesson for us, too. We can also harden our hearts. We can so harden our hearts that it becomes easy to disregard God. It is a dangerous direction when we begin to resist what God tells us to do. We are often more concerned for ourselves, our ideas, our own dreams than we are what God has declared.

Even Christians can resist and harden their hearts. We are moving toward tribulation and God has put us here to be the church. When we start resisting God, we have started in a direction that can only end in tragedy.

23
Babylon the Great
17:1 to 18:24

These chapters confront us with a most solemn subject: the doom of a gigantic international system of religious heresy. This religion of the end times is so close to the truth that millions of people will be deceived by it.

Of course, the most dangerous heresy is the one that sounds the most like the truth. If something is obviously not true we do not have any trouble rejecting it. But, if something sounds good and true and is close enough to the truth that we want to believe it, we can more easily accept it.

In the last days a great religious system will be so close to Christianity that millions will be deceived. There will be a huge ecumenical church and its political counterpart. These chapters describe this for us.

Before we see the perfection of the Lamb and his bride we must see the harlot and the beast. They must be judged first. Final judgment must precede final blessing.

There are two Babylons and one will grow from the other. The beast will control the first and create the second. The religious system will pave the way for the political system. In the beginning the religious system supports the political and is at least tolerated by it. In the end the political Babylon will destroy the religious system altogether.

Religious Babylon

And there came one of the seven angels which had the seven vials, and talked with me, saying unto me, Come hither; I will shew unto thee the judgment of the great whore that sitteth upon many waters: With whom the kings of the earth have committed fornication, and the inhabitants of the earth have been made drunk with the wine of her fornication.

So he carried me away in the spirit into the wilderness: and I saw a woman sit upon a scarlet coloured beast, full of names of blasphemy, having seven heads and ten horns.

And the woman was arrayed in purple and scarlet colour, and decked with gold and precious stones and pearls, having a golden cup in her hand full of abominations and filthiness of her fornication: And upon her forehead was a name written, MYSTERY, BABYLON THE GREAT, THE MOTHER OF HARLOTS AND ABOMINATIONS OF THE EARTH.

And I saw the woman drunken with the blood of the saints, and with the blood of the martyrs of Jesus: and when I saw her, I wondered with great admiration. And the angel said unto me, Wherefore didst thou marvel? I will tell thee the mystery of the woman, and of the beast that carrieth her, which hath the seven heads and ten horns.

The beast that thou sawest was, and is not; and shall ascend out of the bottomless pit, and go into perdition: and they that dwell on the earth shall wonder, whose names were not written in the book of life from the foundation of the world, when they behold the beast that was, and is not, and yet is. And here is the mind which hath wisdom.

The seven heads are seven mountains, on which the woman sitteth. And there are seven kings: five are fallen, and one is, and the other is not yet come; and when he cometh, he must continue a short space. And the beast that was, and is not, even he is the eighth, and is of the seven, and goeth into perdition. And the ten horns which thou sawest are ten kings, which have received no kingdom as yet; but receive power as kings one hour with the beast.

These shall make war with the Lamb, and the Lamb shall overcome them: for he is Lord of lords, and King of kings: and they that are with him are called, and chosen, and faithful. And he saith unto me, The waters which thou sawest, where the whore sitteth, are peoples, and multitudes, and nations, and tongues. And the ten horns which thou sawest upon the beast, these shall hate the whore, and shall make her desolate and naked, and shall eat her flesh, and burn her with fire.

For God hath put in their hearts to fulfil his will, and to agree, and give their kingdom unto the beast, until the words of God shall be fulfilled. And the woman which thou sawest is that great city, which reigneth over the kings of the earth (17:1-18).

Who is this mysterious person, this mysterious woman called Babylon? She is called a harlot, a whore and those who unite with her are said to commit fornication or adultery. It is important to be reminded that in the Scriptures the reference to a harlot or to an adultress or to adultery many times refers to spiritual adultery: people who worship false gods.

We know what God has said about immoral activity and actions. He is trying to remind us that spiritual adultery is just as vicious, vile and unthinkable as physical adultery. This great religious system will be so powerful that the harlot is seen sitting on a scarlet colored beast. That means her power will be so great that it will appear she even controls the beast.

The Antichrist will give obeisance to the woman. It will seem she has promoted him into his position but he will only be using her. In the first half of the tribulation period the Antichrist will condescend to the religious system and will take advantage of its popularity. But in the end he will throw off this religious system.

Verses 7 through 15 explain the beast. He is described as one who was, and is not; and shall ascend out of the bottomless pit, and go into perdition. Doubtless that means the Antichrist who will be killed and then resurrected during the tribulation.

The reference to the ten horns and seven heads reminds us of Revelation 13 and Daniel 2 and 7. Those chapters speak of the political confederation of the end times. The ten kings will rule in the last of the days that usher in the tribulation time itself, until they bring their armies into the battle we call Armageddon. They are going to bring their armies against God himself.

The woman is full of names of blasphemy. This reminds us of the blasphemous nature of government without God. Anytime, anywhere a government is without God, it is a government against God. In history it has always been that way and it always will until the end. That government without God is a government that blasphemes God.

The harlot sits on the people of the world (v. 15). That shows her dominance over them. She will dominate the nations as this system will dominate all peoples. It will be a system apart from Christ that will deny him, a system that will ultimately blaspheme God himself. This system will control and dominate the entire world, including the political spectrum itself.

When we come to the end of the seventeenth chapter we find that the political system turns on the religious system. The government will turn against this worldwide church and destroy it.

God says this about the godless governments of the world: "God hath put in their hearts to fulfill his will, and to give their kingdom unto the beast till the words of God shall be fulfilled" (v. 17).

What a marvelous thing: God accomplishes his purposes even by using his enemies. Even when we think things are out of control, God uses the activities of godless governments to achieve his ends.

It has always been that way. God is still in control; God is still moving history toward his desired conclusion. God is working out his own purposes using godless, evil men.

At the very end of time when the Antichrist will turn on the great religious system and destroy it, he will be systematically doing exactly what God wants him to do. What a tremendous confidence it ought to be for us to realize that God, our God, is a sovereign God. Our God is gracious; he is going to do everything within his power to draw us to himself and lead us to faith in Jesus Christ.

We see that again and again throughout this book. Even in the end times God will use the apparent conquest of evil nations and the Antichrist himself to fulfill his own will and word. So the great religious system will be destroyed.

When we come to chapter 18 the political system will be destroyed. The clock of eternity will wind down; the end of the age will approach.

Political Babylon

And after these things I saw another angel come down from heaven, having great power; and the earth was lightened with his glory. And he cried mightily with a strong voice, saying, Babylon the great is fallen, is fallen, and is become the habitation of devils, and the hold of every foul spirit, and a cage of every unclean and hateful bird.

For all nations have drunk of the wine of the wrath of her fornication, and the kings of the earth have committed fornication with her, and the merchants of the earth are waxed rich through the abundance of her delicacies.

And I heard another voice from heaven, saying, Come out of her, my people, that ye be not partakers of her sins, and that ye receive not of her plagues. For her sins have reached unto heaven, and God hath remembered her iniquities.

Reward her even as she rewarded you, and double unto her double according to her works: in the cup which she hath filled fill to her double. How much she hath glorified herself, and lived deliciously, so much torment and sorrow give her: for she saith in her heart, I sit a queen, and am no widow, and shall see no sorrow. Therefore shall her plagues come in one day, death, and mourning, and famine; and she shall be utterly burned with fire: for strong is the Lord God who judgeth her.

And the kings of the earth, who have committed fornication and lived deliciously with her, shall bewail her, and lament for her, when they shall see the smoke of her burning, standing afar off for the fear of her torment, saying, Alas, alas, that great city Babylon, that mighty city! for in one hour is thy judgment come.

And the merchants of the earth shall weep and mourn over her; for no man buyeth their merchandise any more: the merchandise of gold, and silver, and precious stones, and of pearls, and fine linen, and purple, and silk, and scarlet, and all thyine wood, and all manner vessels of ivory, and all manner vessels of most precious wood, and of brass, and iron, and marble, and cinnamon, and odours, and ointments, and frankincense, and wine, and oil, and fine flour, and wheat, and beasts, and sheep, and horses, and chariots, and slaves, and souls of men.

And the fruits that thy soul lusted after are departed from thee, and all things which were dainty and goodly are departed from thee, and thou shalt find them no more at all. The merchants of these things, which were made rich by her, shall stand afar off for the fear of her torment, weeping and wailing, and saying, Alas, alas, that great city, that was clothed in fine linen, and purple, and scarlet, and decked with gold, and precious stones, and pearls! For in one hour so great riches is come to nought.

And every shipmaster, and all the company in ships, and

sailors, and as many as trade by sea, stood afar off, And cried when they saw the smoke of her burning, saying, What city is like unto this great city! And they cast dust on their heads, and cried, weeping and wailing, saying, Alas, alas, that great city, wherein were made rich all that had ships in the sea by reason of her costliness! for in one hour is she made desolate.

Rejoice over her, thou heaven, and ye holy apostles and prophets; for God hath avenged you on her. And a mighty angel took up a stone like a great millstone, and cast it into the sea, saying, Thus with violence shall that great city Babylon be thrown down, and shall be found no more at all.

And the voice of harpers, and musicians, and of pipers, and trumpeters, shall be heard no more at all in thee; and no craftsman, of whatsoever craft he be, shall be found any more in thee; and the sound of a millstone shall be heard no more at all in thee; and the light of a candle shall shine no more at all in thee; and the voice of the bridegroom and of the bride shall be heard no more at all in thee: for thy merchants were the great men of the earth; for by thy sorceries were all nations deceived. And in her was found the blood of prophets, and of saints, and of all that were slain upon the earth (18:12-24).

This chapter begins, "After these things," i.e., after the things of chapter 17. We see two different things because the events of chapter 17 have to happen before those in chapter 18. John said, "After these things I saw another angel,"—not the same angel who was in chapter 17—but a different angel.

The name of Babylon in chapter 18 is not exactly the same as it is in chapter 17. The Babylon in chapter 17 is destroyed by the kings of the earth, the governments. In chapter 18 Babylon is destroyed by God himself. In chapter 17 the kings rejoice when Babylon is destroyed, but in chapter 18 they weep.

They are miserable in the judgment of God on Babylon. Why are the kings, the merchants and the men of the world weeping over the death of Babylon in chapter 18? Because their hearts, lives, visions and hopes have all been wrapped up in this world. The judgment of God is announced. Nothing is mentioned about the beast, the ten kings, or the governments of the earth. It is an intervention of God and there is worldwide weeping. The people of the world have built their lives on it. When their world collapses—is taken away—nothing but grief and sorrow comes to them. That is the fate of those who build their lives on this world.

Many of us build our lives on this world just as surely as the kings in the end times build their governments on it. We live for the things that we possess, for the things that we can achieve and receive. We live for ourselves and build our lives around the things of this world.

It is always a tragedy when that happens within the Christian community. There are many Christian people who build their lives around the things of this world, this life. Their dreams, their hopes and visions are for here and now.

What is your dream for your life? What vision do you have of the future for yourself? Most of us dream about a house, an automobile, investments so we can be secure in retirement, or a career we can be challenged by and satisfied with. Everything we dream about is this life, this world.

Christ wants us to build our lives upon him—the Solid Rock. In Christ we are new creatures: old things are passed away; all things have become new. The only security in this life is Jesus Christ. When I hear of recession and job layoffs my first thought is to wonder how many people affected by that have built their lives upon their job security, instead of God himself.

If you have given your life to Jesus Christ you are a child of the King. You are his responsibility. There is no action of any corporation that can take you away from the security that is yours in Jesus Christ. But, if you build your life only on the things of this world, it is so easily shaken and taken away.

We serve a God who shakes the world that those things which cannot be shaken may remain (Heb. 12:29). These kingdoms of the world lament and grieve over the death of Babylon the Great because they have built their very existence on this world.

Why is God's judgment upon Babylon so severe? "Her sins have reached unto heaven, and God hath remembered her iniquities" (v. 5). The Bible declares in Hebrews 10:16 that God will make a new covenant with his people, will write his laws in their minds and their hearts, will forgive their sins and remember them no more. But to an evil world, to Babylon the Great, God remembers sins. Her sins rise even to heaven and God remembers. Judgment comes because her sins have reeked clear to heaven. Verse 7 gives us another reason: she has glorified herself and "lived deliciously." She said, "I sit as a queen, and am no widow, and shall see no sorrow."

She sits in arrogant disregard to God, and claims no need of him. She has built her life without God, believing God cannot touch her or deal with her. Because of her arrogance, pride, and luxurious living, judgment had to come.

Verses 12 and 13 give us a whole list of things in the business world of the end times that will be bought, sold, and traded. When we come down to the last phrase it says, "the souls of men."

The world will be so degenerate that the souls of people will simply become a matter of commerce, of expediency. No heart, no concern is shown for people as individuals. People are seen as property, chattel, mortgages. The attitude of Babylon, the great political and social system of the end times, will be such that persons will be insignificant. Only what the market desires will matter.

God declared that he must judge that. The twenty-fourth verse gives us another reason. For "in her was found the blood of the prophets, and of saints, and of all that were slain upon the earth." God will not let the martyrdom of his saints go unnoticed. Judgment will come deliberately from the hand of God upon these people.

In the midst of all this an appeal will be made to God's people (v. 4). It is always the call of God that his people be a separate people. God never intended for us to be swallowed up by the world. The greatest tragedy in this world is Christian people who look, act, and react just like lost people.

God calls for his people to come out from among the evil world and be separate. God's saints can never identify with the systems of this world. We can never make an alliance with the evil about us.

The great tragedy of our day is the compromise, the amalgamation of the church with the system of the world. Instead of being a change agent in our culture, the church often becomes a defender of it. So that in the name of Christ, she perverts the very faith she claims to uphold.

In Nazi Germany many of those who murdered and killed viciously had once been church leaders, active in their own church's tradition. How can that happen among people who claim to believe the gospel?

Here's how: they sell their souls to society. They reason that the church should not have anything to say about this and that. And they merge with the society about them. God put us here to change society, not to condone it. In the end times there will be an appeal to come out from them. Do not be partakers of their sins. Receive not her plagues.

This worldwide lament, starting in verse 9, will be purely selfish. All the nations will be upset over the collapse of Babylon because that is where they made all their money. Take away anyone's source of income and they will be mad about it. These nations, kings, merchants, and seamen will cry in agony. The political world, the commercial world, and the military world will all cry. They will weep because their support is gone.

Their wealth will have been destroyed, and they will grieve for it.

Beginning with verse 21, we have the conclusion of the matter. God cannot be silent forever. God moves to bring judgment not only in the end times but in all times. "A mighty angel took up a stone like a great millstone, and cast it into the sea saying, Thus with violence shall that great city Babylon be thrown down" (v. 21). Notice the recurrence of the phrase "no more": "And shall be found no more at all. The voice of harpers, musicians, pipers, trumpeters shall be heard no more at all. No craftsman of whatsoever craft he be shall be found any more. And the sound of a millstone shall be heard no more at all. The light of a candle shall shine no more at all. The voice of the bridegroom and bride shall be heard no more at all."

The end will have come. Iniquity and violence cannot be tolerated forever without divine intervention. No more mirth and music—entertainers and entertainment will be gone. No mechanic will ply his trade. The tool of the craftsman will be silent. The wheels of industry will stop. Trade unions will collapse. The lamp and the light will have gone out and the streets of the world will be caverns of darkness.

Never again will there be the sound of rejoicing. Judgment will have come because men worshipped wealth and luxury and played the harlot with the gods of this earth. No more, no more, no more!

Chapters 17 and 18 are solemn reminders that God will ultimately judge all evil and rebellion. It may seem that is not so today, but God says the time is coming. Some day the party on earth will be over.

We are in one mad scramble for entertainment and leisure today. The highest paid people in our society are entertainers; they are paid more than the presidents, governors, or legislators, more than physicians who minister to our bodies, teachers who help expand our minds, ministers and other leaders who witness to our souls.

Entertainers take our minds away from reality, yet they are the ones we bow before and honor. Some of us give more allegiance and devotion to them than to God himself.

The time is coming when the music will cease and industry will grind to a halt, when the rejoicing of weddings and celebrations will be heard no more. God himself will intervene. That is the real story within these chapters.

It is all in the future—everything we have been shown. The judgment of religious Babylon, an ecumenical worldwide system has not occurred yet. That system is now being built but not yet completed. The political and social system of the Antichrist has not yet been put together. I believe we are moving that way, but it is not yet a reality.

We are still in a day of grace. Praise God for this day, for the invitation of the gospel. Let us thank God that we have an opportunity to stand apart from the world. The apostle Paul reminded us that we are a peculiar people. We are peculiar because we show forth the praises of our God.

The thing that makes us different from non-Christians is that we live to praise God. That is our reason for being. We live, breathe, and move to give glory and praise to him. In these days of grace God gives us the privilege of linking our lives to him.

God is moving in mighty power in the world. We have the privilege of being a part of it, sharing the gospel of Jesus Christ. Let us give ourselves completely to it, fully committed and obedient to our Lord.

24
The Marriage of the Lamb
19:1-21

The final triumph of good over evil will be a time of great
rejoicing. It will be the final triumph of what was purchased by Jesus' blood at Calvary. At last, the promise of the
ages will be fulfilled.

Praise Given

And after these things I heard a great voice of much
people in heaven, saying, Alleluia; Salvation, and glory, and
honour, and power, unto the Lord our God: For true and
righteous are his judgments: for he hath judged the great
whore, which did corrupt the earth with her fornication, and
hath avenged the blood of his servants at her hand. And
again they said, Alleluia. And her smoke rose up for ever
and ever. And the four and twenty elders and the four beasts
fell down and worshipped God that sat on the throne,
saying, Amen; Alleluia. And a voice came out of the throne,
saying, Praise our God, all ye his servants, and ye that fear
him, both small and great. And I heard as it were the voice of
a great multitude, and as the voice of many waters, and as
the voice of mighty thunderings, saying, Alleluia: for the
Lord God omnipotent reigneth (vv. 1-6).

From the experience of breathtaking victory—seeing the

glory of God and the redemption of Christ completed—a great hallelujah chorus will burst forth from the courts of heaven. It will celebrate the redemption purchased by Jesus Christ at Calvary, now about to be fulfilled in the appearance of Christ with his church in triumph at the battle of Armageddon.

It will be a hallelujah for righteous retribution, for evil will have finally been judged and sin finally been dealt with. Ultimate judgment has come upon the earth. This hallelujah will signify perfect realization for the twenty-four elders do not appear on the scene again. Their praise of God that rings throughout the universe is complete.

The hallelujah of the redeemed will be a hallelujah for the reign of Christ, for the Lord God omnipotent will reign.

Could anything be more majestic than that? God is supreme. Every being in the whole universe, the mighty, the humble, every being will join in that swelling chorus of hallelujahs to God. It will reverberate and roll, echo and swell. It will resound and grow into a mighty waterfall of sound, a thunderous roar. Hallelujah rings through the corridors of heaven and time itself. How tremendous it will be to see the praise of God celebrating the fulfillment and completion of all his redemptive purposes.

I believe that our lives ought to always give praise to God. Everthing we do ought to reflect his glory. Every relationship we have ought to reflect the praise and glory of God. This hallelujah that will ascend and echo throughout heaven ought to be foretold in our lives today.

Prize Received

> Let us be glad and rejoice, and give honour to him: for the marriage of the Lamb is come, and his wife hath made herself ready. And to her was granted that she should be arrayed in fine linen, clean and white: for the fine linen is the righteousness of saints (vv. 7-9).

Not only will we see praise given, but we will see the prize received for the marriage supper of the Lamb. His bride—the church—will have made herself ready. Why does it say she has made herself ready? Isn't salvation entirely by grace through faith? Isn't it without works? How then can the bride make herself ready?

The word *righteousness* could probably be translated "righteous deeds." This is not to be confused with the righteousness of God. We received the righteousness of God when we are saved by faith through the grace of God, through no merit on our part. Here we are dealing with the righteous acts of the saints.

By our Christian lives, we are preparing our wedding garment in which we will stand before Christ, and be received at the wedding feast, the marriage of the Lamb.

Not all Christians are going to be happy when the Lord comes again. It will be embarrassing for some. There are many saints who are guilty of committing unrighteous acts, and they will not be fit garments for God's children.

That is why we must appear before the judgment seat of Christ (Rom. 14:10; 1 Cor. 3:12-15). Jesus will inspect us. We will be tried by fire; if our works and deeds have been built on hay, wood, and stubble, they will be burned away. Only that which is built upon the foundation of Jesus Christ is going to endure. We will stand before the judgment seat of Christ for final inspection, to make ready for the marriage.

The wedding gown will be made up of the good works that remain. God expects us to live rightly as his children in this world. Being saved does not relieve us of the responsibility to live for God.

Compromise, sin, ungodly attitudes, and rebellion have no place in the life of a child of God. In this passage we see the truth. Have we made ourselves ready for him? What garment have we prepared? It is the task of the church and the saints to make ourselves ready.

There are two great events that are described in this chapter. One will be in heaven, the other on earth. One will be a wedding, the other a war. The church and the world both come to the consummation of their ways. The long delayed joy is the happy portion of the church. Judgment, delayed even longer, is the portion of the world.

The Lord Jesus Christ will fill both of these scenes. We are invited to a wedding or a war depending on what we do with Jesus Christ. One thing is for sure, as God's children we are preparing, equipping, dressing ourselves for a wedding feast at a marriage that shall come.

Problem Corrected

> And I fell at his feet to worship him. And he said unto me, See thou do it not: I am thy fellow servant and of thy brethren that have the testimony of Jesus: worship God: for the testimony of Jesus is the spirit of prophecy (v. 10).

John was so enamored by the vision that he fell down to worship the angel. That was an honest mistake. We are guilty of the same thing sometimes. Someone is used of God to draw us to him, and we sometimes focus on that person instead of God himself. We can identify with John. But the angel told him, "Do not worship me, worship God. I am just a fellow servant."

Then we have a great definition of prophecy: "the testimony of Jesus is the spirit of prophecy" (v. 10). Prophecy is not just telling the future, not even telling the truth of God. The real test of genuine prophecy is its relationship to Jesus Christ. The testimony of Jesus is the spirit of prophecy. All prophecy points to him; magnifies him. In its fulfillment, all prophecy results in praise to God through Jesus Christ.

Prince Revealed

And I saw heaven opened, and behold a white horse; and
he that sat upon him was called Faithful and True, and in
righteousness he doth judge and make war. His eyes were as
a flame of fire, and on his head were many crowns; and he
had a name written, that no man knew, but he himself. And
he was clothed with a vesture dipped in blood: and his name
is called The Word of God.

And the armies which were in heaven followed him upon
white horses, clothed in fine linen, white and clean. And out of
his mouth goeth a sharp sword, that with it he should smite the
nations: and he shall rule them with a rod of iron: and he
treadeth the winepress of the fierceness and wrath of Almighty
God. And he hath on his vesture and on his thigh a name
written KING OF KINGS, AND LORD OF LORDS (vv. 11-16).

Beginning in verse 11 is a beautiful description of Jesus
Christ, the King of kings, Lord of lords. Armageddon is about
to begin. Up until this time, Jesus has been directing everything
from heaven.

Now he will intervene directly. He will come down to earth
to complete the work he has begun and establish his kingdom.
"His eyes were as a flame of fire, and on his head were many
crowns" means that he has supreme authority, supreme power.
All of the power of the universe is vested in Jesus Christ.

"And he was clothed with a vesture dipped in blood: and his
name is called The Word of God" (v. 13). Jesus was the Word
of God before the foundation of the world. He has always
been the very expression of God.

But at his next appearing he will exercise full authority in
expressing the Father's judicial attitude. As words are the
expression of the mind and heart of an individual, so Jesus
Christ is the only perfect expression of God. He is the Word of

God. We worship and acknowledge him as the Word of God.

There is so much in this passage about Jesus that is fascinating. "And out of his mouth goeth a sharp sword" (v. 15). The normal place for a sword is on the thigh. It is a strange picture. That sword is the Word of God.

The writer of Hebrews said it is sharper than a two-edged sword (4:12). On his thigh instead of his sword he has his name written: King of kings and Lord of lords. That is all he needs. With the sword he will smite the nations.

With great pomp, splendor, and earthly majesty the armies of the Antichrist and the confederated nations will gather to war against God himself. They will file through the passes and deploy the rich fields of Megiddo. The hillsides that surround the valley of Megiddo will be fortified with the latest weaponry possible.

The Antichrist will have amazing weapons in the hands of all his armies. The ground itself will seem to shake with the hundreds of millions of soldier's feet marching to that valley. The skies overhead will darken with aircraft and up and down the Mediterranean near the Gulf of Suez and the Persian Gulf there will be a mighty armada of naval forces amassed to oppose God.

The final command will be given. Then suddenly, it will all be over. In fact, it will be no war at all: just a word spoken from him who sits upon the white horse and it will be over. With just a word the blasphemous, loud-mouthed beast will be stricken where he stands. Another word and the false prophet, the miracle working windbag will be punctured and will stand silent.

The pair of them will be bundled up and hurled headlong into everlasting flames. Another word, and the panic-stricken armies will reel, stagger and fall dead. All will die: generals, admirals, field marshals down to the least recruit.

How our heart pulses quicken as we read this Scripture of

the descending Christ and his saints victorious. What a day that
will be!

Prophecy Realized

And I saw an angel standing in the sun; and he cried with
a loud voice, saying to all the fowls that fly in the midst of
heaven, Come and gather yourselves together unto the
supper of the great God; That ye may eat the flesh of kings
and the flesh of captains, and the flesh of mighty men, and
the flesh of horses, and of them that sit on them, and the
flesh of all men, both free and bond, both small and great
(vv. 17-18).

Prophecy will now be realized. Nothing like this will have
ever happened before. An angel will call all the fowl that fly in
the midst of heaven and say, "Come and gather yourselves
together unto the supper of the great God." It will be a feast
prepared by God for the fowls of heaven.

The language is revolting and nauseating but it reveals the
awful results of revolt against God. We cannot imagine the
tragedy of rebellion against God. For many centuries, God had
given people opportunity to repent and turn to him. Again and
again, they have blasphemed God and refused to repent. Now,
God will pour out his wrath on the ungodly.

Promises Kept

And I saw the beast, and the kings of the earth, and their
armies, gathered together to make war against him that sat
on the horse, and against his army. And the beast was taken,
and with him the false prophet that wrought miracles before
him, with which he deceived them that had received the
mark of the beast, and them that worshipped his image.
These both were cast alive into a lake of fire burning with
brimstone. And the remnant were slain with the sword of
him that sat upon the horse, which sword proceeded out of

his mouth: and all the fowls were filled with their flesh
(vv. 19-21).

The last verses affirm that the promise of God will be kept.
There will be no natural weapon used against the beast and
the false prophet but their doom is certain (v. 20). The great
hostilities of earth will draw to a close. All the rebellion of
history will come to an end. There is no mention of a struggle.
Nor will we find it in any other prophetic portion of Scripture.

With one sweep of God's mighty hand, they will be taken.
Their armies will be helpless to assist. Then the entire army of
the wicked will be slain. The strength of the nations that
resisted God and rebelled against him will be dashed to bits as
pottery struck by iron: an eternal end to Satan's great society.
The winepress is trodden and a river of blood will fill the land.
The fowl of the air will feast on human flesh. What a pivotal
day that will be!

25

The Millennial Kingdom
20:1-10

A t last we come to the golden age, to the day when justice will prevail, where righteousness will be the rule and not the exception, when Jesus Christ will be King of kings and Lord of lords.

This will be the fulfillment of all prophecy in the Word of God about the kingdom of Christ, that time when God finally answers all our prayers.

He told us to pray, "Thy kingdom come, Thy will be done in earth as it is in heaven" (Matt. 6:10). Finally that day will arrive. Let us examine the millennial kingdom. But first a question: why is Satan going to be loosed again after the thousand years? We will look at the answer presently.

After Armageddon, the millennial kingdom will come. The armies of the world will have been disbanded, the "swords" of war beaten into plowshares.

Jerusalem will become the capital of the world. The throne of David will be there. The millennial Temple will have been built for the nations of the world to come and to worship the living God.

Prosperity will reign from pole to pole: material plenty for all people. Poverty and unemployment will be unknown, disease and decay eliminated. There will be no prisons, no hospitals, no mental institutions, no jails, saloons, or homes for the aged.

Such things belong to the past age. Everywhere the glow of youth will be seen.

Cemeteries will be crumbling relics of the past age and tears will be rare. It will be the millenium. Jesus will be Lord and rule the nations with a rod of iron. His rule will be righteous and everyone will obey. There will be no lawbreakers; everyone will obey the law of Christ. Justice will be perfect. The millennial kingdom will prevail for a thousand years. Satan will be bound and the earth will be perfect.

Its Reality

There are many people who believe there will be no millennial kingdom. The prevailing view among many evangelical scholars and teachers is what is called "amillennialism," or "no millennium." These people interpret the Book of Revelation and this passage very figuratively. They say that it is symbolic of something else and is not literal.

I want to emphasize that there is a reality to this kingdom. It is important to grasp this because it gives us tremendous hope for what God is going to do. The evidence points to a literal kingdom. If you do not believe in a literal kingdom, then Revelation stops at the end of chapter 19 for you.

The events in chapters 19 and 20 are sequential. They build one upon another. For instance, in 19:20 the beast is taken and with him the false prophet. They are cast alive into the lake of fire burning with brimstone. Even those who do not believe in a millennial kingdom believe that will take place.

But look at 20:10. The devil that deceived them is cast into the lake of fire and brimstone where the beast and false prophet are. Chapter 20 presupposes chapter 19 and both chapters indicate a literal series of events.

Any other interpretation that can be imposed upon the Book of Revelation is not justified by the text. It is imported from some other theological prejudice or bias. This literal interpretation of the kingdom was believed by the early church until well into the third century after Christ.

Those who do not believe in the millennium will say that the first resurrection is the spiritual rising with Christ which happens when we are saved. The second resurrection, they say, is the general resurrection of all the dead.

But if we take a passage of Scripture that mentions two resurrections—one said to be a spiritual resurrection and the other a literal resurrection—then we make a mockery out of language and Scripture has no meaning at all. We cannot twist and distort the Scripture like that.

The amillennialists say that since there is no millennium then everything in the Bible that refers to the millennium will take place in this age. Yet Scripture teaches that this age will be a period when Satan runs wild. Jesus' disciples came to him and asked, "What shall be the sign of thy coming, and of the end of the word?" (Matt. 24:3). (We are talking about end times.)

Jesus answered and said unto them, "Take heed that no man deceive you. For many shall come in my name saying, I am Christ; and shall deceive many" (Matt. 24:4-5) . . . "For there shall arise false Christs, and false prophets, and shall shew great signs and wonders; insomuch that, if it were possible, they shall deceive the very elect" (Matt. 24:24).

Now, look at 2 Corinthians which speaks about the end times. "For such are false apostles, deceitful workers, transforming themselves into the apostles of Christ. And no marvel; for Satan himself is transformed into an angel of light. Therefore it is no great thing if his ministers also be transformed as the ministers of righteousness; whose end shall be according to their works" (2 Cor. 11:13-15).

In 2 Timothy concerning the end times Paul declares, "But evil men and seducers shall wax worse and worse, deceiving, and being deceived" (2 Tim. 3:13). In Revelation 12 and 13, we have seen that Satan will be busy in the end days prior to the millennial kingdom.

Yet, the amillennialists say there is no millennial kingdom, so everything pertaining to the millennium has to be experienced in the end times. Revelation declares that Satan is bound up and cast into the bottomless pit that he should deceive the nations no more (20:3).

Clearly, Scripture teaches that in the kingdom age, Satan will be bound, not released. So if you do not believe in the millennium, you have a problem because the end of the age has to be characterized by deception and unbelief.

But the Word of God declares that there will come a time when Satan will be bound. He will be bound and cast into the bottomless pit itself. This means that he will stop deceiving the nations. The amillennial view creates an impossible situation.

Amillennials also say when we come to the thrones (20:4) that it does not refer to earthly thrones. They believe that the reigning of the saints is going to be in heaven, not on earth. It is true that Revelation 20 does not specify an earthly throne. But Revelation 5:10 says that we shall reign on the earth.

There is a big inconsistency in interpretation if you do not accept the fact that the millennial kingdom is a literal kingdom. There are more prophecies in the Old Testament about the millennial kingdom of Christ than any other thing. It is the predominant theme of prophecy. The millennial kingdom must definitely be taken as a reality.

Zechariah declared, "The Lord shall be king over all the earth: in that day shall there be one Lord" (14:9). Then he continued, "It shall come to pass that everyone that is left of all the nations which came against Jerusalem shall even go up from year to year to worship the King, the Lord of Hosts, and keep the feast of tabernacles." (14:16).

Isaiah said, "For, behold I create new heavens and new

earth: and the former shall not be remembered, nor come into mind. But be ye glad and rejoice for ever in that which I create: for, behold, I create Jerusalem a rejoicing and her people a joy. And I will rejoice in Jerusalem, and joy in my people: and the voice of weeping shall be no more heard in her, nor the voice of crying. There shall be no more thence an infant of days, nor an old man that hath not filled his days: for the child shall die an hundred years old; but the sinner being an hundred years old shall be accursed" (Isa. 65:17-20).

In other words, there will come a time when aging will not be as we know it now. Many other references in Isaiah speak of the millennial kingdom and scores of other passages are about this kingdom. And some argue that the millennial kingdom is not mentioned in the Bible!

Its Rule

And I saw an angel come down from heaven, having the key of the bottomless pit and a great chain in his hand. And he laid hold on the dragon, that old serpent, which is the Devil, and Satan, and bound him a thousand years, And cast him into the bottomless pit, and shut him up, and set a seal upon him, that he should deceive the nations no more, till the thousand years should be fulfilled: and after that he must be loosed a little season.

And I saw thrones, and they sat upon them, and judgment was given unto them: and I saw the souls of them that were beheaded for the witness of Jesus, and for the word of God, and which had not worshipped the beast, neither his image, neither had received his mark upon their foreheads, or in their hands; and they lived and reigned with Christ a thousand years. But the rest of the dead lived not again until the thousand years were finished. This is the first resurrection. Blessed and holy is he that hath part in the first resurrection: on such the second death hath no power, but

they shall be priests of God and of Christ, and shall reign
with him a thousand years (vv. 1-6).

The term *thousand years* occurs six times in this passage. It
is not right to pass it off as insignificant or unimportant. The
reality of this kingdom will be for a thousand years.

The first thing that will happen is that Satan will be bound.
An angel with the power and authority of heaven itself will
come down and take hold of Satan, put a chain about him,
hurl him into the abyss and lock him up for a thousand years.
Generation after generation will be born and the earth will
flourish just as it did in Eden before the serpent seduced
humanity. For a thousand years there will be heaven on earth.

Satan has been thrown into a bottomless pit so he can
deceive the nations no more. This kingdom excludes Satan;
called the dragon, the serpent, the devil. A careful study of
those words reveal much about Satan's character.

He is a dragon because of his beastial, maniacal leadership
of the world. He is the serpent because of his subtle nature. He
is the devil because he is a liar and murderer. He is Satan
because he is an accuser, a slanderer, and a deceiver of the
nations. He will be bound and the rule of Christ established.

We will see the coronation of the saints, believers from all
the ages who will rule and reign with Christ. "And I saw
thrones, and they sat upon them, and judgment was given
unto them" (v. 4). The age is coming when the ones who have
been despised by the ages of men will be exalted by the eternal
God. They shall rule with him.

John saw these groups of people: saints sitting upon thrones
which represent the church of all ages; martyrs who have been
beheaded for the witness of Christ. The word *beheaded*
literally means "killed with an ax." They will be killed because
they will not worship the beast or take his mark during the
tribulation period.

The rule during the millennial kingdom will be perfectly righteous. When people sin during the millennium, it will not be because they were deceived by Satan. During the millennium, sin will be because of man's native sin nature.

Its Resurrections

But the rest of the dead lived not again until the thousand years were finished. This is the first resurrection. Blessed and holy is he that hath part in the first resurrection: on such the second death hath no power, but they shall be priests of God and of Christ, and shall reign with him a thousand years" (vv. 5-6).

Notice the resurrections that are related to this millennial kingdom. The rest of the dead do not live again until this thousand years is finished. Those who have part in this first resurrection are called blessed and holy. The second resurrection is when the lost are raised. To say there is a first resurrection certainly implies that there will be a second resurrection.

The Bible definitely speaks of two resurrections: one before the millennium and one after, one of the saints and one of the lost. Years divide the two resurrections. The judgment seat of Christ follows the first and the great white throne judgment follows the second. These will be the resurrection of the saints before the millennial period and the resurrection of the lost after.

Its Revolution

And when the thousand years are expired, Satan shall be loosed out of his prison, And shall go out to deceive the nations which are in the four quarters of the earth, Gog and

Magog, to gather them together to battle: the number of
whom is as the sand of the sea (vv. 7-9).

Now look at the revolution that will take place. We might
think that such a revolution would be impossible. Today we
give great effort to bring about peace on earth. The millennium
will be a thousand years of peace with no poverty, sickness,
civil rights violations, unemployment, no injustice, no one
hungry or cold, no want of any kind.

When the thousand years are over Satan will be loosed to
deceive the nations again and gather them together for battle.
A huge army will be amassed. They will attack the saints in and
around the beloved city of Jerusalem. Then fire will come
down from God in heaven and consume them.

After a thousand years in prison Satan will be turned loose.
He will marshal an army and they will attack Jerusalem. Then
God will destroy them.

After a long, blissful, perfect millennium of a thousand years,
there will be a test of people's hearts. We are tested in every
age.

After a thousand years he will not have changed a bit. In fact
he will have been plotting his revenge for a thousand years. He
will have lost none of this cunning. He will still be the great
deceiver, still the most convincing liar in all the world.

Men and sin will still be the same. As before Satan will know
better than anyone how to get the two of them together! He
will come back for one final fling, to try to strike out at both
God and humanity. Once again, sin will blaze like wildfire. The
kindling will still be there, stacked and dry. Satan will provide
the fire. After a thousand years people will still follow Satan.

In fact, the ideal conditions of the millennium may be one of
the reasons why people will not receive Jesus Christ. The self-
righteous and self-sufficient are always the hardest to lead to

Christ. The man who needs nothing will make no attempt to find God. The man who feels his own sufficiency will never repent and come to God.

It may be that the ideal millennial conditions will build up such an immunity to God, such a self-sufficiency and self-righteousness in the hearts of people that they will make it hard for them to come to Christ.

We are seeing a foretaste of that in America. Let our country come under attack by enemy bombers, let bombs be dropped on Dallas, Kansas City, New York, and Los Angeles, and we would have to keep the doors of our churches open all the time; there would be people crowding in every minute to pray to God.

It is our supposed self-sufficiency that keeps us away from God. Someone has said there are no atheists in foxholes. There are no self-sufficient men when faced by circumstances they cannot handle. The prosperity in this age has been one of the main reasons why it is difficult to get men to come to God. There will be a revolution at the end of this time.

Its Retribution

> And the devil that deceived them was cast into the lake of fire and brimstone, where the beast and the false prophet are, and shall be tormented day and night for ever and ever (v. 10).

Satan is cast into the lake of fire. His rebellion never had a chance at success. Do not think for a moment that Satan has a chance of winning. If you cast your lot against God, you have no chance either.

The revolution at the end of the millennium will be permitted to show that only God can change the human heart and that after 1,000 years of a perfect society with perfect provision and prosperity, people will still follow Satan. Only God can change the human heart. That is why Revelation 20 was written: to show us that the heart is deceitful and more desperately wicked than we can imagine (see Jer. 17:9).

Only the touch of God in salvation can change a person's heart and life. Even a perfect society cannot change human nature. There is nothing in this world that can bring peace to our hearts except Jesus Christ. (And he is not of this world!)

Hell was not created for people. It was prepared for Satan, his demons and angels. The lost man goes to hell by his own choice. God never planned it that way, nor did he desire it (see 2 Pet. 3:9). He does not delight in the death of the wicked. When a person looks at the sacrifice of Jesus Christ and chooses to follow Satan and serve evil, he chooses his eternal home in hell.

If you do not get to heaven, it will be because you reject Jesus Christ. The whole drama of Revelation should lead us to faith in Jesus Christ. Revelation shows us the desperate wickedness of the human heart and that only Jesus Christ can bring forgiveness, peace, and eternal life. The only way is Jesus. Only Jesus Christ can change the heart.

26
The Great White Throne
20:11-15

Who is the person who sits on the throne, from whose face the earth and heavens flee? It is Jesus Christ. The Word of God says that God has committed all judgment to Jesus Christ. God judges no man but has committed it to the Son (John 5:22). All people have an appointment with Jesus Christ. You may think you can avoid that confrontation. We may refuse to receive and trust him, or to believe in him. But we will meet him someday either as our Savior or as our Judge.

We will either know him as the Lamb of God or as the Lion of the tribe of Judah. We have an appointment with Christ. We will see him, face him, and will declare him Lord. Every knee shall bow and every tongue shall confess that Jesus Christ is Lord to the glory of God the Father.

The Drama

And I saw a great white throne, and him that sat on it, from whose face the earth and the heaven fled away; and there was found no place for them. And I saw the dead, small and great, stand before God; and the books were opened: and another book was opened, which is the book of life: and the dead were judged out of those things which were written in the books, according to their works (vv. 11-12).

The lost who have rejected and refused him will stand before him. "From whose face the earth and the heaven fled away" (v. 11) means that everything people have depended upon is gone. Everything on earth people think it takes to be secure will be taken away from them. There will be no possession that people can hold in their hands, no mountain behind which they can hide.

Everything in heaven and earth will be taken away. It will be as though men are standing on nothing with no place to hide. On the throne will be the Judge, the one with nail prints in his hands, scars on his back and his brow, with the pierced wound of the spear in his side.

This Jesus Christ, who was wounded and marked by evil men, will be on his throne. People who have refused to respond to him in every way will meet him as their Judge and stand before him.

The "small and great" means just what it says. No one will be too important to get out of this judgment and no one too insignificant to be overlooked. The great and small will be brought before him. Think of the great sea of faces that will stand before that throne—the lost of all ages.

There will be the reprobate: the confirmed sinner who cursed God, hated the church, the Bible, and Christians. He slammed the door in the face of everyone who tried to witness to him. He claimed there was no God.

The self-righteous will be there: the one who did not feel the need of salvation. He may have been educated, cultured, and self-sufficient. He probably had everything materially he needed. There was no reason for him to turn to God, no thought in his heart for eternity. There was no concern in his life for death, the hereafter or judgment.

The procrastinators will be there. They knew they were lost, and did not plan to stay that way. They knew they needed Jesus Christ but put the decision off until another time. Their favorite word was "tomorrow." Agrippa said "tomorrow" but it never came (see Acts 26). Governor Felix said "tomorrow" but it never came.

It never does. Tomorrow is on Satan's calendar but not on God's. The procrastinator will be in front of the throne to be judged.

There will be many church members there, too. Seldom do more than 50 percent of the church members of any local congregation attend. If a man claims that he loves God and despises the very thing God sent his Son to establish—the church—then chances are he is not saved. Many of those who do come to services have no real concern for what God wants of them.

There are many church members who have met the pastor, but not the Master. There are many who have been baptized in a baptistry but have never been baptized with the Holy Spirit to become part of the body of Christ. There are many who have accepted a biblical philosophy, but nothing more.

Our country is a constitutional republic based on the Word of God. A majority of our laws are supposedly based on the Bible. Those who wrote the Constitution went to the Bible for their guidance and it reflects the Word of God. The biblical basis of our nation should make it easy for someone to accept the Christian way of thinking. It makes sense: be honest, disciplined, diligent, moral and pure.

It makes sense to adopt a philosophy that is so much in keeping with the society in which we live. Many people join the church and simply adopt a Christian philosophy. It sounds right to them and they want to raise their children that way.

God never said, "Believe in the church, and you will be saved." He said, "Believe in the Lord Jesus Christ, and you will be saved." There will be many church members standing before the great white throne.

They will be standing before the throne, the way a person stands before the judge when he is sentenced. Here are the great and the small, the dead of all ages, the lost who have rejected Christ, standing before Jesus Christ for one reason: to be judged according to their works and be sentenced.

The drama will then get both more complicated and clearer. "The books were opened: and another book was opened which is the book of life" (v. 12). One book will be the book of the law. God is going to have the book of his law, what he required. Then there is the book of works which contain what they have done. One by one, lost people will come to the great white throne.

God, with tender, brokenhearted care, will open the book of the law. He will show everyone what is required by God's standard. Then he will open the book of works and point by point, he will go over someone's life and show him at every point where he failed to measure up. He will show them one by one why they cannot enter into heaven.

Then the most tender, heartbreaking moment of all will come. Just to be sure, just so that no one can say that God is not just, he will take the book of life in which are recorded the names of all persons who have ever given their heart to Jesus Christ. That is why it is called the Lamb's book of Life. It is for those who have given their hearts to the Lamb of God.

The Heavenly Father will look in vain for someone's name. At length, when He cannot find it he will close the book. With a broken heart, he will say, "Depart from me, ye cursed, into everlasting fire, prepared for the devil and his angels" (Matt. 25:41).

The lost one will tremble as he hears God's command. He brings excuses and words to defend himself like those in Matthew 7:22: "Lord, Lord, have we not prophesied in thy name? and in thy name have cast out devils: and in thy name done many wonderful works?" And Jesus will say, "I never knew you: depart from me, ye that work iniquity" (Matt. 7:23).

Judgment will always be according to works. Every judgment in the Bible is a judgment of works. Christians are going to stand before the judgment seat of Christ and be judged according to their works. It will not determine whether or not one is saved, but everyone's works will be judged.

The lost person will stand before the great white throne not to determine whether he goes to heaven or hell—that will already be determined by his or her own rejection of Christ—but to be judged according to his or her own works. All sinners have a choice: either a free pardon or a fair trial from God.

I warn you that if you have a fair trial, God will be just. He will judge you according to your works. We may think we are pretty good. But the Bible declares that every man who receives a fair trial will be cast into the lake of fire. Every secret of the heart is going to be laid out in the judgment.

"For God shall bring every work into judgment, with every secret thing, whether it be good, or whether it be evil" (Eccl. 12:14). "God shall judge the secrets of men by Jesus Christ according to my gospel" (Rom. 2:16). "Neither is there any creature that is not manifest in his sight: but all things are naked and opened unto the eyes of him with whom we have to do" (Heb. 4:13).

Everything that has been done in secret, God has written down. At this judgment, everything people have thought, said, done, or failed to do will be in the book. They will not be able to hide it from God. They will be judged according to their works.

That will be the drama of the great white throne: Christ on the throne; the dead, great, and small gathered, standing before him; the books opened, searched, scrutinized; the law expressed, the work shown insufficient, no name in the book of life, judgment pronounced.

The Dead

"The sea gave up the dead which were in it; and death
and hell delivered up the dead which were in them: and they
were judged every man according to their works" (v. 13).

Every grave will give up its dead. One's body may have been
cremated and the ashes tossed to the ends of the earth, but
those ashes will be gathered together. Bone upon bone, each
body will be reconstructed in this resurrection.

Death cannot keep men from God's judgment. Death is not
annihilation. People cannot crawl in the grave and hide from
God because a day is coming when the grave and the sea will
give up their dead. All the dead will stand before him.

There will be a resurrection of the spirit also. "Death and
hell" delivered them up. No one is in hell right now. Hell is for
the body. The bodies have not been united with the spirit.

When a person dies without God, he goes to the place of the
dead, a place of torment and torture called hades. But in the
judgment day, the graves will give up the bodies, hades will give
up the spirits and they will all be joined together. This will be a
literal, bodily, physical resurrection. Men cannot hide from God.

The Damnation

"Death and hell were cast into the lake of fire. This is the
second death. And whosoever was not found written in the
book of life was cast into the lake of fire" (vv. 14-15).

Verse 13 tells us that after death and hell deliver up their
dead, "they were judged." There will be no uncertainty about
it. You can be sure your sins will find you out. Do not be
deceived, God is not mocked. Whatever a person sows, he will
also reap (Gal. 6:7). The judgment of God will come and all
will be judged.

When all the books are opened and every detail of their lives will be exposed. When sinful lives are compared to the law and found insufficient; when the book of life is searched and their names are not there, there will be no mercy. With trembling hand, the angel will write "Lost" across that name.

God is a God of mercy, love and grace. If you want mercy you can have it. If you want love and grace you can have it. If you want forgiveness, you can possess it. If you want eternal life, it is yours. But you must take it now.

"Now is the accepted time; behold now is the day of salvation" (2 Cor. 6:2). Now there is mercy, love, and grace. It is yours for the asking. If you reject it the Scripture says, "Whosoever was not found written in the book of life was cast into the lake of fire" (v. 15). The fire will be real anguish and agony for everyone who experiences it. And it will be eternal.

One thousand years before this time, the beast and the false prophet were cast into the lake of fire. We will come to this moment and they will still be there. Not for a moment or a brief visit, but the smoke of their torment will ascend forever and ever.

Do you know how long forever is? The brief moments of this life have been given to us by the hand of a gracious God for us to receive him. He wants us to enjoy the blessings of eternity with him. But if we reject him, we will find that hell is forever.

Those who have accepted Jesus Christ as Savior will not be at the great white throne. Jesus Christ took our judgment. He bore our shame, our sin and suffering. At Calvary, Jesus cried out, "It is finished." Down through the corridors of heaven, "it is finished" rings until it reaches the hearts and ears of every saint who is in heaven waiting for that day.

God writes across the title deed to every Christian's salvation, "It is finished." There is nothing to add. Jesus Christ bore our sins. "Blessed is the man to whom the Lord will not impute sin" (Rom. 4:8). When we are saved, every sin we ever have committed or ever will commit is forgiven.

When Jesus died, all our sins were future. It was finished on Calvary. Do not trifle with the mercy of Christ. Do not cherish some vague hope of a second chance. Come to Christ and know for sure that you will not have any part of the great white throne judgment.

Everything needed for us to be saved has been done. The deed to eternal life is offered. All that is required on our part is to receive it.

27

The New Heaven
and the New Earth
21:1 to 22:5

These last two chapters in Revelation are two of the most exciting and meaningful passages anywhere in Scripture. I confess that I come to this twenty-first chapter with mixed emotions. Partly, I come with unbridled joy as I realize what God has prepared for us.

It has been a long sometimes dark journey through Revelation. It is good to emerge into the brightness and beauty of God's new day. I rejoice in what I see as the inheritance of every child of God in eternity with Jesus Christ.

But I also feel a twinge of sadness, for we have sensed something of the heart of God. There are many who will not be in the new heaven and the new earth. What a heartache it will be to God. It will be wonderful and blessed for us but think of those who are not there. Doubtless, God will view the consummation of the ages with a mixture of joy and sadness as he realizes those who shall not be present.

We now see a whole new picture. Verse 1 sets the stage: "I saw a new heaven and a new earth: for the first heaven and the first earth were passed away; and there was no more sea." The word *new* means not only new in time but new in kind. It will be a new world, a new heaven, never before seen by human eye. Not since Adam has there been a time when the world was without sin.

Even in Adam's time, the possibility for sin was there but no more. There will be no possibility for rebellion against God in this new heaven and new earth. No more will there be the prospect that rebellion and sin will taint the experience of humanity. This will be a new kind of world, for the first heaven and the first earth have passed away.

"But the heavens and the earth, which are now, by the same word are kept in store, reserved unto fire against the day of judgment and perdition of ungodly men" (2 Pet. 3:7). Why is God waiting, withholding his judgment on the world?

Second Peter 3:9 tells us it is so people can be saved. This is a day of grace. God longs for us to be saved. God has a holy reluctance to bring the end. He desires greatly for people to be saved.

We have been left on the earth to help our Heavenly Father achieve that goal—by telling the Good News. "But the day of the Lord will come as a thief in the night; in the which the heavens shall pass away with a great noise, and the elements shall melt with fervent heat, the earth also and the works that are therein shall be burned up.

"Looking for and hasting unto the coming of the day of God, wherein the heavens being on fire shall be dissolved, and the elements shall melt with fervent heat? Nevertheless we, according to his promise, look for new heavens and a new earth, wherein dwelleth righteousness" (2 Peter 3:10,12-13). "For, behold, I create new heavens and a new earth: and the former shall not be remembered, nor come into mind" (Isa. 65:17).

Everything we hold so dear, everything we understand about this life will pass away. God will create a new heaven and a new earth, and we will not even remember this life. It will come to mind no more.

That is what takes place in the first verse of Revelation 21. God is going to destroy everything that sin has touched.

Everything that sin has defiled will be dissolved.

"And there was no more sea" (v. 1) means that things will be changed. Whether or not it means there will be no bodies of water on the new earth is not clear but whatever it means, it means we will have a new earth.

That sea around Patmos separated John from those he loved. "No more sea" definitely means no more separation!

God's New Creation

And I John saw the holy city, new Jerusalem, coming down from God out of heaven prepared as a bride adorned for her husband. And I heard a great voice out of heaven saying, Behold, the tabernacle of God is with men, and he will dwell with them, and they shall be his people, and God himself shall be with them, and be their God.

And God shall wipe away all tears from their eyes; and there shall be no more death, neither sorrow, nor crying, neither shall there be any more pain: for the former things are passed away. And he that sat upon the throne said, Behold, I make all things new.

And he said unto me, Write: for these words are true and faithful. And he said unto me, It is done. I am Alpha and Omega, the beginning and the end. I will give unto him that is athirst of the fountain of the water of life freely. He that overcometh shall inherit all things; and I will be his God, and he shall be my son.

But the fearful, and unbelieving, and the abominable and murderers, and whoremongers, and sorcerers, and idolators, and all liars, shall have their part in the lake which burneth with fire and brimstone: which is the second death (vv. 2-8).

We have seen the works of man and sin. We have seen how sin has infected the whole human race and how even the whole world is under the curse and bondage of sin.

But now we see God's new creation. God has prepared a literal city. It is not symbolic, not Jerusalem as we know it today. It will be a new Jerusalem—prepared, tailor-made by God for eternity. The word *tabernacle* (v. 3) means "the place where God dwells." We have all tried to get close to God through prayer, Bible study, worship, and the like.

There has always been a sense in which God was somewhere else, that we were separated by our flesh. In the new heaven and the new earth God himself will dwell among us and we will know his presence: divine, holy, almighty, and eternal pervading the new Jerusalem, the new earth and heaven.

Sadness and sorrow seem to be our lot as people. But this new heaven and new earth will be a place where tears cannot come (v. 4). Sorrow cannot exist there: "Weeping may endure for a night, but joy cometh in the morning" (Ps. 30:5). Now is the night of weeping, tears and sin, but God is preparing a new world into which no tears will ever enter.

There will be no death there (v. 4). We are hounded by graves, death and grief in this life. "The last enemy that shall be destroyed is death" (1 Cor. 15:26). Death will be unknown in the new world. There will be nothing to cause pain or infirmity, or physical limitation of any kind (v. 4).

He has made the provision of a perfect full inheritance for us (vv. 6-7). We are his heirs; we inherit all things. This is a full inheritance. Jesus is the Alpha and Omega, the beginning and the end. Everything in this world finds its climax, its meaning and purpose in and through Jesus Christ. In this new heaven and new earth, God will have provided for every need through Jesus Christ.

Some people will not be in this new creation (v. 8). But he is not saying that if you have ever committed one of these sins you will not be there. Everyone of us is guilty of at least one of these sins. We are all liars. At one time or another, we have all been unbelievers.

He is declaring that those whose lives have been characterized by these sins, who have lived a life of unbelief habitually, will not be there. There is a difference in telling one lie and habitually lying. The person to whom lying is a way of life will not be in God's new creation.

In the midst of telling about the new heaven and the new earth, God warns of the need we all have to commit our lives to Jesus Christ.

God's New City

And there came unto me one of the seven angels which had the seven vials full of the seven last plagues, and talked with me, saying, Come hither, I will shew thee the bride, the Lamb's wife.

And he carried me away in the spirit to a great and high mountain, and shewed me that great city, the holy Jerusalem, descending out of heaven from God, Having the glory of God: and her light was like unto a jasper stone, clear as crystal;

And had a wall great and high, and had twelve gates, and at the gates twelve angels, and names written thereon, which are the names of the twelve tribes of the children of Israel:

On the east three gates; on the north three gates; on the south three gates; and on the west three gates. And the wall of the city had twelve foundations, and in them the names of the twelve apostles of the Lamb.

And he that talked with me had a golden reed to measure the city, and the gates thereof, and the wall thereof. And the city lieth foursquare, and the length is as large as the breadth: and he measured the city with the reed, twelve thousand furlongs.

The length and the breadth and the height of it are equal. And he measured the wall thereof, an hundred and forty and four cubits, according to the measure of a man, that is, of the angel.

And the building of the wall of it was of jasper: and the city was pure gold, like unto clear glass. And the foundations of the wall of the city were garnished will all manner of precious stones. The first foundation was jasper; the second, sapphire; the third, a chalcedony; the fourth, an emerald; The fifth, sardonyx; the sixth, sardius; the seventh, chrysolite; the eighth, beryl; the ninth, a topaz; the tenth, a chrysoprasus; the eleventh, a jacinth; the twelfth, an amethyst.

And the twelve gates were twelve pearls: every several gate was of one pearl: and the street of the city was pure gold, as it were transparent glass.

And I saw no temple therein: for the Lord God Almighty and the Lamb are the temple of it. And the city had no need of the sun, neither of the moon, to shine in it: for the glory of God did lighten it, and the Lamb is the light thereof.

And the nations of them which are saved shall walk in the light of it: and the kings of the earth do bring their glory and honour into it. And the gates of it shall not be shut at all by day: for there shall be no night there. And they shall bring the glory and honour of the nations unto it.

And there shall in no wise enter into it any thing that defileth, neither whatsoever worketh abomination, or maketh a lie: but they which are written in the Lamb's book of life.

And he shewed me a pure river of water of life, clear as crystal, proceeding out of the throne of God and of the Lamb. In the midst of the street of it, and on either side of the river, was there the tree of life, which bare twelve manner of fruits, and yielded her fruit every month: and the leaves of the tree were for the healing of the nations.

And there shall be no more curse: but the throne of God and of the Lamb shall be in it; and his servants shall serve him: And they shall see his face; and his name shall be in their foreheads.

And there shall be no night there; and they need no

candle, neither light of the sun; for the Lord God giveth them light: and they shall reign for ever and ever (21:9 to 22:5).

The people in the new Jerusalem will be called "the bride, the Lamb's wife" (v. 9). It will be a literal city, and the people in it will be those who have been redeemed by the blood of the Lamb.

This city is what Jesus has gone to prepare for us. He is carefully planning it and building it. This new Jerusalem has the glory of God for its purpose, not manmade glory, people's ingenuity, or dedication. The glory of the city will be the glory of God.

It will be a truly amazing city, with twelve foundations. On the twelve foundations will be the names of the twelve apostles. It will have a great wall built upon that foundation, with twelve gates. The names written on the gates will be the twelve tribes of Israel (vv. 12-14).

In God's kingdom, the Old Testament saints and the New Testament saints will be united in Jesus Christ. The foundation and the gates are both necessary to produce the beautiful foundation, the beautiful gates, entrances to the city of God.

The great wall will be there as a symbol of the security of the city. There will be no fear, no need to be concerned. This city will have perfect safety and security. Another reason to believe it will be a literal city are the careful measurements, about 1500 miles in circumference (v. 16).

"The foundations of the wall of the city were garnished with all manner of precious stones" (v. 19). It is a beautiful picture. Each kind of stone is listed. To discover a fascinating picture, look up all these stones in the encyclopedia and read the colors and descriptions of each one.

The precise color of each stone is not known for sure but we know generally. One thing is absolutely certain: it will be a place of breathtaking beauty, reflecting the glory of God in a spectrum of brilliant color.

Our God is a God of infinite beauty and the colors of the gems are God's way of emphasizing the brilliance of his own nature and majesty.

Most of these stones are translucent. Imagine the perfect light of the glory of God glowing through all of the stones of the foundation. The streets will be of transparent gold and the walls clear jasper. Imagine how gorgeous it will all be.

"The twelve gates were twelve pearls: every several gate was of one pearl" (v. 21). Imagine a pearl that big! The walls are 200 feet high. Imagine a gate so large it is made of one pearl!

Through pain and suffering the oyster produces the pearl. To protect itself from the pain of a grain of sand, it coats it. Through much pain, in time there emerges a beautiful pearl. Through the suffering, pain, and death of Christ, the great pearl of redemption was produced.

That is the gate to the city. Every time we enter and leave, we will be reminded of the price Christ paid for us, that we are there by his grace, his sacrifice.

When we look at the picture of that city with its light shining through the colors in the foundation, topped by the walls of crystal-clear jasper, we see dazzling beauty in keeping with the glory of God. The glory of the city will be the glory of God. The beauty is more than we can possibly imagine.

The absence of a Temple (v. 22) means that there will be perfect worship. We deal with shadows and symbols now. There will be no need for symbolism in the new Jerusalem because God himself will be the Temple. There will be no need for us to go through ritual because he himself will be there.

And there will be perfect praise, for God will be the light of it. The great men of the nations will bring their glory and their honor to it (v. 24). Men who once had claimed praise for themselves will now praise God, presenting their honor and glory to him. The glory of the nations will be presented as an act of praise and worship: the fulfillment of Isaiah 60:19:

"The sun shall be no more thy light by day; neither for brightness shall the moon give light unto thee: but the Lord shall be unto thee an everlasting light, and thy God thy glory."

There will be perfect security there (v. 25); no reason to fear. The gates will always be open. We will have perfect understanding. There will be no more mystery, no more secrets. We will know the answer to everything we have wondered about. "For now we see through a glass, darkly; but then face to face: now I know in part; but then I shall know even as also I am known" (1 Cor. 13:12). It will be a place of perfect security and understanding.

There will be a perfect environment (v. 27), with nothing to attract men to sin in this city.

There will be real permanence. Rivers in Scripture symbolize prosperity, supreme pleasure, and blessing. This heavenly river (22:1) symbolizes the divine life that will be there: perfect delight, joy, and permanent provision for our eternal lives.

The tree of life will stand there. This is the tree that God forbade in the Garden of Eden. Now, in God's glory and in God's new city, the tree of life will grow abundantly, not just one, but many—lining the streets and avenues. The leaves of the tree will be for the healing of the nations. There will be no disease. The leaves of the tree of life represent health.

There will be no more curse (v. 3) of sin, as we have now in our world. Even creation is bound up in the curse of sin (Rom. 8:19-22). But in heaven there will not be any curse to destroy.

In that city we shall see his face and his name will be in our foreheads (v. 4). This will be the climax of everything.

Heaven's crowning joy will be to see his face. That is what the hearts of his people desperately desire. The climax of God's creation will be this new city; the climax of eternity will be coming face to face with him, forever reigning, ruling, living with him.

What a beautiful permanence there will be about the city which God will prepare. After struggling through the time of the tribulation and all the horrible rebellion of Satan, we have seen the inevitable fruit of sin and hostility toward God.

Now there will emerge a new world, a new earth, a new heaven. And he will present it to us. We shall see him and God himself will be with us through all eternity.

28
Even So, Come, Lord Jesus
22:6-21

This is an incomparable passage. Every word and every phrase blossoms with meaning for our lives. There will be a blessing for those who read, heed, and keep the sayings of this book.

The first chapter says: "Blessed is he that readeth, and they that hear the words of this prophecy" (1:3). The Book of Revelation promises a blessing to those who will read it and a more intense blessing to those who will heed and obey it.

The Word of God is never just information simply to be read or heard. It is to be obeyed! The blessing comes when we read it, hear it, and do it.

This blessing that God promises will be compounded and increased depending upon our response. The more we respond, the more blessing we get. The more we study it and heed it, the more we put it into our lives, the more God blesses us.

There is a larger sense in which we regulate the blessings of God in our lives. As we apply and do what God has told us, God brings an increasing blessing.

This passage tells the return of Christ. Three times we find the phrase "I come quickly" (vv. 7,12,20). Now the word *quickly* does not just mean soon. It could mean soon, but that is not the primary meaning. The word speaks of suddenness.

Once the events about his coming are set in motion, they will occur very rapidly.

In Galatians we read, "When the fulness of time was come, God sent his Son" (Gal. 4:4). That means Jesus Christ was born into the world at the precise moment God decreed it. He was not born a minute too early or too late. In the fullness of time, right on time, he came.

This word *quickly* is in the same vein. He is going to be on time when he returns. He will be coming promptly. God is going to send Jesus Christ back exactly on his own schedule, exactly when he decrees and plans it. There is no cataclysmic event in the world that can cause Jesus Christ to return sooner or later than God wants.

People are not in control of the second coming, and we cannot regulate when God sends Jesus Christ back to earth. We are part of the drama of grace and the drama of redemption that is taking place now, but Jesus will come promptly, on time, when God gives his word.

Christ's Word

And he said unto me, These sayings are faithful and true: and the Lord God of the holy prophets sent his angel to shew unto his servants the things which must shortly be done. Behold, I come quickly: blessed is he that keepeth the sayings of the prophecy of this book.

And I John saw these things, and heard them. And when I had heard and seen, I fell down to worship before the feet of the angel which shewed me these things.

Then saith he unto me, See thou do it not: for I am thy fellow servant, and of thy brethren the prophets, and of them which keep the sayings of this book: worship God. And he saith unto me, Seal not the sayings of the prophecy of this book: for the time is at hand (vv. 6-10).

"These sayings are faithful and true"—that is a good

description of the Word of God. Whenever God says anything, it is faithful and true. His word is sure. These are Christ's words for us.

Original sin came into the world when Satan cast doubt on the accuracy and authority of the Word of God. Eve entertained that doubt and sin obtained a foothold in humanity. Sin actually began as doubt of the authority of the Word of God. It is vital to note that the Bible begins and ends with an emphasis on the authority of the Scriptures, the trustworthiness of the Word of God.

The immediate reference is to the Book of Revelation, but it has a broader reference—all of Scripture. There are other references in Deuteronomy 4:2 and Proverbs 30:6 that contain the same warning about adding to or taking away from the Word of God.

God's word is accurate; its truth has been transmitted, recorded, arranged, and preserved exactly as God planned it. If we do not accept this basic premise, then we have degenerated into nothing more than human reason. If we do not stay with what God says, we make man's word and not God's Word the basis of truth.

The battle over the Bible today is real. If you treat the Bible as folklore, yet still claim to have Jesus as your final authority, you have denied the truth of the Bible. If you cannot accept what the Word of God says, then you must rely on what you think or have experienced.

That is nothing more than rationalism and mysticism and leaves no basis for authority. If the Word of God is not the Word of God, if it is not a sure Word—accurate in every area of God's truth—then the human mind is the measure of truth.

The Bible is not a textbook on anything, even on theology. But wherever the Bible touches any area of knowledge, it is true. When it speaks about science, it is true.

Parents, if you do not believe the history in the Word of God then you have no ground to stand on when you try to teach morality to your children. What makes you think the morality of the Bible is right if the history of it is wrong?

What makes you think the theology of the Bible is right if its world view is wrong? How inconsistent we are. We want our children to be honest. Why? The Bible says so. Why do you want them to be pure? Why do we have weddings in our churches instead of our children just beginning to live together? We go by the Word of God.

But destroy confidence in the accuracy of the Word of God, and you have no basis for such practice or expectation. Here at the end of the book, God declares to us that this is an authoritative word.

Blessed are they who hear and who keep the prophecy of this book. God's Word is accurate in every detail. We must give ourselves to it.

When the angel began to reveal things to John, John was overwhelmed. At the end of this glorious unveiling, John was also overwhelmed in his spirit. His reaction was to fall down and worship the angel (v. 8). But the angel very courteously and gently said, "Do not worship me. I am just like others who keep the sayings of this book. You worship God."

That phrase "worship God" is in the aorist imperative and literally means "worship God only!" Worship God and no one else! This book speaks of God and brings man to His feet in worship.

The Scriptures lead us to God. We do not worship the Scriptures. One does not even have to know the details of the Scriptures to be saved. A man could stumble along the street and find John 3:16 torn out of the Bible and not even know where it came from, and he would know enough to be saved.

We do not worship the Bible. But we who have the Bible

need to revere and love the Bible! We hold it dearly in our hands. God has given it to us to study to see his grand design. Let us diligently do it! We are to keep the saying of this book.

If your view of Scripture does not lead you to fall down at the feet of Christ and God and declare the Bible as his word and submit yourself to its authority, then you are worshiping at the feet of human rationalism and reason. We read further that the sayings of this book are not to be sealed for the time is at hand (v. 10). Daniel was told to seal up his vision till the end of time (Dan. 12:4-9). But Revelation is an open book. It is an unveiling.

Some feel that the Book of Revelation is hard to understand, that it is a dark and forbidding book. That depends on how you approach Revelation. The Book of Revelation should be taken at face value. Do not try to make it all symbolic of some great theological drama. If you do that you are imposing on the Book of Revelation a view that did not exist for many hundreds of years after the time of Christ. Just let it say what God has revealed. Come in faith, and God will reveal himself to you in a very special way. This book is open; it is accessible. It is faithful; it is true. The first thing we see is Christ's Word.

Christ's Return

He that is unjust, let him be unjust still: and he which is filthy, let him be filthy still: and he that is righteous, let him be righteous still: and he that is holy, let him be holy still. And, behold, I come quickly; and my reward is with me, to give every man according as his work shall be.

I am Alpha and Omega, the beginning and the end, the first and the last. Blessed are they that do his commandments, that they may have right to the tree of life, and may enter in through the gates into the city.

For without are dogs, and sorcerers, and whoremongers, and murderers, and idolaters, and whosoever loveth and maketh a lie. I Jesus have sent mine angel to testify unto you these things in the churches. I am the root and the offspring of David, and the bright and morning star" (vv. 11-16).

Christ's return will come very quickly, with lightning speed. Paul declared that Jesus Christ will return in the twinkling of an eye (1 Cor. 15:52). That is faster than we can imagine. We cannot catch a twinkle of an eye.

When he comes again those who are not ready will be caught unaware. He that is unjust will not have time to become just. He who is evil will not have time to become good. He who is filthy will not have time to become pure. It will be that quick.

When death comes or when Jesus comes there will be no second chance. When Jesus Christ comes your destiny and character will be sealed for all of eternity. That is why Jesus magnifies the blessings of obedience (v. 14).

He reminds us again of the people who will never enter into the heavenly city (v. 15). These are they who continue in their sins without repentance and faith and die apart from the grace of God.

Verse 16 has an interesting beginning: "I Jesus." That is an interesting construction. "I Jesus have sent mine angel." It is as if he were saying, "This entire drama is exactly what I wanted it to be. I sent my angel to tell you the things in the churches. I am the root of the offspring of David; I am the bright and morning star; I am the One guiding this scene." Christ is in control!

Christ's Final Appeal

And the Spirit and the bride say, Come. And let him that heareth say, Come. And let him that is athirst come. And whosoever will, let him take the water of life freely.

For I testify unto every man that heareth the words of the prophecy of this book, If any man shall add unto these

things, God shall add unto him the plagues that are written
in this book:

And if any man shall take away from the words of the
book of this prophecy, God shall take away his part out of
the book of life, and out of the holy city, and from the things
which are written in this book.

He which testifieth these things saith, Surely I come
quickly. Amen. Even so, come, Lord Jesus. The grace of our
Lord Jesus Christ be with you all. Amen (vv. 17-21).

The last verses should not come as a shock. God makes his
final appeal to the human race. Can you see how desperately
God wants people to be saved?

Here is Christ's final appeal (v. 17).

That word *come* is one of the grandest words in all the Bible.
Come! We first ran into it in the Book of Genesis when God
revealed that he must destroy the world.

When the ark had been completed, God came to Noah and
said to him and his family, "Come into the ark"; and they came
into the ark of safety (see Gen. 7). They came into the ark of
God's provision.

God has repeated that invitation for people to come. Here in
the very last page of the Bible God once again says, "Come."
How compassionate is God's grace!

It is the Holy Spirit that calls us to come, that draws us to
God. He wants us to come to him. The bride, the church, calls
us to come. The one word that the church ought to be
proclaiming through all of time is, "Come!"

Any church that is not inviting men to come to Jesus is an
insult to God and a blasphemy to the very name of Christ.
"Come": that is the message of the church.

"And let him that heareth say come" (v. 17). As individual
believers we ought to be calling men to come to God. When
we receive Christ we should be inviting others to come. So the
Holy Spirit moves among the earth crying, "Come"; the

church preaches and proclaims "Come"; and individual Christians, like firebrands scattering throughout society, repeat the call.

"Let him that is athirst come. And whosoever will, let him take of the water of life freely" (v. 17). Two invitations are given, one to the one who is thirsty. Isaiah declared, "Ho, every one that thirsteth, come ye to the waters, and he that hath no money; come ye, buy, and eat; yea, come, buy wine and milk without money and without price" (Isa. 55:1).

John recorded the words of our Lord, "Jesus stood and cried, saying, If any man thirst, let him come unto me, and drink" (John 7:37). Come, drink and taste of the Lord that he is good.

Then "whosoever will" may come (v. 17). "God so loved the world that he gave his only begotten Son, that whosoever believeth in him should not perish, but have everlasting life" (John 3:16).

Come! The saddest refrain on the lips of Jesus was about the city of Jerusalem: "How often would I have gathered thy children together, . . . and ye would not!" (Luke 13:34). They were not willing. Whosoever will may come! You may come, if you are willing.

He said, "Let him . . . come" (v. 17). I can say, "Let there be light." But unless someone has his hand on the light switch, there will not be any light.

There was a day when God stood on nothing in the blackness of eternity so dark that not even a pencil ray of light had ever penetrated it. God said, "Let there be light," and there was light (Gen 1:3).

When God speaks, it happens! He spoke the world into existence by the word of his mouth. Let there be light, and there was. The God who said, "Let there be light," and light appeared, says, "Let him . . . come."

When God says, "Let him come," one ought to come. You

can come to God. There is not a demon in hell—not all the forces of evil itself—that can keep you from Jesus. No one can stand in your way.

Let him that is thirsty come. Do you know what it takes for you to come to Christ? You have to be thirsty to want his living water. You must be fed up with the world of the flesh and want salvation. You must have a desire in your heart.

When that desire is there God says, "Let him come." And when he says that, you can come. This is the last welcome of the Bible. Let the thirsty come, let whosoever will come and take the water of life freely.

Those who spurn this invitation will hear from our Lord, "Depart from me, I never knew you" (see Matt. 25:41-43).

Here is the final declaration about the Word of God:

> I testify unto every man that heareth the words of the prophecy of this book, If any man shall add unto these things, God shall add unto him the plagues that are written in this book:
> And if any man shall take away from the words of the book of this prophecy, God shall take away his part out of the book of life, and out of the holy city, and from the things which are written in this book (vv. 18-19).

This is not a new prohibition. Deuteronomy declares, "Neither shall ye diminish aught from it, that ye may keep the commandments of the Lord your God which I command you" (Deut. 4:2). Do not add to it or take away from it.

Proverbs counsels us, "Every word of God is pure: he is a shield unto them that put their trust in him. Add thou not unto his words, lest he reprove thee, and thou be found a liar" (Prov. 30:5-6).

Throughout the Word of God there is this reminder: do not add to God's Word; do not take away from it. Do not disparage God's Word. We must not tamper with it.

Approach it in faith and allow God to bring confirmation out of your faith in that Word. Peter declared that those who are born again are born again by the Word of God (1 Pet. 1:23). He is speaking of the Scripture. The Scripture is the instrument God uses to bring new birth.

We now come to the last words Jesus spoke to this earth, "Surely I come quickly" (v. 20). You will never hear him say another thing audibly until he comes with a shout and the voice of the archangel and the trump of God.

"The grace of our Lord Jesus Christ be with you all" (v. 21). Most scholars believe John was saying, "Be with all saints." How much like God that is. But he is calling for the grace of God upon the saints, not the wicked.

The wicked are blessed just like the saints are today: "For he maketh his sun to rise on the evil and on the good, and sendeth rain on the just and on the unjust" (Matt. 5:45). The wicked are blessed today by the providences of God. God sends the rain and the sunshine. God gives the wicked the same care and blessings that he does the saved.

The call he gives and the conviction he sends to the lost is a blessing. The faithful witness of the gospel of Jesus Christ is a blessing. The prayers of the saints are blessings. But the day will come when there will be no blessing for the wicked, for the lost. After that day has passed, the grace of God will rest only on the saints.

My friend, if you are without Christ today you are still blessed with concerned loved ones and friends and with the gospel. The day is coming when even that grace will not be available to you. How like God it is to end up his Word with grace.

There are two invitations here. In verse 17 there is an invitation from God. He invites men to come and be saved. In verse 20, John is calling him to come to us: "Even so, come, Lord Jesus."